A MASTER CLASS ON BEING HUMAN

A BLACK CHRISTIAN AND A BLACK SECULAR HUMANIST ON RELIGION, RACE, AND JUSTICE

BRAD R. BRAXTON
AND ANTHONY B. PINN

BEACON PRESS
BOSTON

BEACON PRESS
Boston, Massachusetts
www.beacon.org

Beacon Press books
are published under the auspices of
the Unitarian Universalist Association of Congregations.

26 25 24 23   8 7 6 5 4 3 2 1

This book is printed on acid-free paper that meets the uncoated paper
ANSI/NISO specifications for permanence as revised in 1992.

Text design and composition by Kim Arney

*Library of Congress Cataloguing-in-Publication
Data is available for this title.*
Hardcover ISBN: 978-0-8070-0788-4
E-book ISBN: 978-0-8070-0789-1
Audiobook: 978-0-8070-0849-2

FOR KARIS BRAXTON:

Be a leader for . . . righteousness!

FOR AVA SANTANA:

Inspired by your curiosity and creativity.

CONTENTS

INTRODUCTION

*Understand this, my dear brothers and sisters: You must
all be quick to listen, slow to speak, and slow to get angry.*

—James 1:19

The only thing that will redeem mankind is cooperation.

—Bertrand Russell

GOING TO HELL ON A YELLOW SCHOOL BUS

BRAD R. BRAXTON: I used to believe that atheists—people like you, Tony—
were going to hell. In the Christianity of my youth, sermons and altar calls
were climactic moments when "unbelievers" were invited, even compelled,
to "give their lives to Christ" for eternal salvation. Many church leaders
coupled this invitation with a frightening exhortation. They said, "If you
die without knowing Jesus, you're going to hell!"

ANTHONY B. PINN: What you're pointing to, Brad, is a toxic form of authorized hate and disregard spoken with such ease by so many. But, damn, the
number of times I said that line as a young, passionate Christian attempting
to take the world for Christ, and the number of times that line has been used
against me since leaving the church, in particular, and theism, in general.

It takes me back to my early church days in Buffalo, New York. I grew
up claiming that anyone who didn't have Jesus as their personal savior
was going to suffer in hellfire for all eternity. This is what I preached and
prayed, what I heard in sermons and in Sunday school. As a child, I was
so concerned about this, and my potential for falling short, that I still remember nightmares I had about being on a bus to hell. Since, according to

the Bible, I was "born in sin," how could I ever be "good" enough? In my nightmares, I was on a yellow school bus to hell, driven by the devil.

BRAXTON: Tony and I will be examining our deep religious differences in this book, and we will take readers on an educational journey. Thankfully, there will be no field trips to hell on a yellow school bus. Now that we have everybody's attention, we want to back up and explain a bit more about who we are and what we are up to.

Music was a major part of my upbringing as a Christian raised in a black Baptist church in Salem, Virginia. During Sunday worship services, choirs sang lively gospel music as they swayed rhythmically in colorful choir robes. During the Wednesday night prayer meetings, the congregation gathered in the fellowship hall adjacent to the sanctuary for a midweek spiritual checkup, filled with prayers, testimonies about God's goodness . . . and yes, plenty of down-home hand-clapping, foot-tapping music.

PINN: I hear you. I grew up in an African Methodist Episcopal (AME) church, and music similarly marked not only Sunday but much of the week. You are right, and I remember it well. Bible study, youth group, prayer meetings—all involved music, old songs sung to express the trials and victories over the course of that week.

These meetings were without the church organist and pianist, and so we followed the lead of the church mothers who clapped and stomped the rhythm that guided our singing. The music was "raw," but something about that rough-hewn singing spoke to the roughness of life "in the world" when you aren't "of the world." But our Sundays were like yours: robes, timed movement by the choir starting with the procession into the sanctuary, all pointing out the power of music—the poetics of sound—to convey deep religious sentiment.

BRAXTON: Man, this is a serious old-school flashback. The black church mothers in Buffalo and the black deacons and missionaries in Salem. Energized by an earnest evangelical piety that sustained their souls, these church elders in those prayer meetings lifted in a capella form what they called the songs of Zion. You captured it! They did not need any musical accompaniment. These saints had "soul music" wafting through their voices as they melodiously sang traditional Christian songs such as:

Give me that old-time religion.
Give me that old-time religion.
Give me that old-time religion.
It's good enough for me.

PINN: It was good for Paul and Silas. Yep, I remember that one. It brings back memories.

BRAXTON: I'm sure it does. Like many traditional Christian hymns, this song about "old-time religion" was an abbreviated Bible lesson. The verses in the song recalled the "old-time religion" that was good for Paul and Silas, the prophet Daniel, and the Hebrew children, all of whom were important biblical characters.

While the early verses of the song glanced backward to the biblical past, the last verse of the song pointed forward to our eternal future. With a swelling crescendo, we rejoiced that "old-time religion" would eventually take us to our new heavenly home:

It will take us all to heaven.
It will take us all to heaven.
It will take us all to heaven.
It's good enough for me.

Even though I cherish (and continue to draw upon) many aspects of my Christian heritage, I must be honest with you. Old-time religion was *not* interested in taking *all* people to heaven. Be very clear: heaven was exclusively reserved, according to the theology of my Christian upbringing, for Christians. By extension, this meant that *everybody else* was going to hell. The list of the hell-bound was lengthy and included people from all other religious traditions, and the list certainly included "misguided souls," like humanists and atheists, who had the unmitigated gall to deny God's existence.

PINN: Now we're getting down to the nitty-gritty. For the Baptist faith you encountered and the Methodist faith that shaped my early years, there was a strict divide—a strong distinction between those who are favored based on their embrace of right knowledge and those who are damned. And when I was young, and involved in church ministry, I couldn't appreciate the idea that there were other paths to a healthy and morally centered life. It had to be my way—my faith and my perception of that faith. As I think about it, this position held a certain negative tension: someone from a marginalized group dealing with marginalization by marginalizing others. Heaven vs. hell provided a quick and graphic way of marking this difference.

BRAXTON: You're telling the whole truth when you talk about marginalized groups marginalizing others. It's a vicious cycle.

We black Christians sang fervently about going to heaven, while passionately believing that most of the world was going to hell. Not hell as depicted in Dante's classic medieval poem *The Divine Comedy*, with its nine concentric circles of increasing woe and misery. Rather, in the Christianity of my childhood, we confidently (or, should I say, arrogantly) assumed that we were included, and unbelievers would eventually experience a time, place, or space of "eternal exclusion."

PINN: You raise an interesting issue. Both of us seem to have experienced a religious world that made a strong distinction and provided a geography of well-being vs. punishment; the details of this place of punishment were vague.

Heaven, of course, included all the good stuff we wanted and didn't have. But hell wasn't so clearly articulated. Maybe that was by design in that it freed the imagination to fill in the gaps, to situate hell as the housing for all our fears and anxieties. And near the top of that list of fears were those who didn't hold to our beliefs, who challenged our way of being in the world through an embrace of their own. I'm on the other side of this geographic divide now, but I remember my earlier thinking and beliefs.

BRAXTON: Like you, Tony, I have been on a long spiritual journey. Having left behind various problematic aspects of my Christian upbringing, I now embrace a progressive, radically inclusive Christianity informed by my profound experiences with people from diverse religious, spiritual, and ethical traditions such as humanism. At present, I am not really concerned about heaven and hell. I am, however, passionately concerned about how we humans can do better on earth right now.

PINN: Agreed, Brad. I moved from being an evangelical Christian preaching hell and a strict (really unrealistic) moral code; you moved toward a more progressive mode of Christianity. In either case, it's really a matter of having grown into a greater sense of engagement, of possibility—exposure to larger worlds, in part, through our shared movement through PhD programs in religion and our spending many years teaching diverse students about religion.

I was warned, when going off to college and again when going to divinity school, not to lose my Jesus. Well . . . we know how that turned out. While higher education doesn't "take your Jesus away," for both of us, something about it fostered curiosity that pushed beyond the cocoon of our early religious convictions.

BRAXTON: Brother, you're spot on. I was fortunate to grow up in a home where my father (a Christian pastor and social activist) and my mother (a Christian educator and musician) held education in the highest esteem. I have precious childhood memories of the awe I felt standing in front of all those books in my father's study in our house. There were shelves and shelves of theological books, biblical commentaries, manuals on church administration, and binders holding sermon manuscripts, already preached.

As I matured intellectually and began the academic study of religion—first as an undergraduate and then as a graduate student—my father spoke joyfully to me, using that old black Christian motto: "Son, just keep some burning with your learning." In other words, learn all you can *and* keep the fires of a genuine love for God and for people ignited on the altar of your heart.

On the one hand, my religious upbringing passed down to me a distinctive religious geography with firmly fixed coordinates of who was an insider and who was an outsider. Yet on the other hand, my parents encouraged me to push beyond the boundaries of my known and native theological world. By fueling my love for learning and my love for people, my parents gave me permission to explore difference—different cultures, practices, and belief systems—without fear or shame.

So, I have no desire to "convert" you or "save" you from damnation. On the contrary, I am eager to listen to and learn from you, as we together walk a path of illumination on what it means for us—*all* of us—to be better people.

PINN: I'd say we both came to recognize—in part through open conversation with difference—the need to think the world bigger, to find opportunity for exchange that expands the possibilities for life in light of both our commonalities and strong distinctions.

BRAXTON: Absolutely! And this is what we want this book to embody, in form and content: dialogue that courageously probes our deep differences about serious topics, with the ultimate goal of promoting constructive engagement, enhanced understanding, and more compassion among people with different identities, beliefs, and practices.

Let me also add this. Despite the impressive technological advances in our society, many of our educational institutions, cultural organizations, and religious and philosophical traditions do not equip people to encounter and embrace difference in healthy ways. Consequently, difference becomes an occasion for trauma—like the subconscious distress you experienced as a child disturbed by night visions of a trip to hell on a yellow school bus.

Difference need not trigger trauma or incite violence—whether it is the violence of religiously "pious" parents hurling harmful words at a transgender child or the violence of politically "pious" nations hurling rockets at each other because they share geographical borders but not philosophical beliefs. Hopefully, this opening exchange between us reveals why we are so passionate about the positive embrace of difference. Throughout the book, we do what we have just done. Chop it up, back and forth, in vigorous dialogue that never *backs away* from our significant differences.

PINN: Yes! And before we dive in, I want to make certain readers "don't get it twisted." This book isn't simply about religious disagreement. Since the topic of disagreement is more complex and consequential than we sometimes understand, this book is also about the broader well-being of our social world and our democracy.

Some of the most worrisome challenges endangering the world and the survival of democracy are tied to differences in belief, different understandings of morality, and different ethical assumptions. These are some of the very things that Christians (like Brad) and humanists (like me) struggle with, even if our struggles are on a smaller scale. So, by examining the differences—and even battles—between Christians and humanists, we might gain clearer insight into the troubling impulse undergirding many crises in our nation and throughout the world: the inability to have honest exchanges and discuss our differences *for real*. Diverse groups of people urgently need to cultivate the ability to communicate with each other in ways that move beyond winning at all costs.

WHY WE WROTE IT, AND WHY YOU SHOULD READ IT

The body of the book consists of the kind of dialogue you have just been reading. But we are going to briefly put the dialogue aside and talk more about the motivations and aspirations for this book.

One of us, as you know, is a Christian (Braxton). One of us is a secular humanist (Pinn). Persuaded that the embrace of difference—not the elimination of difference—is an effective classroom for learning to be better humans, we have joined forces in this book. We have no interest in uniformity.

Spoiler alert! By the end of the book, we do not reconcile our differences in the name of a bland mutuality. Our distinctive ways of thinking and doing—shaped by Christianity and humanism, respectively—retain their sharp edges. However, instead of using those sharp edges to harm each other, we use those edges to unravel and cut through knotted and conventional thinking about significant social issues.

We both have reached a mature phase of our lives, a time in life's journey when introspection and retrospection are common. Our musings on the world given to us and the world as we will leave it occupy more of our mental energy than they did decades ago. While we hope many vibrant years of life lie ahead, neither of us takes anything for granted. Thus, *legacy*—in a word—is the energy animating the collaboration in this book.

We both are eager to amplify opportunities for well-being that are more robust than those we inherited. In a small way, we want to leave our families, friends, and communities a model of involvement and exchange that reflect the best of our intellectual and communicative possibilities. Using our talents and skills, we want to encourage the (re)shaping of interaction between diverse groups of people in productive ways.

Moral frameworks and ethical commitments enable people to make meaning from their lives. Yet these frameworks and commitments can also create gaping chasms between people. Intense warfare occurs not only between hostile nations but between hostile family members living under the same roof who have drastically different religious or philosophical principles and practices. Even if ambassadors to the United Nations never read it, we want this book to create more ambassadors for moral courage and intellectual curiosity, who will unite their families and communities while maintaining respect for the significant differences in their families and communities. If you are comfortable asking tough questions about serious philosophical, cultural, and religious issues and want to enlarge your scope of dialogue partners, this book was written just for you.

MOVING FROM COMBAT TO CONVERSATION

Christianity and secular humanism have for centuries existed in opposition. The theological-philosophical self-understanding of each tradition is based in part on antagonism and aggressive statements of difference. For example, many Christians assume that secular humanists, by definition, lack moral correctness, which is—according to Christians—available only through belief in a divine authority that shapes and monitors human activity. Consequently, some Christians even contend that disbelief—as represented by secular humanism—is the source of moral and ethical decay in the United States and the reason our country has lost its global status and "divine favor."

On the other hand, many secular humanists insist that religion—and Christianity is high on this list—is the source of irrational behavior and "tribal" violence that have hampered human well-being. Said simply, many humanists believe that ending religion is a crucial step toward ending humanity's most challenging problems.

The discord between Christianity and secular humanism will probably continue along its current trajectory. We, however, believe in a more interactive model that allows for fruitful critique and affirmation. This model also might empower us to improve our collective life, while devoting significantly less time to belittling, verbal jousting, and attacks meant to nullify either Christianity or secular humanism. In short, we are not interested in the one-upmanship typifying many contemporary intercultural and interreligious conversations. According to the zero-sum mentality of that combative approach, the validity of one tradition is secured by depicting other traditions as vacuous or vile.

We, instead, seek to expose the assumptions undergirding the arguments of both Christians and secular humanists in a spirit of intellectual rigor and compassion. Our exploration is rooted in a shared accountability for, and responsibility to, the world as it is, as we find ourselves in it, and as we work to shape it for the better.

We are not suggesting that dialogue, or even mutual understanding, is a panacea for unjust social interactions and arrangements. We, however, are firmly convinced that a probing, good-natured exchange of ideas can clarify perspectives and assumptions that function below the surface of theological-philosophical tirades. In a world saturated with social media, tirades are easy clickbait that attracts people to digital platforms and echo chambers where their assumptions are reinforced and rarely, if ever, investigated—let alone interrogated. Tirades often harden hearts and shut minds precisely when softer hearts and open minds are needed to foster more benevolent interactions.

Our interactive approach is not a Pollyannish call to simply recognize ourselves in the "other." Rather, we seek in this book to model the possibility of fruitful exchange that accounts for, rather than masks, our differences. Accordingly, our exchange may begin to eke out an alternative vocabulary and grammar of collective life that extends beyond the reach of our limited worldviews. Such a move will not dramatically change the world. Constructive exchange between secular humanists and Christians will not abolish injustice. This type of constructive exchange, however, might reduce the "noise" that prevents an acute focus on the larger, death-dealing issues impairing the world.

A ZONE OF EXCHANGE: A PIVOTAL MOMENT OF LEARNING FROM EACH OTHER

We share a professional world—the study of African American religion—and our paths have crossed often during events in that world. However, opportunities for full engagement in light of our personal-professional identities as a Christian and a humanist have been limited. Sure, we have talked—typically in passing and without occasion to ask questions, offer critique, and exchange ideas in a sustained manner.

All of this changed during an encounter at The Open Church of Maryland, where Braxton is the founding senior pastor. The Open Church is a community of progressive Christians who value probing dialogue and are not afraid of disagreement or a counterpoint to their belief systems. Pinn was the speaker for the online Sunday service at The Open Church of Maryland in July 2020.

In his presentation at The Open Church, "Thoughts on African American Humanism," Pinn offered a compelling fifteen-minute autobiographical narrative of his journey from the theism of his childhood to the humanism he now espouses. He launched the presentation with a provocative question that has indelibly influenced his personal and professional life: What can you say about God in light of suffering in the world?

During the talk, Pinn defined a humanist as someone who is "suspicious of supernatural claims" and does not "hold to the belief that there are gods or god." Yet a humanist believes that "humans are morally and ethically responsible for each other, for life writ-large, and for the world in more general terms."[1]

After Pinn's presentation, Braxton facilitated a robust dialogue where congregants engaged Pinn with their questions and observations. At the conclusion of the dialogue, La Tanya Simms, a member of The Open Church's board of directors, summed up the experience by posting in the Zoom chat box: "This is a master class on being a better human."

Based on our experience, this level of conversation is unusual, but we have found it so beneficial. It pushed us, informed us, and challenged us. Moreover, it motivated this project. Shortly after the event at The Open Church, we talked and began writing this book.

HOW TO READ THIS BOOK

We wrote this book during intense moments of the COVID-19 pandemic and before the widespread availability of a vaccine. Meeting in person was not an option. Delaying this project was also not an option. President Donald Trump's vitriolic rhetoric and the tensions of the 2020 presidential election intensified the palpable anxiety already in the air. The times were deadly but also filled with opportunity to think and do differently. We had to respond to the moment . . . in the moment.

Recognizing the potentially harmful dynamics that could erupt in a dialogue between a black Christian and a black secular humanist, we set ground rules to guide the exchange. The goal from start to finish was never to win points through "gotcha" moments. Instead, we aimed to express ourselves in ways that allowed us to cut through the stereotypes of our respective communities.

In an ideal world, we would have written this book sitting in a coffee shop over the course of many meetings. In the meetings, we would have recorded our conversations and later transcribed them. The harsh realities of the COVID-19 pandemic forced us to replace our preferred approach with a different option: email. Email communication was a way around the restrictions of social distancing and travel and also enabled us to incorporate the project more nimbly into the rhythms of our personal and professional schedules.

To maintain the coffee shop feel, our weekly emails to each other were casual but informed, fervent but humorous, bold but considerate. Instead of producing mini-research papers that might allow us to hide behind other people's arguments, we became vulnerable and shared thoughts, feelings, stories, and memories about the strengths and weaknesses in Christianity and secular humanism. For us to have a down-on-the-ground and keeping-it-real dialogue, a tidy string of scholarly essays advancing the arguments of abstract "believers" or "nonbelievers" simply would not do. We had to explore what might happen if Brad and Tony just kept "chopping it up" week after week, with no pretense but plenty of passion.

We also limited the time frame for our weekly responses to keep the conversation fresh, as if we were chilling at that coffee shop with a hot beverage and a toasted bagel. There were occasional gaps in our communication—longer than usual response times, as one or the other of us pondered a bit longer about remarks received or questions raised. Nevertheless, the approach worked and enabled us to listen to each other—*really listen* to each other. As we responded to and riffed on our distinctive worldviews, we used the time between exchanges to carefully consider the perspectives of the other rather than preparing the next battle plan to overwhelm the other.

As you read through our conversations in this book, what should you do? We hope *A Master Class on Being Human* will encourage deeper thinking about difference or affirm your view of difference not as a problem to solve but an opportunity to embrace. When difference is defined as a problem, difference must be eliminated—you must think as *I* think, see the world as *I* see it, move through the world in line with the values and commitments of *my* group. But when difference is considered an opportunity, it enables a broader perspective on human circumstances. It affords precious occasions to learn from others, refine our thinking, and adjust our doing.

We believe this takes place when we open ourselves to conversation—to *listening*, not just hearing. With hearing, we all too often catch just enough to develop our counter-position—pay enough attention to counter the claim being made. *Listening,* we believe, entails a particular openness to vulnerability and discomfort—to the possibility of shifting our thinking, or at the very least, to justifying our claims in light of the good point made by the other. Consequently, we can create and nurture communities where agreement is not mandated, but honest communication, which clarifies and edifies, becomes the norm. Audre Lorde wisely advised in *Sister Outsider*, "Difference must be not merely tolerated, but seen as a fund of necessary polarities between which our creativity can spark like a dialectic."

AN OVERVIEW OF OUR EXPERIMENTAL "FINDINGS"

We decided to address seven themes. We determined the themes by culling from a longer list of issues with social importance to both of us—issues related to our moral and ethical commitments as expressed within the particular framework of our philosophical-theological orientation. The chapter titles are the overarching prompts that we used to initiate each discussion.

Prompt 1 considers the meaning(s) and function(s) of religion and examines key terms and themes (e.g., religion, authority, community, hierarchy, injustice). It also presents our complex engagement with religion in that Pinn is a secular humanist with a sense of religion (and experience with the church in particular), and Braxton is a religious person but not in a traditional (restrictive) sense.

Prompt 2 examines the "nones," the colloquial term for a large and growing group of religiously unaffiliated people in the United States and around the world. Conversations about the "nones" frequently focus on certain groups of young white people who are moving beyond their connection with churches. These conversations neglect the growing number of people of color who claim no particular religious affiliation. The prompt seeks to correct this omission by focusing attention on black "nones" and their moral and ethical commitments to social justice.

Prompt 3 investigates significant philosophical and theological frameworks of our respective traditions. As black scholars keenly aware of injustice, we focus on moral evil and how it is defined and explored within Christian and humanist circles. We employ two scholarly categories: *theodicy* (What can we say about God in light of moral evil, or in short: Is God good?) and *anthropodicy* (What can we say about humans in light of moral evil, or in short: Are humans good?). We also engage other probing questions: Is human suffering redemptive, or capable of teaching important lessons? Is it possible to use the Bible as an instrument for liberation instead of a weapon for domination?

Prompt 4 moves from a general discussion of moral evil to a specific conversation about black death (the prolonged and concentrated assaults on black bodies and communities that result in the premature death of black people). We investigate a range of questions: What is black death? What causes black death? Can we reduce black death in ways that promote black life? Additionally, we discuss the relationship between race and racism and consider whether science and spirituality offer resources for black people to resist philosophies and social systems that disregard their humanity.

Prompt 5 examines two related conceptual frameworks—"hope" and "future." In this prompt, we wrestle with whether hope is justified and whether any talk of the future is related in realistic ways to the ongoing struggle for social justice. To avoid abstraction and naivete, the prompt situates the discussion in current and recent events, such as the COVID-19 pandemic, ceaseless episodes of antiblack violence, and the presidential elections during 2008–2020. Pinn eschews hope as a useful concept in social struggle, replacing it instead with an ethic of resistance, framed in terms of the persistence of possibility. Braxton embraces hope as a vital instrument for social advancement and advocates for hope's internal, external, and eternal dimensions.

Prompt 6 analyzes one of the most influential social movements in the twenty-first century—Black Lives Matter (BLM). Since BLM emerged during the presidency of Barack Obama, we interpret the broader social context in the United States immediately prior to and during his presidency. In response to the continued disregard for black humanity, BLM rapidly grew from a social-media hashtag to a social revolution. After establishing this interpretive framework, we address various questions including: What does BLM achieve? Does it possess religious (theistic) overtones and draw from certain religious assumptions of the civil rights movement? In what ways is BLM more intersectional and pragmatic in terms of its philosophies and strategies?

Prompt 7 considers a question that provokes considerable disagreement and heated rhetoric: Does (or should) religion have a public role? In evaluating religion's public role, we realize that religion for many Americans is an inextricable part of the "democratic experiment" in the United States (as expressed in aphorisms such as "America is a 'Christian' nation."). Yet we question whether the special status of religion, and particularly Christianity, is warranted and useful. Our assessment of religion's public role—for good or ill—engages a diverse set of cultural resources, ranging from biblical texts about Jesus to rap lyrics from Tupac Shakur.

To maintain the "mood" and "feel" of conversation throughout the chapters, we avoided detailed attention to secondary sources, limiting ourselves to a reference style more consistent with casual talk rather than formal academic publications. However, at the end of the book, we listed some authors and texts mentioned in our exchanges.

As noted above, the goals for the book are modest. We hold no illusion that it will radically change patterns and practices of animosity built over centuries. Humanists and Christians will continue to be at odds. But perhaps this project will challenge some of the problematic patterns and pedagogies that fuel the hatred (which is not too strong a word) between these groups—and offer an alternate strategy for engagement.

CLASS IS ABOUT TO BEGIN!

In bell hooks and Cornel West's pioneering dialogue book *Breaking Bread* (to which we are indebted), West reflects on the responsibilities of black intellectuals:

> Black intellectuals must realize that the creation of "new" and alternative practices results from the heroic efforts of collective intellectual work and communal resistance which shape and are shaped by present structural constraints, workings of power, and modes of cultural fusion.[2]

In an attempt to create "alternative practices" sympathetic to democratic exchange and appreciative of cultural and religious differences, we joined forces in this book and tried our best to do some "collective intellectual work." We discovered a refreshing solidarity in the midst of our profound differences.

Engaging difference—let alone understanding and appreciating it—can be an awkward and even frightening experience. Fear not! Our dialogue attempts to lessen the awkwardness and remove the fear.

In this book, we engage, seek to understand, and appreciate each other's differences. As you—whether you are a devout believer or a dispassionate skeptic—eavesdrop on our dialogue, we happily enlarge the classroom so that you can join us in the ongoing lesson of learning how to be a better person.

Without your valuable input and positive influence in the communities where you live, work, and play, the lesson plans for this class will remain woefully incomplete. Now that you are here and ready and willing to teach and learn along with us, this master class on being human can begin. Ding! Ding! Class is in session.

NOTES

1. Anthony B. Pinn, "Thoughts on African American Humanism," presented at The Open Church of Maryland (July 12, 2020), https://clovermedia.s3-us -west-2.amazonaws.com/store/d4ee997e-f904–43b1–9e27-ae4d0893f608 /45d32e81c7/720p.mp4.
2. bell hooks and Cornel West, *Breaking Bread: Insurgent Black Intellectual Life*, 25th-ann. ed. (New York: Routledge, 2017), 145.

WHAT IS RELIGION, AND DOES IT HELP OR HARM?

Brother Brad—

COVID has changed my routine. I used to do my best to get to the gym on campus in the morning, but that's no longer an option. So, I do what I can at home with my limited equipment, grab a bite to eat, and make my way to the computer. Second cup of coffee near the computer, I get underway. Properly caffeinated, I'm ready to go. Let's do this! Attached please find my initial response to the prompt: What is religion, and does it help or harm? Looking forward to reading your thoughts.

Cheers,
Tony

> Tony,
>
> Thanks for sending this. I'm eager to see where the journey takes us as we wrestle with these provocative questions. As I may have shared with you, I'm a morning person. I usually get up no later than 3 a.m. and try to ride my Peloton bike in the apartment by 6 a.m. I cycled and lifted weights this morning. That workout prepared me for another workout: responding to the weighty thoughts of Tony Pinn. LOL.
>
> Best,
> Brad

.   .   .

ANTHONY B. PINN: We have similar backgrounds. We have both occupied the pulpit and wrestled with the nature and meaning of life, and how religion—black religion—might aid our effort to understand life's dynamics in light of transhistorical ideals and claims. And something of this religious context shapes our movement through the world for good or ill. But despite those commonalities, we are likely to disagree regarding the nature of this religion we shared, at some point, and whether it is a helpful or harmful orientation.

Concerning the nature and meaning of religion, my thinking has changed over time. I've gone from thinking in terms of institutions, doctrines, and creeds that shape the geographies of engagement and reflection we have called "traditions." My concern grew to include humanism as an orientation with functions that replace "traditions." While some might disagree, it seemed to me that humanism became a type of alternate religious system. Mindful of this, I found it was no longer possible to define (or theorize) religion with markers that privileged theistic orientations, primarily the black church. I needed a more inclusive way to think about religion that accounted for conflict and contradiction.

Instead of privileging institutional forms, I began to think about religion as a field of exchange that centered on the effort to name and address moral evil in the form of injustice. This allowed me to think in terms of commonalities between theistic and nontheistic orientations, and to do so without negating their distinctions. I argued that religion is a quest for complex subjectivity—the tool by which we seek to wrestle with the fundamental questions of existence. This theorizing of religion has held for me for a good number of years, although more recently I've modified it a bit.

Regarding whether religion is helpful or harmful, I would argue it is both. When addressing certain modes of injustice, religion renders invisible other structures of disregard. For example, the black church addressed racism but for a long time failed to address sexism. And when addressing sexism, it often failed to address other modes of violence—such as transphobia.

In the name of fairness, the same is true for nontheistic orientations that often belittle theists and turn a cold shoulder toward the "religious." Many nontheists argue that if theists want to believe "fairy tales," they deserve the consequences of that belief. Additionally, to be nontheistic in orientation isn't a safeguard against being sexist or homophobic, for example.

BRAD R. BRAXTON: Your comments provide an excellent introduction and framework for our dialogue. The allusion to pulpits makes me reflect on how influential preaching has been in my life. In my interrelated roles of theologian and pastor, I have spent countless hours preparing to preach, preaching, and evaluating my preaching and the preaching of others.

I wrote every sentence of my PhD dissertation while serving as the senior pastor of Douglas Memorial Community Church, a vibrant, socially engaged congregation in Baltimore, Maryland. During the three-year span of researching and writing the dissertation, I preached twice, occasionally three times, on most Sundays. The dissertation research and writing were intellectually arduous. Yet the weekly attempt to provide powerful, polished sermonic language that nurtures a congregation amid its joys and sorrows was as intellectually demanding as anything I have done as an academic researcher and author.

My reflections on preaching have significantly shaped my thinking about religion. Thus, permit me to offer some thoughts about preaching because my reflections can be extended and generalized to encompass some of my broader thoughts about the nature of religion.

Preaching is a multidimensional, communal deed. Preaching at its best, especially in various black contexts, is an artful, choreographed dance involving a congregation and a preacher using heads and hearts to interpret and transmit values, to grapple with life's meaning and purpose, and to (re)negotiate constantly the contours and responsibilities of their participation in the congregation and the larger human family.

PINN: Brad, what comes to mind immediately is *God's Trombones* by James Weldon Johnson. As a humanist, Johnson is concerned with the sermonic tradition that isn't tied to its theological claims. Rather, he points to something you're highlighting: the poetic quality of expression, the way that words are used to shape and reshape worlds of possibility and meaning. The black sermonic tradition is a dynamic mode of communication that cuts across what is and engages moral imagination as a marker of what can be despite conditions, and it reads against circumstances.

BRAXTON: Absolutely, Tony! Preaching can be a marvelous form of po-etic expression. The Greek verb *poieō* means "to create" and gives us the English word "poetry." Accordingly, the artful stitching together of words, images, intuitions, and feelings in the preaching moment can, indeed, create "new worlds," or at least, new and more capacious perspectives on our existing world.

Furthermore, my description of preaching highlights the importance of interdependent communal actions or deeds. As an event, preaching includes the preacher (a religious leader), the congregation (a community defined by certain boundaries), the sermon (a ritual expression of worldviews and interpretations of texts, stories, and traditions), and the culture (broader relationships, beliefs, practices, and communal arrangements that comple-ment or contravene the congregation's values and worldviews). Preaching assembles all these actors and factors in the quest to discern and enact ways of life that promote noble thinking and altruistic living.

Properly understood, preaching is not an authoritarian imposition of meaning upon a passive community. Preaching instead invites a variety of voices—the preacher, the congregation, and ancient and contemporary texts, traditions, and practices—to articulate and implement a vision for people to flourish and be free.

PINN: I'm curious how this works—the resistance to preaching as "an au-thoritarian imposition of meaning upon a passive community." How does this play out when the physicality of the preached moment seems to set apart the preacher? The way the preacher occupies space within the pulpit suggests distinction—with the congregation gathered in pews. Something about this indicates passive engagement along the lines of the academic "banking model" (in which the teacher or expert "deposits" knowledge into "passive" students).

I'm not sure how the physical arrangement of the sermon suggests mu-tuality beyond the process of call-and-response. The preacher picks the text, the preacher frames the argument, the preacher states the importance of the lesson and the takeaway. True, those listening—and I emphasize *listening*—can accept or reject what is delivered, but they don't challenge or add to the sermon in real time. Perhaps you can help me understand what you mean by that statement I've highlighted—the mutuality you claim. How does that dynamic engagement take place? What aspects of the physical space of the sermon suggest your philosophical interpretation about the sermon?

BRAXTON: Your concerns about the physical arrangement of the preaching moment and the messages that arrangement conveys are germane. In responding to your concerns, I hope to further explain why the community is such an integral part of my understanding of preaching in particular and of religion in general. When communities are at their best, they counteract some of religion's potentially harmful effects.

Preachers are a part of the community, not "heroes" who swoop in from outside to "save" or "enlighten" people. Often the people to whom we tell the story told it first to us. This is especially the case if preachers are preaching in communities where they were raised or they have lived and been nurtured for some time.

For example, I'm mindful of this when I return to my hometown to preach. My father and mother served as key leaders at the First Baptist Church in Salem, Virginia, for thirty-three years. I received my ministerial license and ordination in the black Baptist tradition in this church and was nurtured spiritually in the broader community in Salem. Whenever I return to my hometown to preach, I'm preaching to certain people who have known me all my life. Their values and commitment to their religious practices provided an indispensable foundation for my moral development.

PINN: I agree with you in theory: "Preachers are a part of the community, not 'heroes' who swoop in from outside to 'save' or 'enlighten' people." Nevertheless, how do the performance of the preached moment and the configuration of ministry support this assertion? The culture of ministry displays the preacher as distinct, as "special," as having a more intense and insightful vertical connection.

The organizational framing of "church" also works against this argument since there is a hierarchy of significance, with the minister at the top. The minister is, indeed, a part of the community. However, the minister has a distinctive relationship. The minister is the most visible, authoritative component of the community, with whom authority rests to decide and to speak on behalf of others. There's no reason to assume that community is, by its nature, egalitarian.

BRAXTON: Your concern about potential imbalances of power between congregations and ministers is well-taken. As you know, some Christian denominations have more formal (and rigid) hierarchical structures than others. Depending on the particular ecclesial structure, the potential for misalignments of power is more or less a theoretical and practical challenge.

My formative years and professional ministry have occurred largely in so-called free-church traditions, where churches are autonomous even if they are part of a larger denomination. For instance, I was raised, licensed, and ordained in a black Baptist church affiliated with the National Baptist Convention, USA. The centrality and agency of the congregation were affirmed in various ways, thereby demonstrating that ministers and the congregation were partners and mutually accountable to each other.

I experienced my call to ministry at age seventeen. I shared my call with my parents first, then later with my home congregation. More than a year elapsed between the public announcement of my call and the invitation to preach my initial sermon and receive my ministerial license. During this period, the congregation and I further discerned my intention to be a minister.

The initial sermon is a rite of passage in many black churches, and some churches formerly referred to it as a "trial" sermon, indicating the need for the would-be minister to provide persuasive evidence of a call and commitment to ministry. This momentous and joyful occasion involves the delivering of a public sermon to the congregation, after which the congregation endorses through its vote or sanction that the potential minister has the characteristics and budding skills to be an effective leader. After this communal affirmation, the minister receives a "license," signifying that the minister is an emerging leader authorized to perform limited ministerial functions.

After I preached my initial sermon, the chair of the deacon board, along with my father, who was the pastor, offered poignant comments that I remember to this day. They said, "Brad, the same congregation that gives you this ministerial license can also take it away." They were impressing upon me that power in the ministerial office is not simply vertical (i.e., based on the minister's relationship with God). The power dynamic is also horizontal (i.e., based on the minister's relationship with the congregation). They were also affirming that God speaks to and through the congregation just as God speaks to and through the minister.

Furthermore, I have been blessed to serve in my pastoral ministry with marvelous church governing and ministerial boards. These boards, which consist primarily of congregationally appointed laypeople, are typically referred to as deacons/stewards and trustees/directors. The leaders on these boards work collaboratively with the ministerial leadership in all areas of congregational life. The boards are a wellspring of invaluable wisdom, and they also offer a check and balance on the unfettered use, or abuse, of ministerial power.

It's also worth noting that adage many black pastors know well: "In black churches, people vote in two major ways—with their feet and their purses/wallets." In other words, churches are voluntary organizations. Thus, apart from two key resources, namely the people's presence and their financial support, many ministers would be preaching outdoors to the birds and squirrels. My understanding of preaching in particular and religion in general pays great homage to the role of the congregation/community.

As I was saying, some of these congregants were my Sunday school teachers when I was a child. Many good things about religion entered my life because of the "saints" in my childhood community. The community played an important and healthy role in helping me discern that my skills could be used effectively in professional ministry. Also, the community "set me apart" and ordained me to be a "gospel storyteller" commissioned to share good news and encourage others. And it's a particular honor when the community that commissioned me invites me back to tell them the gospel story afresh.

PINN: I agree that members of the community play a role in encouraging the development of ministers. This was my experience as well. However, what are the markers they see—the signs they claim—indicating someone should be in ministry? The "call" to ministry can be an arrangement of particular social markers of significance and "specialness" that play into the sense of the minister as a special figure—unique and uniquely qualified.

In the free churches you highlight, a hierarchy of significance persists, with the minister atop the hierarchy. Even these free churches aren't free of the social coding of gender that informs both "secular" and "sacred" power structures. To be "free" is an organizational arrangement that isn't necessarily free from larger social arrangements.

BRAXTON: I understand your theoretical concern here, but the actual practices and mechanics of congregational ministry can mitigate the concern. Ministry, as with other professions, requires certain basic skills and dispositions, as well as skills and abilities acquired through education and practice in communities.

Let me illustrate it this way. When teaching emerging ministers in my introduction to preaching course in divinity school, I say jokingly to the students on the first day, "If the mention or sight of blood makes you faint, you probably shouldn't go to medical school. Similarly, if you're unwilling to talk in public, maybe divinity school and professional ministry aren't for you. Effective public speaking is a key skill in ministry. So, let's learn how to do it with excellence and finesse."

This is my humorous way of indicating that each profession has some rudimentary aspects to it, and the development of certain competencies is important. Congregations play a significant role by discerning if potential ministers have various traits and skills, including, but not limited to, empathy, humility, active listening skills, management capabilities, oratorical abilities, and the intellectual curiosity and acumen needed to grapple with religious texts and traditions.

As noted earlier, I was licensed by my home congregation in 1988 after my first year as an undergraduate at the University of Virginia. I didn't become a fully authorized or ordained minister in my denomination until three years later, in 1991. In the intervening years, I completed a BA degree at UVA, where I majored in religious studies. Rigorous education deepened my intellectual understanding of the history and practices of religion in general and Christianity in particular.

In my ordination process, a panel of seasoned ministers publicly examined me on major themes, doctrines, and practices of ministry for nearly two hours. During the examination, one minister asked me, "Can you provide evidence that someone has accepted Christianity on the basis of your preaching?" In other words, my ordination was not predicated upon me being "special" but rather on the basis of my ability to be an authentic and persuasive witness for a defined set of religious beliefs and practices. Had I not been able to confirm in the presence of the community that people in the community had assented to Christianity through my ministry, I would not have been ordained.

In many religious traditions influenced by African cultures (black Christianity being one), there is a delicate balance between the authority of religious leaders and the community's authority. In traditional African cultures, tribal chiefs and other religious leaders are catalytic agents of sacred energy that can empower the community. Many black Christians consider preachers as catalytic agents. Preachers don't "own" this sacred energy; they're stewards and facilitators of it. Thus, the authority of the preacher is a cultural umbilical cord connecting black ministers with Mother Africa.

PINN: I hear what you're saying, but it doesn't address sufficiently my concern. My argument isn't simply theoretical. It's practical and played out in the plight of church members who are women and non-cisgender. The hierarchy isn't simply thought; it's practiced—arranged to impinge upon the opportunities afforded to folks in churches. You present an "ideal" case, but it doesn't represent the larger tradition, which undeniably disadvantages women, for example.

If this weren't the case, womanist critique, for example, would have faded away. But the ongoing work and critique in womanist scholarship target an ongoing problem. So, I have to respectfully disagree. This call for commonality is more "wishful" than authentic. Don't we have to be mindful of the different ways that authority is established in "traditional African cultures," and how the preacher is called and selected in the North American context? They aren't identical. Consequently, one doesn't speak to the dynamics of the other.

BRAXTON: Both of us are allies with our womanist colleagues, and we have benefited immensely from their audacious critiques of religiously sanctioned injustice, including sexism and heterosexism. To put it bluntly, I have said often in my lectures and sermons that many black churches should "spend at least thirty days in hell doing penance" for how they have mistreated girls, women, and LGBTQ communities. Therefore, we must confront unflinchingly the pernicious inequity and injustice in black churches. Nevertheless, I'm trying to articulate how more equitable conceptions of shared authority in religious communities might alleviate these problems.

Now, let me address your point about North American and African contexts. There, of course, are differences. I'm not arguing that these contexts are identical. The long history of scholarship on African cultural retentions in diasporic contexts is, in my understanding, based on the delicate balance between similarities and differences. In other words, there are discernible concepts and practices rooted in continental African cultures that are retained and yet transformed as they emerge in African diasporic contexts such as the United States.

One of my former students from Nigeria taught me that in many African contexts the authority of the preacher is *not* carte blanche. There are important checks and balances provided by the congregation and/or community. This student informed us one day, in my introduction to preaching course, about African ecclesial practices that underscore the community's ethical responsibility to ensure communal well-being in religious practices such as preaching.

PINN: The African preacher in what context? Which denomination? There's nuance here that should be recognized.

BRAXTON: If memory serves me well, this story emerges from a Nigerian Methodist context. This student said that some African congregations are empowered to play an active role if the congregation senses that a preacher is struggling in the sermon that day. If the sermon is not edifying the community or is veering significantly from beneficial discourse, a community intervention would be common and even expected. While acknowledging respect and appreciation for the preacher, congregants would, nonetheless, interrupt the sermon and politely ask the preacher to leave the pulpit with these words: "Please come down, Preacher. Today, you do not have the word."

This story reminds us that the preacher is not the sole arbiter of what is true and beneficial for the community; neither is the community a passive recipient, devoid of ethical obligation to assert its authority when the best interests of the community are not being served. Those words—"Please come down, Preacher. Today, you do not have the word"—are not meant as a lasting rebuke of the preacher. The preacher would be invited to speak again, and on the next occasion, the preacher, hopefully, would be a more faithful conduit of communal edification. Those words instead are a vivid reminder of the need to constantly discern how religious actors and actions are functioning for the good or ill of the community.

PINN: I'm not certain how this collective response and correction challenge the authority and special status of the preacher. The preacher is still set apart to give the sermon. In your example, the community offers a critique, but critique doesn't constitute the dismantling of authority and assumed special knowledge. Think in terms of the critique of an academic monograph. Anyone can provide a review or critique, but that doesn't negate the assumed expertise (and special status) of the scholar who wrote the text. The hierarchical arrangement is able to accommodate input.

BRAXTON: We often talk about hierarchy as if it is inherently inferior, and egalitarianism as if it is inherently superior. As you noted above, nuance and context matter here.

PINN: You'd need to provide me with examples of hierarchies that avoid these dilemmas. By its very nature, hierarchy privileges and disadvantages. Hierarchy is vertical in nature.

BRAXTON: Your comment about "the dismantling of authority" is broad-brush, theoretical language. This language doesn't pay enough attention to examples of shared authority and power in many religious traditions. I've presented examples earlier concerning mutual accountability in some religious communities I know.

In appropriate contexts, I'm a proponent of "functional hierarchy," even as I eschew "essential hierarchy." For instance, during my grueling but ultimately successful sojourn through skin cancer a decade ago, I benefited from functional hierarchy. I submitted to the care of a skilled oncologist and an accomplished plastic surgeon at Northwestern Memorial Hospital in Chicago and the professional medical team supporting them. The doctors had authority and special knowledge that contributed to my well-being. They were not "essentially" different or better than me in any existential way. They, however, had acquired through learning and practice highly specialized knowledge and skills, which they utilized to help me move from disease to wellness.

I also was a cocreator of my wellness in that I was an informed patient throughout the process. I consulted with medical experts in my network and read medical literature on treatments for my type of skin cancer. Insights gained from these outside sources led to key suggestions that aided my doctors, even amid their considerable expertise.

Similar things are at work in ministry. Ministers are not "essentially" different from others in the community, but through learning and practice, they can facilitate spiritual wellness. Ministers, who are doctors of the spirit, also benefit from congregants who are informed "patients," ever willing to secure a second and even a third opinion.

PINN: I have to resist you labeling my argument "theoretical." Although you're not dismissing my argument, you're categorizing it in a way that diminishes its reach and impact. Dismantling authority isn't a theoretical consideration any more than your "functional hierarchy" is merely theoretical. It's an idea brought into the world of practice. So, it's a matter of praxis. I'll need to see models of this shared authority that aren't victimized by social codes that disadvantage certain populations by practice or omission.

Also, I'd argue that the authority of doctors and ministers isn't the same. The authority of the doctor is guarded by scientific method and verifiability. This is not the case for ministry and the authority of the minister. And, more to your last point, ministers are essentially different. Everything about the practice and performance of ministry speaks to distinction. Martin Luther's call for a greater equity in terms of the practice and performance of faith didn't dismantle the ministerial rank.

With all due respect, your metaphor misconstrues the comparison between medical doctors and ministers. The doctor's commitment to health and well-being is monitored and can be challenged. For example, the doctor's professionalism is conditioned through the reality of malpractice insurance, which speaks to the ability to challenge with consequences. Where's the equivalent for the minister? The doctor is required to have a certain level of training and ongoing certification. What is the equivalent for the minister?

BRAXTON: With all due respect right back at you, you seem determined to define ministry by its worst characteristics. Thus, your depictions sometimes feel more like a "grievance" than an evenhanded evaluation acknowledging both strengths and weaknesses. In my earlier comments, I offered real-world vignettes exemplifying checks and balances on the exercise of authority in congregational settings.

Furthermore, as a profession supported by thousands of years of practice, ministry possesses various formal and informal professional development opportunities, including divinity school and seminary curricula, training institutes and conferences, and internships and apprenticeships. For example, Martha Simmons, a trailblazing black homiletician and minister, created an innovative national mentoring project—Women of Color in Ministry—that provides robust opportunities for women to expand their networks and hone their professional skills in ministry.

In this part of our dialogue, I feel no need to "defend" the profession of ministry. Rather, I am trying to advance a textured discussion of how I understand religion and certain religious practices such as preaching. In that regard, the feminist biblical scholar Elisabeth Schüssler Fiorenza has shaped my thinking about the ethical import of religion in general and Christian rhetoric in particular. Like Schüssler Fiorenza, I am committed to rhetorical practices and communal configurations that support radical democracy, emphasize egalitarianism, valorize different identities and perspectives, and legitimize the sharing of power. Schüssler Fiorenza argues that for those of us who believe in God the key question is: Do our conceptions of God promote liberation and well-being for as many people as possible?

So, whether talking about preaching or my broader conception of religion, I am keenly interested in communal practices that foster democracy and justice. Religion, for me, involves cultural (and often communal) *practices* as much as it involves beliefs. These practices have the potential to foster ethical awareness and accountability. Undoubtedly, communal religious practices can become authoritarian, exclusionary, and harmful. But communal religious practices, like other cultural practices, can sponsor noble and abiding ethical commitments in both individuals and groups.

PINN: I wonder, however: Does religion constitute a cultural force that offers something that can be duplicated—without some of the liabilities—by other cultural institutions and practices? Is there a reason we maintain religion, other than habit of practice and tradition?

BRAXTON: The quest to find meaning and purpose and experience the joys and responsibilities of community can occur in many cultural institutions and practices. Religious communities have no copyright on this. Yet I suspect that other cultural institutions and practices—and any new ones we create— would still struggle with some of the difficulties that attend religion. In other words, are you suggesting that religion is inherently more prone to misuse than other cultural practices? If that's your argument, what's your evidence?

PINN: I hear you; let me clarify my point. There is a significant difference between the ability to challenge and correct organizations that are horizontally oriented and organizations, like the church, which are vertically oriented. The rules of engagement and the framing of knowledge for the two are different—the former is more susceptible to reason and logic while the latter claims an authority and knowledge that supersede human logic. Horizontally oriented organizations operate on human reason, logic, and law. Organizations like the church operate on faith in a transcendental "Grand Unity," which is another way of naming an overarching meaning behind our relationship to and life within the world; some might call it God and the workings of God.

BRAXTON: Religion is not inherently superior to other cultural arrangements and practices for addressing existential issues. Neither is religion any more prone to misuse and abuse than other cultural practices.

PINN: No, it's not more prone to misuse. However, my concern is with the ability to correct for this misuse.

BRAXTON: In my earlier examples, I referenced mechanisms for mutual accountability to curb the misuse of power. As you mentioned, many cultures maintain religious practices due to habit and tradition. In some instances, the continuity is important for transmitting healthy values upon which societies are maintained. On other occasions, those habitual traditions stifle innovation and freethinking and vilify diversity in extremely destructive ways.

Furthermore, many cultures continue to embrace religious traditions because these traditions codify the strivings of countless generations, including our present generation, to address quintessential human questions such as:

1. Who are we?
2. What does it mean to be human?
3. Why are we here?
4. To whom are we accountable?
5. What practices, values, and goals should guide our individual and communal existence?
6. Where, if anywhere, are we going?
7. Does life have lasting, penultimate, or even ultimate meanings?

PINN: Yes, I agree those are the questions religion seeks to answer. For some years, I've labeled this the "quest for complex subjectivity." However, there's little reason to assume this quest is always productive or positive. We should pay attention to scholars of religion, like Robert Orsi, who encourage us to understand the ways that religion can produce harm and destruction. For example, the black church's productive work on racism did little to dismantle its long and explicit history of homophobia.

BRAXTON: Yes, we must consider religion's destructive capacity. The appalling promotion of homophobia by black churches is an example of that destructive energy.

I am also heartened by how some black Christian theologians are using the tools of religion to dismantle homophobia. More than twenty years ago, in her groundbreaking work *Sexuality and the Black Church*, the theologian Kelly Brown Douglas asserted that homophobia—not homosexuality—is the "sin" that should concern black churches. Homophobia is sinful because it separates people from one another, and it frustrates a sense of wholeness by leading people to believe that LGBTQ people are a lesser part of the beautifully diverse human family God has created.

Let me comment further on the creative and positive aspects of religion. Religion, at its best, unleashes creative energy by encouraging us to connect multiple ways of being, knowing, and doing, including, but not limited to, the affective, the cognitive, the intuitive, the aesthetic, and the kinesthetic. Contrary to market-based approaches that often reduce human worth to quantitative measures, religion intentionally explores the qualitative, intangible dimensions of human life. In the quest to wrestle with moral quandaries and promulgate wisdom and beauty, religion understands that life is not a reproducible spreadsheet but an irreducible kaleidoscope.

PINN: I appreciate and understand what you're saying, but I'm still left wondering what you mean by religion. Is it synonymous with the Christian faith? Is it sui generis? What exactly is this religion preached by the preacher?

BRAXTON: My understanding of religion is not limited to Christianity or any theistic tradition. Neither is religion sui generis with respect to other cultural practices. Religious sensibilities emerge as much, if not more, through the ceremonies people enact, the artifacts they create, and the informal stories they tell beyond the confines of their formal religious spaces and structures. By focusing keen attention on religious practices, I'm interested in a term you referenced earlier, namely praxis.

By praxis, I mean the cyclical and mutually beneficial relationship between practices and theories. Since praxis undergirds my approach to religion, I neither devalue practice as inferior to theory nor dismiss theory as irrelevant to practice. Various religious practices, whether theistic or nontheistic, can purvey moral wisdom and intellectual insights and serve as hospitable spaces for individual and communal enhancement. For example, the foodways of religious communities (e.g., how religious people prepare common and/or ritual meals) and the aesthetic practices of religious communities (e.g., how religious people work with textiles, precious metals, stones, and other materials to adorn their bodies and their ritual objects) can reveal more about sacred meaning than the formal interpretation of scriptures and traditions can elucidate.

PINN: I wouldn't disagree with what you're saying. However, you're suggesting a communal dimension to religiosity—to the meaning of religion—that isn't necessary from my perspective. If we think about religion as a quest for complex subjectivity, it can take place within the context of community, but this isn't a requirement.

BRAXTON: You rightly detect the communal emphasis in my understanding of religion. Yet I'm *not* excluding the individual dimensions of religion. A considerable amount of my religious practice has occurred in the beauty of solitude. On many mornings, while the moon is dancing and the sun still sleeping, I have knelt at a personal altar at home, lit candles, meditated, prayed, and read scriptures and devotional writings in the attempt to connect with sacred energy within and beyond me.

I also approach my scholarly vocation as a form of religious practice. As we both know, scholarly activities such as reading and writing involve serial and protracted solitude. The homiletician Fred Craddock suggests that it's a blessing when one's desk becomes one's altar. My attempts at intellectually honest and clear writing have made me more of a priest perhaps than my performance of traditional religious rituals such as weddings, baby dedications, and funerals.

PINN: This is intriguing; please say a little more on this point.

BRAXTON: I reference again the journey of writing my doctoral dissertation. My dissertation advisor and beloved mentor, Carl Holladay, is an extraordinary and compassionate teacher, unrelenting in his commitment to precision and excellence. He expects these things of himself and of his students. He insisted that I write one chapter of my New Testament dissertation three times until I got it right.

The revision process was arduous, especially since the chapter was about fifty pages long. When I eventually got it right, he proudly exclaimed, "This is what it means to be a doctor of the scriptures. You are entering a venerable tradition of scholarly interpreters of these invaluable texts, and the details of your interpretations matter a great deal." Across many days and years at my desk by myself, I have learned how to slow down and handle "holy things" with care and appreciation. So, when performing holy work at altars—whether officiating a wedding in a church sanctuary or writing a book in my study at home—I approach the task with priestly precision and reverence.

Engaging and contributing to the ever-expanding body of writing and knowledge are holy tasks indeed. In her marvelous essay "Writing as a Spiritual Discipline," the theologian Stephanie Paulsell insists that impactful writing arises from a spirit of generosity and the desire to inform and enrich people.

So, I value the individual dimensions of religion. Yet it's important to emphasize the communal aspects and the embodied practices of some religions. A communal emphasis is a corrective to the tendency to define religion too narrowly as a matter of individual belief and practice, with little or no reference to how these beliefs and practices influence other people.

PINN: I'm not certain religion—as we've both defined it—is synonymous with this process of intellectual inquiry. This may be a stretch. There is a shared wrestling with deep inquiry, but these modes of inquiry have different obligations and are "charged" in different ways. The audiences and the long-term ramifications of "success" aren't the same. Religion claims metaphysical concerns that aren't present (certainly not in the same way) in academic investigation. Religion claims to be explicitly subjective in its work. Scholarship aims for "objectivity" and analyses that extend beyond the author (even though the claim of objectivity is false).

BRAXTON: Permit me to respond first to your critique about the intertwining of intellectual inquiry and religion. I'll then return to my argument about religion's communal dimensions.

Across the millennia, many scholars and artists have cited religion as the inspiration for, or the context of, their scholarly or artistic productivity. So, I wonder if my parallelism here is as much of a "stretch" as you suggest. The metaphysical concerns animating the work of some scholars and artists serve as a catalyst for, not prohibition to, intellectual rigor and artistic excellence.

Even your terms for religion such as "complex subjectivity" and "field of exchange" accommodate the parallels that I'm drawing. Why should religious people not be allowed to attach religious or metaphysical significance to their scholarship or art, especially if these scholars and artists adhere to canons of excellence determined by each intellectual discipline or artistic pursuit? The subjectivity of religious and scholarly endeavors (at least within the broad field of the humanities) opens space for a poetic and playful comparison between these endeavors.

Let me now return to my comments about the communal and public dimensions of religion. Depictions of religion's public role in the United States are often truncated to how "authorized" male religious leaders interpret sacred texts and traditions, frequently to the exclusion and detriment of females and gender nonconforming people. So, I'm interested in amplifying communal religious spaces where female agency and nonbinary gender perspectives are determinative and valuable.

For instance, when examining the religious practices of Native Americans, the cultural studies scholar Andrea Smith reminds us that Native American culture is rooted in orality, like African American culture. Storytelling is a vitally important action in these cultures. The stories recounted in venerated religious texts and traditions are not the only repositories of religious insights. Sacred stories exist beyond temples and altars. Sacred stories are also created and transmitted, for example, as religious women braid their daughters' hair in living rooms in the morning and organize political rallies on street corners in the evening.

PINN: I want to exercise caution here in that there are distinctions to be made. For instance, the scholar of religion Tink Tinker suggests that the terms of religion and theology do not operate in Native American contexts as they do for Europeans. How does your argument account for these distinctions?

BRAXTON: It's important to honor the distinctions that reflect diverse cultural identities and worldviews as well as different understandings of community boundaries, cosmology, epistemology, and rituals. Therefore, I mentioned earlier in our discussion religious leaders, the congregation/community, diverse ritual expressions that involve stories, myths, and symbols, and the relationship between the community and the wider culture. These are indicative, not exhaustive, placeholders for the manifold actors and factors that often constitute religious traditions. Yet the distinctive ways that each religious tradition emphasizes, minimizes, or improvises on these and other factors is what makes the study and embrace of religious pluralism so powerful and important.

PINN: I'm not certain this constitutes religious pluralism, which involves equity concerning religious experiences and an awareness of competition and conflict among traditions. I'm not sensing this in your discussion.

BRAXTON: My understanding of religious pluralism is committed to equity. An equitable approach makes room for competition and conflict that arise through these different religious traditions. My sense of equity also highlights another "c" word that does not receive enough emphasis, namely "curiosity." At The Open Church of Maryland, where I serve as the founding senior pastor, we enthusiastically embrace religious pluralism in the name of intellectual and moral curiosity. The question we often ask is: What will we not know or value if we do not listen to and learn from religious, spiritual, and ethical traditions beyond our own?

Without an embrace of pluralism, approaches to religion can quickly become an exercise in "holy hubris"—a self-righteous certainty about what religion means that ignores one's limited scope. Pluralism, according to the homiletician Joseph Webb, is a liberating call to uncertainty, which entails an awareness of the limited nature of our perspectives.

Truth held in a *vise grip* often leads to the *vice* of arrogance. Arrogant religion tends to be extremely dangerous. On the contrary, by *opening* our hands and hearts, we make it possible to grasp, and be grasped by, larger truths—truths in our own traditions and truths that emanate from other traditions.

PINN: I agree about the potential pitfalls you highlight, but I'm not certain pluralism is the proper framing. That framing doesn't adequately neutralize the tendency to normalize a particular tradition as the hermeneutical lens. One can still center Christianity and claim pluralism. The study of religion requires a framework that more fully decenters the normativity of any given tradition. However, this isn't typically done, and there is often resistance when it occurs.

Think, for example, in terms of black religious studies, which is often reduced to black church studies. Pluralism is often shrunk to mean more shades of the same. We need frameworks that more adequately center the existence of competing and contradictory structures of thought and practice. This requires a vocabulary and grammar that aren't drawn so heavily from any one tradition. We have yet to create such a language and its rules.

BRAXTON: Sign me up, Tony, for the project of decentering "the normativity of any given tradition." I trust that our probing dialogue will aid that project in some small way.

Let me say a bit more about how I understand religion. To employ language from the womanist scholar Stacey Floyd-Thomas, religion, for me, is not a "neck-up (i.e., disembodied)" or "ivory tower (i.e., elitist)" enterprise. Religion is about the folk, not just what the folk believe, but also how the folk engage in practices to create what is good, beautiful, and true. These practices vary widely and include preaching in pulpits, community-building efforts around dinner tables, and social activism on street corners, to name but a few.

PINN: Your reference to Stacey Floyd-Thomas's description tells me where you think religion "lives," but it doesn't tell me what you think religion is. Although, for example, you mention Native American and nontheistic patterns, you seem to make certain conceptual assumptions concerning religion, its location, and its intent. I appreciate your insights about religion perpetuating both good and harm, but I'm left wondering what you mean by religion.

BRAXTON: I'm puzzled why you remain unclear about my conception of religion. We have somewhat similar understandings of religion, but we use different language to define it. I understand your term for religion—"complex subjectivity"—and what you convey by it. Yet the term can lend itself to abstractions that diminish the flesh-and-blood vitality that makes religion so fascinating and complex.

PINN: Yes, the quest for complex subjectivity is an abstraction and involves theorization. It attempts to capture a general impulse and framing. Yet it doesn't diminish the "fleshy" nature of religion; it seeks to understand what undergirds that "fleshy" dimension.

BRAXTON: I'm as interested as you are in "complex subjectivity" and the diverse ways that people seek meaning and address existential dilemmas. Yet as a practitioner and scholar of religious practices, I situate this "complex subjectivity" in deeds and rituals.

PINN: This isn't a point of disagreement. Religion as a quest for complex subjectivity is an effort to theorize—to get behind the "deeds and rituals" that interest you. However, the quest for complex subjectivity can't be reduced to complex subjectivity as if this subjectivity is achieved.

The "quest for" is vital. That's my point; religion involves an effort not a conclusion. This is where we might disagree. You're thinking about what religion achieves, and I'm thinking about what religion aims for (but misses). We're using the same language, perhaps, but we seem to mean something different by it.

BRAXTON: I appreciate the attempt to delineate our differences. Yet you may have somewhat misconstrued my position. My understanding of religion also makes room for mystery, the ineffable, the unknowable, error, and incompletion. In the words of the Apostle Paul, that consequential first century theist who wrestled in 1 Corinthians 13 with the nature of love, "we see through a glass, darkly." Irrespective of the presence or absence of God(s) in our respective worldviews, our perception of reality remains limited and is always subject to enhancement and correction.

Although I am deeply invested in the positive possibilities of religion, I am fully aware of religion's considerable capacity to inflict harm. From the slave castles in Ghana that held tortured Africans in the eighteenth century to Robben Island in South Africa, which imprisoned twentieth-century anti-apartheid freedom fighters, to the fundamentalist Christian pulpits in the twenty-first century that oppress women and vilify LGBTQ people, religion has played—and continues to play—a horrible role in genocide and the mistreatment of diverse groups of people.

Across history and around the world, women have often experienced most acutely the despair and destruction that religion can inflict. In many conversations with Martha Simmons, for example, she has deepened my understanding of how women have been omitted from history and depicted as irrelevant and dispensable.

Considering this genocidal impulse, which occurs especially against women, scholars such as Martha Simmons and Mercy Oduyoye in Ghana have prioritized for me this question: Does religion make women's lives better or worse? As the son of a black woman, the husband of a black woman, and the father of a black woman (all three of whom have religious sensibilities), this question for me is not a matter of abstract speculation but a flesh-and-blood invitation to honestly assess both the positivity and pathology that religion can foster.

PINN: This important question persists, but I wonder about an answer that maintains a deep and abiding regard for the harm done and those to whom it is done.

BRAXTON: In a world pulsating with cultural diversity, we must bear in mind that religion has both mediated grace and motivated genocide. Approaches to religion that fail to address the oppressive impulses sponsored by, and even contained in, religion will be whitewashed tombs—antiseptic exteriors masking death and corruption below. On the other hand, by honestly addressing and nullifying these oppressive impulses, religious communities can animate the death-defeating power of liberating love and holy hope that are central concerns in many religious traditions.

PINN: This begs the question: What suggests that the benefits of religion outweigh its liabilities? Does the harm done indicate an intrinsic quality to religion that will already and always point toward harm—toward the demonizing of difference and the theological justification for so doing?

BRAXTON: As noted earlier, I don't believe that religion is unique in terms of the good that it can do nor the harm that it can inflict. You queried earlier whether I think religion is sui generis, but it appears at times that you are making that claim. You seem to suggest that religion needs to be "set apart" from other cultural practices because it inherently has more potential to do harm than other practices. I'm not convinced of that claim. Any cultural practice, under the weight of arrogance and xenophobia, can become a weapon of mass destruction.

PINN: I disagree. I'm not understanding religion as a "thing" but rather the opposite. Doctrines, creeds, rituals, and structures aren't religion. They are the historical manifestation of a particular impulse. Religion is that under-lying impulse—that quest. It isn't a "thing"—it's a quest.

Thus, I'm hard-pressed to understand how I'm suggesting religion is sui generis. For the sake of argument, if I wanted it set apart, that wouldn't make it sui generis. Rather, it would make it marginalized, restricted, or stigma-tized. Religion can harm (as can other cultural structures of engagement). It isn't inherently "good" or "bad." My concern is that theistic expressions of the religious make transhistorical claims and advocate for epistemological uniqueness that hampers critique and correction.

BRAXTON: This clarification is helpful. I misconstrued some of your earlier comments and thought you might be singling out religion as inherently more destructive than other cultural practices.

PINN: Thank you. That may be the argument of the "new atheism," but it isn't my argument. For me, religion is simply one structuring of meaning that has the potential to expose us to (and justify) destructive patterns of thought and behavior. But, again, it's not the only one.

BRAXTON: Is the limiting of critique and correction inherently a by-product of theistic religions, or is it a by-product of fundamentalism? By fundamentalism, I mean an overall approach to reality that transforms culturally conditioned criteria for truth and relevance into universal criteria. Furthermore, fundamentalism vigorously—sometimes violently—compels acceptance of those criteria and demonizes diversity. There are ways of adhering to theism, atheism, and/or humanism that do not involve fundamentalism.

Fundamentalism—whether expressed through science, philosophy, or religion—hampers the critique and correction which we both believe are important for moving communities toward justice and flourishing. For instance, white supremacy has functioned as a type of fundamentalism in the United States for centuries. Various theists—who believed that humanity's connectedness under the parentage of God disallowed one group to dominate other groups—offered important critiques of America's social and political fundamentalism. So, extremism and absolutism, not theism per se, are often what prevent debate, constructive dissent, and the healthy embrace of diversity.

PINN: I don't think we can restrict this to fundamentalism. That is much too easy and too narrow. The issue is larger than that. To be free of fundamentalism—whatever we mean by that—isn't to be free of this dilemma and danger. It simply means a different ideological expression of the same danger.

You mention white supremacy, but let's add to that its inner logic of white privilege—neither of which is demolished by wiping out fundamentalism. I would also raise questions concerning your projection of theism and its egalitarian impulse. We have so many examples of nonfundamentalist theism that do the opposite—that provide a more liberal (even progressive) framing of a similar disregard. I don't see a way to free theism from such a challenge. For me, it always remains suspect.

WHAT ABOUT BLACK "NONES"?

Tony,

Amid the madness we witnessed this week, I hope you are well. The events of this week—from Warnock's election to the Capitol insurrection—will be grist for our mill as we write. On January 6, colleagues and I spent the day planning how our school would celebrate Martin Luther King Jr. Day—an annual holiday commemorating the US's arduous, ongoing voyage toward democracy and inclusive justice. For years to come, January 6 will now be a grim annual reminder that the headwinds of hate and pathological patriotism have always threatened to steer the ship of state severely off course, if not completely wreck it.

Best,
Brad

> Hi Brad—
>
> Another day during COVID finds me taking advantage of the small bit of comfort that comes from sitting at my desk—writing and avoiding for a brief time the news of more death and political hatred. These are dangerous times—but with some moments of possibility, like the election of Warnock. One of the high points for me is this exchange with you.
>
> Cheers,
> Tony

■   ■   ■

BRAD R. BRAXTON: I approach the topic of black "nones" with appreciation and curiosity. Before going further, it might be useful to discuss who we are talking about when we use the term.

ANTHONY B. PINN: The term includes any population not easily absorbed into existing religious frameworks. But there has been limited attention to diversity and distinctive opinions and orientations among "nones."

BRAXTON: As I understand it, "nones" has become shorthand for a large, diverse group of religiously unaffiliated people in the United States and around the world. Included in this umbrella term are people who are ada-mantly opposed to religion and consider it to be a categorically misleading or false phenomenon. People in this category might agree with the philosopher Karl Marx when he referred to religion as the "opium of the people." In other words, religion is a "drug" that distracts people from addressing the real sources of, and solutions to, their unhappiness.

The "nones" also contain people who remain open to religion and/or spirituality broadly defined. Yet these people are disconnected from religious communities for many reasons, not the least of which are the harm and division often perpetuated in the name of religion. People who embrace a growing sense of secularity are another vital component of the "nones." Does my characterization of "nones" resonate with you? I welcome your clarifications and corrections now and as our dialogue proceeds.

PINN: There is much in what you say that rings true for me. Like you, I think the "nones" include a range of perspectives, but they typically share a suspicion, if not rejection, of traditional, institutionalized religiosity.

Additionally, "nones" maintain moral and ethical commitments to jus-tice. However, they don't ground these commitments in transhistorical claims. They, instead, connect their justice commitments to a sense of well-being not mandated by divine figures but by material life and the human capacity for doing justice. Also, much of the attention concerning "nones" revolves around certain generations of white people and their move beyond the church. Conversations often neglect the growing number of black and brown people who claim no particular religious affiliation.

BRAXTON: Thank you for highlighting the growing number of black and brown "nones." By underscoring these groups, we add texture and complexity to the characterization of American religiosity. As you rightly suggest, media coverage and scholarly examination of religion in the United States often ignore the role that race/ethnicity has played, and continues to play, in creating nuances within and between cultural groups. For example, white (evangelical) Christianity is often assumed to be the default religious position and any "deviations" from that are considered relatively unimportant, or even suspect, by some segments of American society.

We saw a version of this in the historic runoff election that sent Raphael Warnock, a Christian pastor and scholar of religion, to the United States Senate as the first black United States senator from Georgia in 2021. His opponent (Kelly Loeffler) characterized Warnock's black liberation theology as "radical" or "deviant." Such mischaracterizations of black religiosity fail to acknowledge how large numbers of white people intertwined race and religion in "radical" or "deviant" ways to brutalize black people throughout American history. When defending their personhood against the onslaught of white supremacy, many black people intertwined race and religion as an instrument for self-expression and social liberation.

PINN: I agree with you. The misrepresentation of black religious thought here is similar to the attacks on Reverend Jeremiah Wright during Obama's campaign in 2008. However, I wonder about our push against black theology being called "radical." Isn't it? Wasn't the intent to produce theological reflection that challenged the assumptions of white supremacy as the religion of the United States? Doesn't this objective cut to the foundational nature of US life? Hence, isn't it radical? In terms of white supremacy, black theology by extension *is* deviant. So, we need nuance here.

Our rightful rejection of the critique offered by Warnock's opponent is not a rejection of the label "radical" or even "socialist." Weren't Reverdy C. Ransom (of the AME Church) and Ida B. Wells (a Baptist) radical? Ransom was even a self-identified socialist. Instead, we are rejecting the underlying normalization of whiteness and how whiteness seeks to protect itself by misusing the label *radical*. We give up too much if we spend time justifying ourselves and our radical thought in ways that allow whiteness and white privilege to remain the normative grammar and vocabulary of life.

BRAXTON: Dr. Pinn, you're doing some fine teaching and preaching here! What else can I say but "Amen!" The term "radical" is a most appropriate descriptor for the avant-garde work of ancestors such as Reverdy C. Ransom and Ida B. Wells, as well as the audacious aims of black theology.

I imagine that people in our respective circles have occasionally labeled some positions that you and I espouse as radical. While I will never even come close to making the pioneering contributions, or enduring the significant sacrifices, of the ancestors, I consider it a badge of honor when people label me as a radical. The term actually refers to the courage and curiosity to deviate from a status quo that often vilifies and victimizes so many people.

PINN: All I can offer is a secular "Amen!" LOL.

BRAXTON: Undoubtedly, some radical thoughts and actions are destructive and decimate life and positive possibilities. On the other hand, many radical thoughts and actions facilitate what the social ethicist Walter Fluker once described to me as "creative destruction." In other words, things sometimes need to be brought down before they can be built anew. Unfortunately, in our current political climate, dominant forces craftily use terms such as "radical" to avoid serious dialogue about the merits of cultural perspectives and public policies.

PINN: I agree with you: the rather casual use of the term "radical" has reduced its impact and significance.

BRAXTON: Many Christians, especially certain white evangelical Christians, have used the term "radical" as a weapon against black and brown people and organizations and initiatives that address racial injustice. These same Christians simultaneously endorse the *radical* inhumanity, for example, of the Trump administration's immigration policies that have caged Latinx children in the borderlands of our country and viciously separated families.

Furthermore, since we're writing this current exchange only a few days after the insurrection at the United States Capitol, we need to highlight the *radical* indecency of some conservative Christians during the Trump administration. These Christians enabled Trump prior to the insurrection, and they provided support—whether implicit or explicit—for the fiasco on January 6, 2021.

PINN: Rather than calling it "radical" indecency—although I get your meaning—I might simply say their radicalism was terrorism. I wouldn't want to lend any assumption that their terrorism was meant as sociopolitical transformation or an act meant to cut to the root of a problem. Those two positions—transformation and cutting down to the root of circumstances—involve a thoughtfulness or mindfulness that isn't present in conspiracy-theory-driven and hate-fueled Trumpism.

BRAXTON: Thanks for the important clarification. We must, indeed, call the January 2021 attack on the Capitol what it was—terrorism. Using the right terminology enables us to have more honest public conversations about our disparate approaches to terrorism based on the skin color, nationality, or religious identity of the terrorists. As we move past the twentieth anniversary of the 9/11 attacks on the United States, it remains to be seen if the United States has the political and moral wherewithal to vigilantly root out terrorism when the perpetrators are white people who read the Bible instead of brown people who read the Qur'an.

PINN: Good point! It also demonstrates how segments of the population are willing to destroy democracy and install in its place white supremacy in the guise of liberty denied. In this way, the Civil War isn't the last example of white supremacy as national infrastructure for politics.

BRAXTON: As I say often in my sermons and lectures, the term "conservative Christian" makes no sense to me. Radical moral and political impulses motivated Jesus and his teacher John the Baptizer. Their radicality was rooted in noble attempts to break the cycle of imperial violence. However, many of these white evangelical Christians seem willing to utilize violence to replace democracy with imperialism.

The emphasis on black and brown "nones" not only decenters whiteness, it also decenters Christianity in necessary ways. On those rare occasions when public conversations focus on the religiosity (or lack thereof) of people of color, there is again a working assumption that Christianity is the default position of these groups. As we know, the American religious landscape is much more diverse than this, especially among younger generations.

PINN: That's an excellent point! When the black and brown "nones" are recognized, it forces a more expansive sense of the competing ways that these communities have sought life meaning.

BRAXTON: During my service as the director of the Smithsonian's Center for the Study of African American Religious Life, our team examined the escalating religious diversity among black millennials, which includes a growing segment of black "nones." My colleague Teddy Reeves, a Christian minister and scholar in the millennial generation, is the creator and curator of "gOD-Talk: A Black Millennials and Faith Conversation."

This creative initiative explores how black millennials interact with religion, diverse communities, social media, and the environment. It also seeks to amplify the voices of leading black millennials, including activists, entertainers, entrepreneurs, athletes, scholars, religious leaders, and politicians. When naming the program, Teddy purposefully used a lower case "g" for the word "gOD" to symbolize how this millennial dialogue would transgress traditional understandings of what is sacred.

We launched the dialogues in Los Angeles in August 2018 and convened in several other cities, including Atlanta, Chicago, and Dallas. As you recall, Teddy invited you and me to join the "gOD-Talk" dialogue in Dallas in January 2020 as "village elders." In the Dallas dialogue and the other three dialogues I witnessed in Los Angeles, Atlanta, and Chicago, I was struck by the candor of the millennials' sometimes-scathing critiques of religion. These black millennials were also willing to remix and merge various religious, spiritual, and ethical traditions to build more inclusive and equitable communities.

PINN: I agree. Rather than the allegiance to "tradition" that often marks our generation, millennials are much more pragmatic and concerned with function: What does a religious system offer? Additionally, they are more willing to blend the sensibilities of traditions to develop approaches to life that reflect their particular needs.

BRAXTON: Let me now underscore why I appreciate the "nones" in general and black "nones" in particular. The "nones" have enlarged and enriched my moral and ethical frameworks and vocabulary. I was nurtured spiritually in a moderate, black evangelical Christian worldview that shaped my understanding of right and wrong, both in terms of personal conduct and social responsibility. Although that worldview facilitated my moral formation in important ways, it also foisted upon me a problematic dichotomy and a restrictive vocabulary.

In the black evangelical worldview of my upbringing, there existed two primary social groups, namely those who were "in the church" and those who were "in the world." When I was growing up, it was unbecoming and even "dangerous" to be labeled "worldly" because "worldly" thinking and behaviors were morally suspect and could cause one to miss "being saved" from sin and consequently experience future damnation. According to one mantra that I often heard in my formative years, "*Good* people don't go to heaven, only *saved* people do."

PINN: Interesting. That dichotomy also shaped many of my formative years. However, in reflection, it was a slippery distinction. "Being in the world" is more a mindset of opposition than any actual "geography." Wouldn't paying our bills, going to movies, listening to music, participating in the political process all involve being in the world and, to some degree, being guided by an embrace of the world?

"Being in the world" is a doctrinal-theological distinction that shifts and changes over time based on sociohistorical need. This distinction produced an ongoing anxiety, derived from the need to manage proper involvement over against improper involvement based on scripture and church doctrine. This damaged the joy of living, replacing it with a fear of hell.

BRAXTON: Even as an adolescent, I recall my discomfort when such simple binaries were tossed around. The statement "Good people don't go to heaven, only saved people do" seemed arrogant. Those uttering the statement, of course, typically assumed that they were "saved" and belonged to the crowd that was acceptable to God. Yet even as a young person, I was mindful that the Bible reserved some of its most intense critiques for persons exhibiting self-righteous behavior.

As I became increasingly aware of the practices and worldviews of the "nones," they revealed to me the narrowness of my ethical frameworks. Many "nones" are deeply concerned about personal and social responsibility, the eradication of injustice, and the well-being of the environment. As a result of the "nones," I began challenging some of the orthodoxies of my religious upbringing. If these "good people" who are trying to do "good things" on earth are not fit for heaven, well then maybe heaven is not as good a place as I once thought it to be.

PINN: I agree with you; the social justice concerns of "nones" recorded in quantitative studies and public engagement raise questions concerning where one finds, and becomes committed to, "righteous" moral and ethical frameworks. The "nones" significantly push against theistic concerns with the "after" life and instead give attention to the quality of "this" life. The "nones" are also contesting the markers of what it means to be "good" and what keeps us being "good." Furthermore, as you note, this raises questions concerning the nature and meaning of religiosity as a guiding orientation for "good" living.

The preoccupation with "heaven" and the "after" life is one of the more evident conceptual problems in theism (and some modes of Christian theism in particular) highlighted by the "nones." Similarly, the effort of many churches (across diverse ethnicities) to capture young people's attention (including "nones") also emphasizes some of the difficulties with church thinking and doing. For example, how do churches overcome their problematic thinking on sexuality? How do they move beyond a topic we have covered before—destructive hierarchies of authority and permission—to embrace the more egalitarian inclinations of the "nones"? What are churches (or Christianity in general) willing to give up in order to be "relevant"?

BRAXTON: Your comment about the "nones" and sexuality is pertinent. In preceding generations, two competing and problematic impulses have often defined many public conversations in the US concerning sexuality. One impulse is *sexual repression*—the relentless denial of sexual pleasure or blatantly ignoring sexuality in general. A second impulse is *sexual obsession*—the relentless (and often thoughtless) pursuit of sexual pleasure at all costs. Yet sexuality—one of the most mysterious, delicate, and powerful dimensions of human experience—deserves public conversations characterized by positivity, depth, and nuance.

PINN: I agree with you. Sexuality demands more serious attention within "religious" and "secular" circles. However, these tough conversations require us to develop first a different and healthier relationship to embodiment. In both religious and secular circles, we are suspicious of the body. This manifests itself in our grammar/vocabulary and practices of restriction or in our grammar/vocabulary of excess, to play off your language. Both entail an anxious engagement with embodiment.

The problematizing of embodiment for the religious and the secular differs. I'm thinking here of the philosopher Michel Foucault and what he says about the regulating of bodies. This has to do with the maintenance of the state through the molding and managing of embodiment. For the religious, let's say black Christians, for the sake of argument, the suspicion stems from flawed theology and a narrow reading of scripture.

BRAXTON: Younger "nones" as well as some younger religiously affiliated people are enhancing public conversations concerning sexuality by overtly connecting sexuality to moral/spiritual meaning. Through this connection, these groups are addressing the problematic impulses we are highlighting. Rather than repress or obsess about sexuality, these groups are encouraging us to situate sexuality in deeper intellectual and ethical frameworks.

In these frameworks, sexuality is more than biology; sexuality is also a matter of anthropology. In other words, our sexual identities and actions reveal distinctive aspects of what it means to be human. Sexuality can also be a matter of spirituality. In other words, our sexual identities and actions may define our quest to connect with sacred power inside us, between us, and perhaps beyond us.

PINN: This also includes a sense of sexuality as fluid.

BRAXTON: You're right. The "nones" of the millennial generation and Generation Z are publicly engaging a broad range of sexual topics. These groups are linking these topics to broader issues of religion, community formation, and social justice. These sexually related topics include but are not limited to: embodiment/body image, fluid and nonbinary gender and sexual identities, LGBTQ moral and civic equality, erotica, marriage/partnered relationships, reproductive rights, surrogacy, and sexualized trauma (e.g., the Me Too movement and the pedophilia crisis in religious communities).

PINN: We've seen some of this play out through Black Lives Matter—and its sense of justice.

BRAXTON: When connecting sexual topics to larger frameworks of meaning, these younger groups may appeal to traditional religious resources (e.g., religious texts and traditions). Yet to your earlier point, the "nones" are also boldly expanding their canon of authoritative resources (e.g., music, movies, literature, and social media influencers) that/who inform their ethical perspectives on embracing their bodies, and the bodies of others, in affirming ways. When sexuality is viewed in a positive manner, it promotes healthy dialogue that examines the broad range of experiences that define the human desire for connection and intimacy.

As you rightly suggest, some churches need to relinquish their rigid, puritanical perspectives on topics such as sexuality if they want to reclaim any relevance for a wide assortment of younger groups. These churches must understand that younger groups are not advocating for a "lawless" approach to, for example, sexuality, in which "anything goes." On the contrary, these groups are often engaging in principled discussions about sexual ethics that underscore that the "laws" about sexuality written by ancient biblical communities may not be the most relevant or effective contemporary guides for the "righteous" use of our bodies.

PINN: I find your use of two phrases intriguing: "'lawless' approach" and "anything goes." Isn't a "lawless" approach precisely what the "nones" intend? The removal of state regulation on women's bodies, for instance, and the "decriminalization" of modalities of sexuality and sexual expression that don't fit social norms might be examples of this. From the vantage point of state regulation and social normativity, this would seem like anything goes. And if the "nones" were to mean "anything goes," couldn't that simply entail a freedom on the part of consenting adults to express themselves in ways that bring and give pleasure? Would we necessarily have to reduce an "anything goes" conversation to modes of conduct such as pedophilia?

BRAXTON: I appreciate you excavating the deeper connotations of terms such as "lawless." For example, as an advocate of women's reproductive choices, I support the removal of state regulation on women's bodies, while also wishing for a world where there are fewer abortions. In other words, I wrestle with this question: How do we proceed with the complex moral and political calculus that eliminates or reduces certain legal regulations in the service of enhancing positive life circumstances of various groups?

PINN: We do this on one level by assuming people are equipped to determine what happens with their bodies. With the issue of a "pro-choice" stance, for example, we follow the lead of women in that conversation rather than having women's bodies monitored and controlled by policies generated through a masculine impulse.

BRAXTON: When people possess resources to enact positive outcomes for themselves and others, they generally pursue those positive outcomes. Some positive outcomes, in this instance, might include the expansion of economic opportunities and healthcare options for women, a decrease of unintended pregnancies, and enhanced investments in placing children who are in foster care systems in more permanent community/family structures that promote their long-term well-being. So, the lessening of "laws" should not be construed as an abandonment of serious moral reasoning about complicated issues concerning embodiment.

PINN: Agreed. It will also be helpful to limit how theological grammar and vocabulary and religious organizations guide these conversations. These are issues best addressed through a more "secular" or religiously "neutral" stance. Perhaps we could employ a grammar and vocabulary of moral and ethical obligation that is more expansive and devoid of a retributive impulse.

BRAXTON: You also mentioned pedophilia. This is a criminal and moral dilemma where an intensification of legal regulations may better serve the common good. Pedophilia is especially heinous because it results from a predatory imbalance of power, where adults violate children. So, there are times when the state's regulations serve to protect the innocent from perpetrators.

Yet the intensification of "legal" laws must also be accompanied by an intensification of our broader "moral" laws, whereby we as a society make the safety and well-being of children one of the greatest achievements of our civilization. We cannot simply seek to deter "criminality." We also must incentivize the highest manifestation of civility.

PINN: This must be parsed in terms of particular dimensions and dynamics of collective life—particular laws? Particular policies? Particular communities?

BRAXTON: Financial budgets are actually "moral spreadsheets." Our spending priorities typically reflect our highest values. If we really valued the physical and emotional well-being of children as much as we say, we would pay kindergarten teachers multimillion-dollar salaries instead of paying such salaries to professional athletes.

In earlier moments of my life, my goal might have been to "convert" the "nones" to my way of thinking. Now, ironically, I am grateful to the "nones" for how they have "converted" me from narrow ways of framing what it means to live an ethically committed and purposeful life.

PINN: I'm curious: What are some particular ways the "nones" have influenced and informed your theological thinking? What have you surrendered in light of their orientation? What have you altered in response?

BRAXTON: One example immediately comes to mind. The "nones" have prompted me to reevaluate the social and political significance of certain religious rituals. Rituals in Christianity such as holy communion can be so divisive and restrictive. These rituals allow access to some, while denying access to others. In a world where so many people struggle with hunger and food insecurity, it is problematic that some churches use a food ritual like holy communion to symbolically erect a dogmatic fence around resources, even symbolic resources.

PINN: That's an interesting point. I also wonder, however, about other implications of communion. Does communion's symbolism suggest yet another embrace of suffering as a sign of usefulness or purpose? Are there ways this ritual further damages the "sacred" nature of the body by reducing it to a certain type of utility? Isn't it possible that communion points to the limited value of the body, objectifying the body in a particular (theological) way?

BRAXTON: I agree with you to a point. There are certainly ways of viewing communion that devalue the body. When we consider Jesus's crucifixion as an "atonement for" or "cleansing of" our sins required by God, we can promote a "cult of sacrifice." This problematic theology makes the appeasement of a disembodied deity more important than our tangible efforts to affirm and preserve our bodies.

PINN: It's more than a "cult" since there aren't connotations of marginality associated with this sense of atonement. But I get your point.

BRAXTON: Yet communion can actually be a ritual that heightens the appreciation for embodiment. As a political ritual, communion, to me, is a serious, provocative invitation from Jesus, a revolutionary prophet, for his followers to earnestly consider what the fight for justice might require. Our bodies are valuable, and the pursuit of restorative justice is also valuable. Given the persistent nature of evil systems such as imperial governments, we, at times, might need to willingly risk our precious bodies for the sake of a precious freedom.

PINN: Does it depend on which Gospel account one privileges? Is Jesus always the revolutionary? Hence, is the consumption of his body always a sign of participation in progressive, socially and politically oriented transformation?

BRAXTON: You raise excellent questions here. The synoptic Gospels (Matthew, Mark, and Luke) characterize Jesus more as a social and religious revolutionary than the Gospel of John. So, I gravitate more to those three Gospels.

There is a crucial detail in one biblical story of Jesus's final meal with his followers that doesn't receive enough attention. As a child, I listened with rapt attention to my father as he presided every month at the communion table and recited Jesus's stunning declaration in Matthew 26:29: "I tell you, I will never again drink of this fruit of the vine until that day when I drink it new with you in my Father's kingdom."

Jesus acknowledged that hand-to-hand combat with empires could be deadly. Yet he anticipated a time of revolutionary newness where a different kind of meal would be served. Accordingly, it might be incorrect to call communion the "last supper," since Jesus believed that there would be another supper, a banquet in the future that would signal the triumph over injustice and domination.

So, I'm open to new kinds of mythmaking, storytelling, and ritualizing that can bring together the "nones" and religiously affiliated people. Yet I encourage Christians (and others who might be interested) to inquire if there are portals of possibility in certain existing rituals that might point us in promising directions, even as we attempt new forms of mythmaking.

PINN: I still wonder about the ability to create—or the need for—such a totalizing process of meaning making. What does such a push say about difference? Wouldn't it be enough to say that despite our theological differences we share a concern with struggle against injustice—and assume that struggle is our "common" ritual?

BRAXTON: The ultimate communion is a banquet where we "drink wine in a new way" (an image connoting joy, fellowship, and fullness). We don't have to wait around for some futuristic "heaven" to create and enjoy some of this newness.

What if we perpetually sent RSVPs to create new forms of "communion" and community? In these new formations, we, when appropriate, would lay our bodies on the line for justice with the hopes that we also can create more spaces for diverse bodies to "drink wine in a new way" together, undisturbed by divisive forces that seek to kill both our bodies and our spirits.

PINN: I hear you, but I can't get over the way the ritual of communion you seek to transform is still a marker of redemptive suffering. For me, this is an issue.

BRAXTON: Communion is also problematic for me when it is interpreted as a marker of "atonement" and "redemptive suffering." Yet considering our earlier discussion, I am a "radical" black theologian committed to progressive thought. So, a key theological task is the transformation of problems into positive possibilities.

In addition to other professional duties, I serve as the chief diversity, equity, and inclusion officer at St. Luke's School, a coeducational Episcopal independent school in New York City. The school is culturally and religiously diverse and deeply committed to diversity, equity, and inclusion. We have a considerable number of staff, students, and families who are religiously unaffiliated.

Since the school is Episcopal, the serving of holy communion/eucharist is a regular feature of one of the two weekly chapel services. In this religiously diverse context, I consistently encourage our school community to think about how this "food ritual" can be used to speak to the broader, perhaps shared, ethical concerns of a diverse constituency, rather than viewing it as a "sacrament" that reinscribes a Christocentric narrative.

PINN: Can communion really serve this larger purpose? And, although I get what you mean, wouldn't an effort to extend its meaning also entail an expansion of Christianity's role in the lives of those who make no claim to it? Can it really be said to speak to "shared ethical concerns" without running the risk of it becoming a normalized performance of a totalizing concern and identity? In order to get to your aim, couldn't we also simply say communion works for some, but it has no significance for others—and allow members of the community to opt out of that ritual? Is there some sort of agreement—or other condition—required in order to enroll or work there that makes presence during communion a requirement?

Perhaps instead, the people not interested in communion could involve themselves in other school-sponsored performances of community concern and relationship, other approaches to an appreciation for the liberating potential of embodiment. Couldn't they appreciate the Episcopal orientation of the school without a universalizing of that particular ritual? Aren't there other moral and ethical frameworks that could facilitate a sense of connection within the community?

BRAXTON: Tony, in this instance, you and I are in total agreement. When I started working at the school, I was surprised to discover that holy communion/eucharist was a prominent feature of one of the weekly chapel services. St. Luke's School does a marvelous job of fostering the intellectual and moral formation of children. Yet the universalizing of that particular Christian ritual is a concern for some staff, students, and families (including me).

The school and St. Luke in the Fields Church, which founded the school, are now independent entities. Yet these two institutions still coexist harmoniously in the same block in New York City's West Village. For a host

of complicated institutional and theological reasons, holy communion/
eucharist persists as a ritual in the school, even though some of us have ad-
vocated that it should be removed. Or, as you mentioned, at least a robust
set of options should be extended to community members to disrupt the
normative nature of Christian identity and practices.

Even as a senior administrator at the school, some things are beyond
my control. Thus, I use whatever occasions I can to intervene, and my in-
terventions are funded by my progressive theology and my solidarity with
the "nones."

PINN: What does this mean in terms of the interpretive tools we then use?
What do we privilege when making determinations concerning what stays
and what goes? And, because this sort of work will come with disagreement
and resistance, what is an acceptable level of discontent?

BRAXTON: In a recent chapel talk at the school, I suggested that "holy
communion" should not be something that we *take* (ingesting the elements
of bread and wine in a specific Christian ritual). On the contrary, "holy
communion" should be something that we *make* together as we seek to
foster inclusive communities where differences are celebrated. The word
for "communion" or "fellowship" in the Greek New Testament is *koinonia*.
So "nones" are inviting me to rethink, reformulate, and even relinquish
certain practices and perspectives in the hopes of sharing more koinonia
across diverse religious boundaries. I often ask myself these days: How do
we transform the Christian communion table into a radically inclusive
welcome table?

PINN: I appreciate your point, but the vocabulary used to express it is
limiting. For example, "more koinonia" would still suggest an expanding
framework tied to the linguistic expression of a particular community and
text—the apostolic church. Doesn't what you suggest also require a rethinking of the language we use to express these connections and boundary
crossings?

BRAXTON: I'm already doing what you're suggesting, namely rethinking
language. This rethinking process is in its preliminary stages and will need
to shed any baggage that weighs it down as the journey proceeds.

Etymologically, many terms that we might now associate with Christianity, such as "justice"/"righteousness" (*dikaiosune* in Greek) or "good news"/"gospel" (*euangelion* in Greek) predated Christianity. In some instances, these were terms that the Roman Empire used. Consequently, such terms carried oppressive overtones for those minoritized communities that the Romans oppressed, such as the African-Asiatic communities colonized by Rome in ancient Israel/Palestine. These ancient Jewish and Christian communities "recycled" and reimagined the meaning of these terms and used them afresh to construct anti-imperial ways of thinking and living.

A similar process can happen with "communion" or "fellowship" (*koinonia*). Attempts by first century Christians to infuse language with new meaning were not immune to hegemony, divisiveness, or failure. As diverse, twenty-first century groups containing theists and "nones" attempt our own linguistic reimagining, we also will meet with successes and failures. The process is asymptotic. Like a line moving infinitely closer to the curve but never touching it, we should edge ever closer to more inclusive ways of talking and creating community. Although we may never obtain our ultimate goal, we become better and stronger through the process.

PINN: Mindful of this, I have a question: What dimensions of our language—our modes of communication and the content of that communication—are we willing to surrender for the sake of a collective composed of conflicting values and moral claims?

BRAXTON: Your incisive question points to the complex calculus of give-and-take, of negotiation and adaptation, that is required when building genuinely inclusive communities.

In addition to appreciating how the "nones" are influencing my theological thinking, I'm also curious what they might teach us about the formation of more inclusive communities. As you know, I've helped to establish an inclusive congregation/community in Baltimore—The Open Church of Maryland. As a result of the COVID-19 pandemic, we moved all our worship services and congregational gatherings to an online format where we made considerable room for community dialogue. As people from various parts of the country have found The Open Church online, I'm struck by how important a sense of openness is to those who are connecting with us.

On one recent Sunday when we welcomed visitors during the online service, a visitor said she literally typed the words "open church" in her internet search, and our congregation popped up. The "nones" may be an important source of wisdom about what it means for us to create open communities, whether secular or religious, because now more than ever people are eagerly searching for open spaces and places that create a sense of belonging.

PINN: There's a problem here. Although I appreciate your effort to rethink community, it seems to me one of the lessons we've learned from the "nones" is a depreciation of formal gathering (e.g., church worship). They tend to think more expansively about gathering and ritual, and I'm not sure that it can (or should) be boiled down to transformed Sunday worship, even within radically rethought churches. Such a move might damage the "openness" and radical sense of community the "nones" suggest (if they don't advocate for this explicitly).

My fear is that such a move renders the understanding of the "nones" within traditional structuring of the religious, when their orientation is a push against that exact framing. They claim, in general, no particular religious affiliation, and I'm not certain how one captures that in church community and ritual.

BRAXTON: Let me be clear. My rethinking of community, as flawed and incomplete as it is, involves more than transforming the nature of, and rituals associated with, weekly gatherings (although that transformation is important). At the heart of my "open" theology are efforts to reconstrue how social power is understood and might be shared in more democratic ways.

The Open Church is more about radical democracy than even radical theology. The Open Church is an experiment in radical openness. Thus, with respect to The Open Church, the key word for me is "open," not "church." I frequently say to the supporters of The Open Church that we should soon move assertively to drop the term "church" from our name. In other words, as we pursue radically inclusive forms of community and the democratic sharing of power, the term "church" will increasingly become too restrictive a label to contain our expansive aims.

PINN: Wow! This is intriguing. Help me understand what you mean by "open" and how "democracy" functions in this context. Could you say a little more here?

BRAXTON: Openness involves a willingness to move beyond the "off-limits" signs of traditionalism and provincialism. The open mind and heart transcend preconceived cultural, religious, or political boundaries. Thus, people committed to a moral mandate of openness are driven by ethical earnestness and intellectual curiosity into previously unthinkable conversations about unconventional topics with seemingly unlikely conversations partners.

As we are moved beyond our comfort zones, we begin to realize that otherness—other perspectives, other practices, other people—should not be vilified. Others can instead be the *open* channels to a greater apprehension of what is good, beautiful, and sacred. Therefore, dialogue and inquiry are key methods at The Open Church.

PINN: This is really interesting! How does one set the ground rules for this type of engagement? Isn't it also possible, however, that being pushed beyond our comfort zones can also result in a backlash—an affirmation of narrow practices of thought?

BRAXTON: Healthy intercultural communities should constantly assess whether, and to what degree, they are fostering the habits of democracy. One of those habits is the constant effort to demystify how power works (e.g., who has it, for how long do they have it, what are the checks and balances on the exercising of it?).

For example, the financial dealings of any community can easily become a place where power dynamics are not as transparent and accountable as they should be. Thus, from the first moment that I received financial compensation from The Open Church, the amount of my annual compensation has always been public knowledge. Additionally, many new members of our community are stunned, in a good way, when they have attended our business meetings and witnessed how open and transparent we are about the fiscal matters of the community.

PINN: Fantastic! This is very unusual but inspired.

BRAXTON: As another pragmatic example, permit me to mention the bylaws of the community. When developing the governance rules, we inscribed democratic impulses into the document. The community's "Dream Keepers" (the board of directors) and I collaborated to create the bylaws, and the broader community affirmed them. Even unofficially renaming the board at The Open Church the "Dream Keepers" was an attempt to foster a broad, shared ownership of the community's well-being.

Neither the Dream Keepers nor I lead autocratically. We, along with the community, revere the dream of radical inclusion, and together we seek to put flesh and blood on that dream. Rather than narrowly characterizing democracy by the action of voting, our bylaws emphasize how practices of collaborative spiritual discernment—prayer, preaching/teaching, scripture study, fellowship, dialogue, consensus building, and receiving the counsel of experts and wise persons—foster dialogue, deliberation, and democracy.

I will quickly note three other things. First, while we have policies and procedures, we also highly value those relational activities and skills that allow discernment to occur (e.g., dialogue and consensus building). Second, rather than arrogating power to avoid democratic voting, the Dream Keepers and I seek to exercise our power derived from the community to bring issues back to the community for their consent or dissent. Third, an emphasis on these first two factors has enabled us to be a community that only has one major "vote" each year—the vote on how the fiscal resources of the community are budgeted and disbursed.

Furthermore, since we value youth input and involvement, young people have voice in all our meetings, and those who are sixteen and older have a vote. We figured if someone is old enough to accept the moral responsibility of driving a car, they should be more than capable of assisting us with how to use our financial resources in wise and efficient ways.

PINN: This is intriguing. What is the typical (and initial) response of folks coming to The Open Church from other congregations with a more rigid and hierarchical model of leadership? Has there been any pushback in terms of these practices? I see the positive development this entails, but is there a down-side? Is there room for atheism in The Open Church? How "open" is open?

BRAXTON: People are surprised and delighted by the openness of our prac-tices at The Open Church. During the community's ten-year history, we have received little, if any, pushback. Instead, we regularly receive positive feedback.

Let me say it plainly: *Open* for us means OPEN! When I wrote the vision statement more than ten years ago, I purposefully included the following line in anticipation that humanists and atheists would be an integral part of our community:

> [The Open Church] is a wide place where "Abraham's family"—Christians, Jews, and Muslims—can dialogue with Buddhists and Bahá'is and where Hindus can dialogue with Humanists.

So Tony, since there is plenty of room at The Open Church for humanists, what are you waiting for? The members of The Open Church eagerly anticipate your arrival. LOL. The front door is open. The back door is open. The windows are open. The ceiling is open. Our hearts and minds are open. Come in whenever you want, any way you want, and stay for as long as you want.

PINN: That's mighty open! Ha-ha!

BRAXTON: I want to comment briefly on your earlier point about the "nones" and formal religious gatherings. I wonder to what extent, if any, the COVID-19 pandemic transformed previous critiques of "formal gatherings" that both the "nones" and religiously affiliated people offered. In other words, the social distancing of the pandemic may have shown us how much we took for granted the power and importance of our formal and informal gatherings.

PINN: Good point.

BRAXTON: Let's return now to our fascinating musings on openness. As I say often to my pastoral colleagues, churches that remain "closed" in their theologies and principles will eventually close. One need only consider the dwindling influence of many churches in contemporary Europe. In their heyday, churches in Europe were so vital, and their leaders wielded great social influence. Now the public impact of some European churches and religious leaders are hardly perceptible.

PINN: I'm not certain this is a good example or something to which we should aspire. These churches you mention "in their heyday" also perpetuated great harm—restricting life and punishing those outside this framework. Tied to these churches is a damaging sense of orthodoxy that we should avoid. From the second century CE on, the struggle for "orthodoxy" and dominance by the apostolic church has resulted in great harm.

The "nones" offer a counter lesson. From my vantage point—and that of many "nones"—this decline in the "public impact" of churches and church leaders isn't to be lamented but celebrated. It has meant the potential for greater participation in the public arena and a more expansive sense of moral and ethical well-being.

BRAXTON: When musing about the public role of churches, whether in previous centuries or this one, I unequivocally critique all abuses of power and harmful orthodoxies. My point is that churches that widen the aperture of their theological approaches and ethical concerns may be able to engage in more expansive, constructive conversations in the public square.

In the United States, many mainline Christian denominations, such as the Episcopal Church, the Presbyterian Church (USA), and the United Methodist Church, are facing significant decline that is forcing them to consolidate or close many congregations. Other Christian communities, including certain black denominations and Pentecostal/charismatic denominations, remain numerically solid. Nevertheless, the integrity of their public presence is compromised by at least four stubborn factors: (1) the promotion of sexism; (2) the lack of social justice engagement; (3) the inhospitality, and even hostility, toward LGBTQ people; and (4) the reticence to embrace interreligious collaboration. These four factors, along with a growing perception of Christianity's social irrelevance, compel many people to opt out of religion altogether.

PINN: I want to challenge this characterization. It's misleading to suggest the "nones" are "nones" only as a matter of negation. Many of these "nones" have grown up in secular households, for example. Your statement suggests that if churches get themselves together the "nones" will join them.

I hear in that—and it makes me a bit uncomfortable—an assumed centering of church thought/practice that the "nones" push against. They aren't simply (or primarily) rejecting Christianity (as if it's the only religious orientation available to them). They're rejecting theism more generally and are embracing human accountability that is more expansive than the language of theism. The assumption that getting church "right" will create an influx of the "nones" misunderstands that population and its orientation.

BRAXTON: I'm not so focused on getting church "right." I'm focused on getting "community" right.

PINN: I wonder, in your context, what the difference between the two is—particularly in light of the innovative thinking of The Open Church?

BRAXTON: In some ways, "church" is still a meaningful part of my heritage, lexicon, and worldview. But neither the linguistic term "church" nor the sociological experience of "church" typically possesses the malleability to encompass the radical diversity that I champion. Admittedly, the term "community" is nondescript and unimaginative. Yet its vagueness can be a gift because it allows us to stretch and reconfigure the term in nontraditional ways, thereby creating more opportunities for engagement among people with different perspectives and practices.

I might invite The Open Church soon into a linguistic thought experiment. In our public communications, we often refer to ourselves by the initials TOC. I might ask the congregation to consider this proposal: Is it time for us to replace the word "Church" with the word "Community" in our name? For branding purposes, we would still be "TOC" of Maryland, but that would now stand for "The Open Community" of Maryland.

In this experiment, we would not be playing around with words. As you and I know, words and images possess great power to catalyze or curtail imagination. The goal would be to empower the congregation to assess whether we are living as fully as possible into our commitment to foster a sense of belonging that transgresses narrow boundaries.

PINN: This is interesting! But what criteria would be used to assess this "living as fully as possible into our commitment"? What would be an acceptable level of discontent with(in) the community?

BRAXTON: In The Open Church's logo, we symbolize the aspiration for a capacious community that transcends the restrictions often associated with "church." When creating the logo, we purposefully avoided traditional Christian iconography (e.g., crosses and sanctuaries). Instead, in the circular space of the capital "O" in the word "Open," our graphic artist created a picture of a beautiful, broad meadow.

Community, in my estimation, is akin to a broad meadow. I'm passionately committed to fostering broad, meadow-like spaces and experiences, where people can luxuriate in the diversity of what is cultivated, while also appreciating the commonalties within the shared landscape.

Furthermore, I'm not trying to offer a restrictive characterization of the "nones" defined by negation. Yet when engaging with some "nones," they have expressed appreciation for The Open Church's attempts to reimagine communal life. This reimagining makes room for a wide assortment of people, some of whom are oriented toward theism and some of whom are not.

Also, I realize that some "nones" are choosing more "secular" forms of fellowship and spiritual enrichment. With increasing regularity, I hear stories of people who now receive more spiritual nourishment from their Sunday brunch conversations in restaurants than in their Sunday liturgies and sermons in sanctuaries. People are flocking to restaurants to find food and fellowship and nourish the body and soul—because they often are unable to find substantive spiritual food in some traditional forms of religion.

PINN: Here's a point of strong disagreement between us. I think the "nones" point to the possibility of collective life beyond the reach of a particular religious orientation. This isn't simply a secularized mode of "worship." So, I don't see the decline of these churches as something to lament or a problem to fix. Instead, it's a positive, evolutionary development that allows for a reimagining of the public arena and the nature/meaning of community; this reimagining enables new ritualization of life and community, a new grammar of wonder, and an alternate politics of moral and ethical development.

Perhaps organizations like the church don't have the ability to meet the current need along the four issues you highlight. Therefore, my question is an uncomfortable but important one: Is it possible that churches have served their purpose, and we need to move beyond churches and develop new organizations for housing our profound questions concerning existence? As I noted earlier, the "nones" aren't simply reacting to the failure of churches. Their creativity isn't restricted to that, and many of them aren't recasting themselves against churches or other forms of theism.

BRAXTON: Your weighty question creates no discomfort in me whatsoever. I have grappled with versions of it for more than a decade. In a momentous phone conversation in 2008 with the radical Christian theologian Christopher Rowland, one of my beloved mentors, he insisted that churches, by and large, could no longer advance the revolutionary aims that animated Jesus's ministry. His audacious assertion has informed my approach to community building.

As committed as I am to The Open Church endeavor, I have always referred to it as an "experiment." By definition, experiments run the risk of failure. Churches that are oriented toward radical inclusion can play a meaningful role in promoting the open, progressive society you and I envision. Yet if the evidence of the experiment at The Open Church, for example, proves otherwise, I will gladly join you in the bold and necessary enterprise of "moving beyond churches."

Since I'm deeply invested in the formation of inclusive communities, I have much to learn from the "nones," and I'm eager to partner with them. In these perilous times—when life is constantly under assault from divisiveness, disease, and death—religiously affiliated and unaffiliated people need to unite, learn from, and support each another in the creation of inclusive and equitable communities. The ability to unite, amid principled differences of opinion and approach, may unleash fresh moral energy that the world sorely needs.

PINN: I agree with you concerning the need for conversation, collaboration, and mutual respect. However, what isn't clear to me is what Christians, and other religious communities, are willing to give up in order to prepare for the "creation of inclusive and equitable communities"?

BRAXTON: While I can't speak for other communities, I'm pleased to be in a religious community that is taking an inventory of what might need to be relinquished to form more inclusive and equitable communities. For instance, at The Open Church, we aren't creating a culture of indoctrination. Instead, we are establishing a culture of inquiry, where deep questions, not dogmatic answers, are the motivating energy.

PINN: This was apparent that Sunday I spent in conversation with The Open Church.

BRAXTON: It's kind of you to say this, Tony. Your visit with us at The Open Church was a watershed moment for us. As usual, your teaching that day was brilliant, provocative, and invitational. You invited us to think more broadly about the beliefs of others and to interrogate more deeply our own cherished beliefs. Members of the community talk often about how morally elevating it was to be in space where a humanist was challenging many long-standing Christians to go broader and deeper in their moral discernment.

I'm so pleased that you sensed our commitment to openness. This commitment may be one reason why a key leader at The Open Church—who is a queer, white agnostic/atheist—is a vital part of our community. Indeed, she is a member of our board of directors. She subscribes to few, if any, of the transcendental beliefs that certain members of the community profess. Yet the earnest and messy effort to create spaces where theists and atheists can cohere and conspire for goodness is especially appealing to her. The Open Church is trying to put flesh and blood on your earlier, very suggestive term—"a grammar of wonder."

PINN: Could you say a bit more here? For example, in light of the key leader you mention and the full range of religious orientations present, how would you describe The Open Church's theology? Or is theology no longer an adequate way to name the principles held as central to the church's self-understanding and presentation?

BRAXTON: "Theology" broadly defined remains a fitting term for many at The Open Church. The term is also operative for me. Yet I, perhaps more than others, am comfortable moving beyond the language of theology. Irrespective of whether and how we employ that term, people in our community have a vested interest in fostering a sense of newness, and there is an eagerness for capacious spaces to envision the "what if" of different ethical possibilities.

The social ethicist Emilie Townes insists that to be called "beloved" is to say an emphatic "Yes!" to God's "What if?" In other words, what might our communities look like if we genuinely believed that we are recipients of God's grace and love? The Open Church is attempting to speak that emphatic "yes" to God's or the universe's "what if" by proclaiming that each of us—all of us—have sacred worth. In my estimation, The Open Church is a "what if" community—a vibrant, diverse, daring group of people who are *open* to possibilities for partnership and power-sharing that we may never have imagined at first.

As you aptly call attention to what Christians must relinquish, I'm interested in hearing what you believe the "nones" must relinquish in the service of creating robust, reimagined communal spaces, where neither theistic nor secularistic dogmas rule.

PINN: Good point. Let me talk in terms of humanists and atheists. I think we humanists and atheists must give up a posture toward the world that is already and always confrontational. Working with theists will require engaging in exchange without assuming the need for defensiveness and apologetics. We also should push beyond critique of theism to a more complex understanding of theisms. We need to step away from the "new atheism" and its rather toxic—from my vantage point—engagement with culture and religion.

In short, humanists and atheists need to be more open to exchange in a way that seeks to understand and appreciate a range of perspectives, to approach theists by first working to appreciate what they believe theism offers them. This would entail moving away from a mission of de-conversion. In essence, we need to move beyond the wish of wiping out religion. That isn't possible nor is it desirable. We instead need to collectively work to reduce the harm nontheists do in the world and the harm theists do in the world.

BRAXTON: Wow! Your powerful words inspire my head and heart! It also would be fascinating for you to talk in more concrete terms about how you think the "nones" are creating and embodying "new ritualization of life and community, a new grammar of wonder, and an alternate politics of moral and ethical development."

PINN: I think this happens as "nones" seek to ritualize the ordinary activities and moments of life. For example, the way in which a walk in the park, a gathering with friends, an organized and peaceful protest all speak to the making of meaning. The grammar of wonder has to do with an appreciation for the diversity of mundane life as its vibrant element that calls us beyond ourselves. (Theists might call this the "sacred.")

Additionally, the respect for the environment and the materiality of the universe, which pulls us beyond ourselves and our limited take on community, speaks to a new ritualization of materiality that doesn't require tradition, god, or gods. This alternate politics of moral and ethical development is expressed in the inspired work to safeguard despised communities such as transgender communities, our elders, and so on.

Morality and ethics here aren't premised on particular sacred texts or a range of religious creeds culled from these texts but from the demands of justice: What practices and principles will help us be well and whole? I think a key example of all of what I've tried to name here is Black Lives Matter (as expressed in some of its early written documents). It's also what Ethical Culture and the Unitarian Universalists have tried to do but without the same level of public appeal and success. Houston Oasis—a community of nontheists (one of many Oasis groups)—tries to promote community based on this model. Although it's past its high point, Sunday Assembly also tried to forge community and a sense of morality and ethics along these lines.

BRAXTON: Thanks for sharing these marvelous examples. And, in support of your previous observation, it would be inspiring if more forums existed for diverse groups of "nones" and religious folks to listen to, and learn from, one another without any "conversion coercion" or fear of destructive conflict. So much positive heat and light can emerge when we earnestly explore commonalities, while also unapologetically confronting the creative conflicts that exist between us.

THEODICY (IS GOD GOOD?) AND ANTHROPODICY (ARE HUMANS GOOD?)

Brother Brad—

As soon as I finished up some administrative work—the never-ending emails—it was time to get back to our project. Attached you will find some opening words related to prompt three. I could have kept writing—there's so much to say—but I thought I better get the document to you and let the conversation begin!

Cheers,
Tony

> Tony,
>
> Thanks for sending this. Like you, I just waded through a barrage of emails so I could clear my mind to engage this tough topic. My favorite mug is filled with some freshly brewed coffee, and I'm settling in to see where the dialogue takes us this month. Intellectual and moral growth require our heads and hearts to stretch. Well, Brother Pinn, I'm growing for sure because our dialogue is s-t-r-e-t-c-h-i-n-g me!
>
> Best,
> Brad

■   ■   ■

ANTHONY B. PINN: So much of what we've discussed—particularly in light
of the ongoing disregard we encounter—raises the question of theodicy.
As you know, Brad, I've long been interested in the metaphysical quagmire
associated with this issue, as well as the existential paradoxes fostered by
attempts to answer the challenge. Simply put, it goes this way: What can
be said about God in light of human suffering in the world?

This question framed so much of my early development as a theologian.
In retrospect, it also defined much of my childhood response to church and
ministry, particularly concerning the conduct of black life faithfully amid
ongoing misery and black death. The question captured my attention during
my master of divinity program and became a concern for my required thesis.
Although my personal belief system changed, the question persisted for me
during my PhD work and was the topic for my dissertation and first book
(*Why, Lord? Suffering and Evil in Black Theology*).

As is common knowledge in our circles, Brad, the absurdity (I'm using
the term as Albert Camus uses it) of the question and the effort to answer
it informed my movement into black humanism. The late William R.
Jones tutored me, informally through attention to his work and formally
through conversation. He helped me give scholarly form to this shift in my
perspective—a perspective that shaped much of my writing and thinking
over the past thirty years.

Theodicy, for me, is tied to our conversation regarding the role of religion in the public arena later in the book. I remain convinced that any
effort to mediate suffering—as theodicy requires—short-circuits forceful
critique of and challenge to moral evil in the forms that impact us most. In
other words, theodicy in black thought encourages—if it doesn't require—a
compromise in at least two ways:

1. *Redemptive Suffering*: The dilemma can be resolved by finding merit in
   suffering, either as pedagogically beneficial or as justified punishment.
   There is ample consideration of this resolution in black thought—
   even from otherwise radical figures like Bishop Henry McNeal Turner
   (African Methodist Episcopal Church), who argued that God allowed
   enslavement as a means to secure for Africans the Christian faith and
   acquaintance with a "civil" form of government that could then be

taken back to the continent and used to uplift Africa. For him, this thinking was grounded in scriptures such as Psalm 68:31: "Ethiopia shall soon stretch forth her hands to God . . ." The problem, according to Turner, was that Europeans tried to make slavery, which was a temporary training station, into a permanent institution.

2. *Mystery*: We don't know the mind of God.

William Jones insists that both of these resolutions ignore the possibility that God—if there is one—doesn't like black people. Black Christians, of course, read themselves through the narrative of the Israelites, not the Canaanites. When addressing the second response—mystery—interpreters often turn to the Book of Job, where God allows Job's suffering. You know this story better than I do, but to support my argument, let me say just a few words.

Readers of Job know through the backstory that Job is without blame. This is precisely why he suffers. Job and his friends search for God's logic in this misery—the loss of all, including Job's children. His friends quickly turn to Job's misdeeds as the answer. Yet Job resists. What did he do?

Ultimately, Job will question God, although questioning is overstated language here. Job is more subdued than that; God's response is a blistering statement of metaphysical superiority that negates Job's right to pose a question. Ultimately, readers often assume that God's allowance of suffering is left to mystery. But is it really?

Readers know that God allowed it to prove something about God's character—to demonstrate God's righteous dominance and that love is based on who God is rather than what the faithful have. This is odd, isn't it? No, it's tragic. Only Job's wife has a sense of the integrity of life and the limited range of options we have for demanding recognition of our agency against our circumstances. She makes black moralists and humanists proud!

With that said, my takeaway from the story is the utter failure of a response to theodicy. The response in the Book of Job to theodicy damages human integrity, denies the "realness" of our existential circumstances, and forces a type of "silence." And, by extension, the effort on the part of black Christians to find meaning in misery works against any claim of advancing the well-being of black people. It's a compromise whose very nature diminishes our being.

Well, that's my initial take on it, and I've gone on too long. I'm sure your perspective is a bit different.

BRAD R. BRAXTON: Tony, you mention biblical texts like the Psalms and the Book of Job in your poignant reflections. Thus, some "aerial" comments on the Bible seem appropriate. Yet along the way, I'll certainly bring it "down on the ground," especially concerning the Bible and human suffering.

The Bible is more pliable than humanists like you and many of my conservative Christian friends give it credit. It feels like I must "wage war" here on two fronts. With you, I want to uphold the Bible's possibilities as a resource to sponsor positive public engagement. With my conservative Christian friends, I want to highlight the problems that the Bible creates for positive public engagement, especially for those who take it seriously as a canonical text to guide thought and practice in the contemporary moment.

Nuance about a simple and overlooked aspect of the Bible is important. The Bible is not a uniform, singular book but a collection of diverse books, or a "library." Indeed, it is a library that was written and arranged across more than one thousand years and in different cultures and languages. And just like the many libraries where you and I have spent countless hours, the biblical library contains different genres and even conflicting voices.

Canonization implies a ratification of plurality and even conflicting opinions about the complex issues the Bible addresses. The Bible incentivizes debate by canonizing in its very pages examples of debate. The ancient writers and later compilers of the Bible may have been wittier, nimbler, and more courageous in their thoughts about interpretation than some contemporary theologians who in pedestrian fashion argue for the "inerrancy" and "infallibility" of scripture.

PINN: That is partly the issue for me. Black Christians—all Christians— affirm the ongoing merit of documents based on a "ratification" that doesn't consider their context. We need instead a radical interrogation and contextualized interpretation that frees readers to endorse and reject "sacred" texts based on current relevance. The Bible is important for what it might offer in terms of moral and ethical insights, but it's no more important than texts generated by current communities—no more important than Toni Morrison's writings, or Richard Wright's, or Nella Larsen's, or W. E. B. Du Bois's, and the list goes on.

BRAXTON: Your generalizing language about Christian engagements with the Bible, and more specifically black Christian engagements with it, raises concerns for me. By painting with such broad strokes, are you overlooking that you and I may agree more than we disagree concerning the Bible's role in these matters? By extension, depending on the particular humanist and black Christian communities we're talking about, there may be more congruence than dissonance in how our respective communities view the "authority" and role of classic moral texts such as the Bible.

PINN: There is considerable agreement between us. But the points of disagreement are substantial and a vital dimension of engagement. I get your point; however, I don't think it's a reach to claim all Christians, in appealing to the Bible, are applying moral and ethical codes generated within a context foreign to them.

BRAXTON: Your assertion about Christians "applying moral and ethical codes generated by a context foreign to them" seems forced or overly fretful. When readers from one historical era engage texts from another historical era, there is always a merging, or perhaps collision, of different moral codes and worldviews. Progressive interpretation doesn't involve a wholesale "applying" of ancient codes that completely dismisses contemporary codes. Conversely, I'm not endorsing a wholescale applying of contemporary codes that completely dismisses the historical codes of the Bible.

My training in hermeneutics (the art and science of interpreting texts and cultures) has fostered in me a profound respect for history. Thus, humility is a necessary virtue for culturally responsive interpretations of classic moral texts like the Bible. Contemporary readers should approach the Bible (and other classic texts) with an intellectual and moral openness. This openness enables us to engage more fully the experiences, wisdom, and weaknesses of the writers of these texts and the stories and customs the texts convey, so interpretation is not a mindless "applying" of "foreign" ethical and moral codes.

Similarly, my training in homiletics (the art and science of preaching) has instilled in me a yearning for contemporary relevance when I interpret biblical texts. The Bible certainly contains ancient history, but ancient history isn't the Bible's ultimate subject. The heart of the Bible's message revolves around God and other existential themes such as the nature of human beings, the blessings and challenges of family life, and the boundaries of our ethical connections and commitments to one another.

PINN: Your training certainly produced a nuanced reading of scripture—a range of related materials against which scripture is read. However, is this the case for other interpreters? There are clear examples of appeals to scripture—perhaps without context or historical analysis—that support very troubling moral and ethical claims and limitations. There's also another problem to highlight: the Bible is not a text written with our particular social world in mind. It responds to the "arrangement" of life that isn't our "arrangement" of life.

If interpretation involves a more selective application, what criteria are we to employ? On what basis do we select certain meanings and oppose others? Isn't it likely we do this based on our particular needs and perspectives? If we're pulling scripture into the contemporary context, what do we use to weigh the validity of any given interpretation? And if the litmus test involves our current need and sensibilities, why privilege the Bible at all?

BRAXTON: You correctly assess some of the significant challenges—even dangers—associated with biblical interpretation. The biblical scholar Krister Stendahl suggested that the public handling of the Bible (and other religious texts and traditions, I might add) is a matter of public health. Across the millennia, imperialistic readings of the Bible have released in the body politic the toxins of tribalism and terrorism resulting in exploitation and genocide.

On the other hand, liberating readings of the Bible have inoculated many weary souls from the virulent effects of bigotry and systemic oppression. Mindful of the ethical import of religious texts and rhetorical practices, I teach interpretation and public rhetoric as important acts of liberation ethics. Here I'm thinking about scholars like womanist ethicist Katie Cannon—someone familiar to both of us.

So, I belong to the school of thought that highlights liberation and well-being as key criteria for evaluating in your words "the validity of any given interpretation." And let me be abundantly clear: the meanings and practices of liberation and well-being are themselves the result of, and are subject to, interpretation.

PINN: I see your point. However, what do we say to and about those outside this school of thought? Even amid this important movement toward well-being, there are embedded markers of disregard. Attention to antiblack racism through the moral and ethical lens of the Bible exposes the Bible's sexism. And attention to sexism through the same lens exposes other modalities of disregard in the Bible.

This is certainly the case with any culturally conditioned source material. However, unlike more secular materials, we have limited epistemological vantage points from which to assess the intended meaning of the biblical text. This isn't simply because of the age and point(s) of origin for biblical narratives but also because of claims to a type of transcendental presence guiding the Bible. How do we control for this? Perhaps the answer is a hermeneutic of irreverence where the needs and conditions of the community of concern take priority over any discussion of the integrity of the text?

BRAXTON: When Christians debate among themselves the meanings and ethical implications of biblical texts, one group will often discredit the interpretation of another group with a trite retort: "Well, that's just your interpretation." The unspoken presumption of that weak critique is that the group offering the critique has something more durable, more real than "interpretation." That group has "the truth." Yet what is "truth" for one group may be "trouble" for another group.

The interpretive debates depicted above happen all the time in mundane matters of daily living. For example, as a sports fan, I'm amused by the heat and light of current "debates" on cable TV shows about who is "the greatest" National Basketball Association player of all time: Michael Jordan or LeBron James. This debate, of course, is a form of entertainment and has no bearing on major issues of public well-being.

Yet we seem more capable of grasping a key interpretive insight when the stakes are lower; namely we are already engaging in interpretation *even as we seek to settle debates*. Thus, the "objective facts" of Jordan's six NBA championships and LeBron's four (to date) NBA championships are weighed differently by various groups based on how they interpret their understanding of NBA history. Was Jordan's NBA era of the 1980s/1990s harder or easier than Lebron's NBA era of the 2000s? Is it more significant to win six championships with one team or four championships with three different teams?

To paraphrase the apt adage of the literary critic Stanley Fish, facts do not determine interpretations. Instead, interpretations often determine what we consider the (persuasive) facts to be. This is all the more prevalent when we take it up many notches and engage classic texts with significant public import like the Bible or the US Constitution.

There is no "Olympian" vantage point that gives us the "ultimate truth" of these texts. Instead, with our feet of clay firmly planted on the ground, we *interpret* to delineate our conceptual frameworks; we *interpret* as we employ those frameworks to determine the persuasive facts; we *interpret* as we marshal those facts in dialogue with, or in contestation of, other persuasive facts; and we bring those many interpretive moves and "facts" into the public square in order to persuade each other of the "truth" of the matter. Since I wanted to explore in my professional pursuits the interplay between interpretation and public persuasion, I decided as a doctoral student years ago to couple my research and writing in biblical studies with my research and writing in homiletics.

PINN: I appreciate your sensitivity to these issues and acknowledge how you add complexity to interpretative patterns. Still, I wonder how this is resolved by homiletics—when I would think of that as the expression of those claims in order to produce "disciples" rather than a fundamental critique or challenge. What do we say to and about those who don't align themselves with your progressive mode of scholarship? How does the average reader develop this nuance?

BRAXTON: Thanks for the incisive questions. Before addressing some specific aspects of homiletics, permit me to speak about the broader intellectual field in which homiletics sits: practical theology. Practical theology provides a sturdy platform to engage serious issues like theodicy.

Activities like preaching, praying, and social activism are more than mindless mechanisms for "producing disciples." Let me also say for the record that producing disciples is not inherently problematic. As teachers, you and I are in the business of producing disciples. The Latin word *discipulus* (which gives us the English word "disciple") means "a student" or "one who learns." We train our students not to be parrots but disciples, persons who can engage *and interrogate* various schools of thought and practice.

When teaching practical theology, I remind students of the Greek word *pragma,* which means "deed" or "event" and supplies our word "pragmatic." Accordingly, practical theology is a type of inquiry concerned with the profound moral and cultural knowledge conveyed by deeds or practices.

I taught a course in 2016 at Harvard Divinity School, Preaching, Healing, and Justice, where students witnessed firsthand the ethical significance of performing religious practices with intellectual sophistication and emotional finesse. In the final assignment of the course, students were asked to preach a funeral sermon and create a funeral liturgy for one of the recent victims of police-related lethal force: Rekia Boyd (Chicago), Michael Brown (Ferguson), Tanisha Anderson (Cleveland), Eric Garner (New York City), Freddie Gray (Baltimore). Regrettably, were I to teach the course again, the list of victims of police-related lethal force would have to be expanded to include more recent examples, such as Breonna Taylor and George Floyd.

Violence (especially state-sanctioned violence) and the untreated trauma of that violence in so many communities are stubborn ethical dilemmas. When dealing with a dead body in a casket, grieving families in a religious sanctuary, protest-hardened social activists on the streets, and the eavesdropping electronic ears of social media, public leaders realize that ethics and theodicy are not abstract topics but embodied enterprises. Many students in the course acknowledged the relevance and specificity of the assignment required integrated ethical thinking that plumbed the depths of their emotive intelligence and aesthetic imagination as much as it probed their cognitive intelligence.

Homiletics—a discipline very comfortable with religious claims—has empowered me to ask a pertinent question about the Bible and scholarship on the Bible: So what? Once the ancient biblical sources have been sorted, the grammar has been parsed, and the social contexts of ancient Judaism and ancient Christianity have been reconstructed, so what? What did the Bible's religious claims *mean* to these ancient communities? How did these religious claims impact daily life in these communities? Regardless of whether I believe those claims, I, as a humanities scholar, am curious to know how large swaths of people in other historical eras understood key dimensions of human existence.

Furthermore, homiletics has compelled me to ask the "so what" question in an even more contemporary manner. The homiletician in me reminds the biblical scholar in me that ancient history is not the only history. The ancient meanings of a biblical text, to the degree that we can grasp them, never halt a text's interpretive trajectory. Biblical texts have living, ongoing histories and meanings, which inform the lives of millions of contemporary people. Might the poetic claims about human nature found in the Bible and other religious and cultural traditions constructively impact public debates about the opportunities and dangers of contemporary intellectual and cultural practices?

PINN: I appreciate the "so what" question. But the question already assumes some utility, some value in the biblical text. Does the Bible, for example, offer insights that can't be gained—with fewer contextual-social world issues—from other sources? Again, my question, another version of the "so what" question you've offered: Why invest this particular text with an authority and power that over-determine the moral and ethical framing of contemporary life?

BRAXTON: As a homiletician, I ask the "so what" question in other ways. What difference, if any, should Hebrew Bible texts such as Joshua and Judges make to the discussion of "just war" theories or postcolonial struggles of Indigenous Peoples around the world? These Hebrew Bible texts tell problematic stories about the Israelites occupying lands that were inhabited by Indigenous Peoples. Conquest and colonization do not become "holy" just because people may have believed that "God" commanded them to do so.

What difference, if any, should Pauline texts make to the discussion of gender justice and the role of women in society? There is evidence in Paul's writings that he valued the leadership of women in advancing his fledgling house-church movement as it grew under the imposing shadow of the Roman Empire (e.g., Philippians 4:1–3). Yet Paul's patriarchal pronouncements in other writings counteract these otherwise brilliant glimpses of egalitarianism (e.g., 1 Corinthians 11:1–16 and 14:26–36). So, I encourage readers of classic moral texts to neither wholly deify, vilify, or apply these texts. Instead, I invite a humble, curious engagement that considers the worldviews of both the text and contemporary readers.

Let me speak briefly to the excellent question you raised: "Why invest this particular text [the Bible] with an authority and power that over-determine the moral and ethical framing of contemporary life?" I wonder if social liberation and diversity are furthered not by "eliminating" the Bible but by "relativizing" it. I have in mind here the last scene in the movie *The Book of Eli*, starring Denzel Washington. The movie tells the story of a complex brother, Eli, who carries a complex book, the Bible, on a journey to make a new world after the cataclysmic destruction of the old world.

After many twists and turns, Eli ensures that the Bible makes it "out west" to a library where the Bible can be safeguarded and appreciated. In the final scene, the Bible is placed on a shelf alongside other classic texts such as the Qur'an. In this movie, the Bible is both castigated as a weapon that destroyed a previous world and appreciated as an instrument that might help to create a new world. This final scene may suggest that the Bible and other classic texts serve humanity best when they are brought into respectful conversation with one another and not when one text is considered preeminently important or determinative.

Thus, I'm happy to bring the Bible into equal dialogue with other texts, traditions, rituals, and critiques offered by the likes of James Baldwin, Langston Hughes, and Lorraine Hansberry, or a twenty-first-century black female atheist such as Sikivu Hutchinson, or the *babalawos,* those religious leaders in African-derived traditions such as Santería. Do my musings here on the broader mechanics of interpretation raise other questions and concerns for you?

PINN: Thanks, Brad. This is informative concerning how the professional— the trained scholar and preacher—understands and uses the Bible, but is this perspective common? In other words, is the "so what" question offered beyond the classroom and the (informed) pulpit? I still wonder about the central position of the Bible as applicable *beyond* the confines of individual orientation toward life.

BRAXTON: Unfortunately, the perspective I'm highlighting is not as common as I would want. I'm using my public platforms to advocate for it as often as possible.

In the beginning of this conversation, you summoned a towering scholar and ancestor, William R. Jones. I want to summon another towering scholar and ancestor, Cain Hope Felder. Felder served as professor of New Testament language and literature at Howard University School of Divinity. Many black biblical scholars—including me—benefited mightily from his work and example. In 2019, he transitioned to the ancestral realm after decades of pioneering scholarship and teaching that highlighted black people's powerful and peculiar engagements with the Bible.

Felder's most enduring professional contribution was his service as the editor of the landmark book *Stony the Road We Trod: African American Biblical Interpretation*, a collection of essays by trailblazing black biblical scholars. The book's title—a direct citation from the second stanza of James Weldon Johnson's famous poem "Lift Ev'ry Voice and Sing"—is apropos to our dialogue about theodicy. By alluding to these words from Johnson's poem, the book's title connotes the challenges that black scholars have overcome in academic arenas where white supremacy remains potent. The book's title also points to a deeper cultural reality. Black engagements with the Bible are well acquainted with the "stony roads" and rough sides of the mountain that have typified black existence in physical places and cultural spaces that are hostile to black people.

PINN: For James Weldon Johnson, the religious involves a cultural world— signs and symbols housed within cultural codes that have some meaning to people. But it isn't an endorsement of the theological claims undergirding those codes. As we've discussed, Johnson wasn't a theist, so you're pointing to ways that the song has been interpreted as opposed to theological claims on his part.

BRAXTON: As a culturally responsive interpreter, I respect history. Thus, I appreciate you consistently highlighting that Johnson wasn't a theist. Also, I believe that texts are "alive" and have trajectories that include, but are not completely determined by, the biographies and beliefs of their authors.

As you know, there is a saying in literary studies: "The death of the author is the birth of the reader." In other words, once authors set words on a page, they "die" in that they can no longer control how readers might interpret those words. Thus, in writing, authors "die," and readers are "born," creating meanings that may be an extension of, or in contradiction to, the meanings the author might have intended.

Furthermore, as a troubadour of black tragedy and triumph, Johnson pays homage in "Lift Ev'ry Voice and Sing" to metaphysical beliefs that are central within significant strands of black life, even if he was agnostic about, or a disbeliever of, those beliefs. In Johnson's poetic vision, when the world is right, liberty will reverberate not only among people but also into the heavens and beyond. Social justice celebrates the distinct identities and possibilities of every voice and seeks to unite those voices in ways that replace cacophony and chaos with harmony and healing.

PINN: Johnson wasn't an agnostic; he was an atheist. There are notable implications regarding an atheist speaking about the cultural value of the sermonic style. He tamed the theological assumptions of the grammar and vocabulary of the sermon. Instead, he highlighted the cultural and social power of the poetic to encourage a rethinking of the world and our relationship to it. I could say more on Johnson as well as other black humanists and atheists who tamed the theological claims of black religion to highlight the cultural meanings. But I'll stop and move on with a general response.

Yes, there is a poetic hopefulness here, but I interpret Johnson's song in relationship to the blues, for instance, where a more sober depiction of collective life is offered. The blues acknowledges hope but attaches it to the faulty efforts of humans and celebrates defiance as a mode of freedom. The blues also examines possibility within a social context of continued demise. What do we make of the hope in Johnson's anthem considering the ongoing racial disregard that defines this nation? How do we respond to the questions of theodicy and anthropodicy, which incessant injustice forces us to confront? In other words, what do we make of life once the song comes to an end?

BRAXTON: Whether or not Johnson believed that God had brought black people "thus far on the way," he realized that many black people believed in God's providential leading. Yes, I'm pointing to how black people have interpreted Johnson's poem, and I'm also noting that Johnson's poem is itself an interpretation of the beliefs and practices of many of the black people on whose shoulders he stood. So, it doesn't strike me as inappropriate when black people do to Johnson's cultural production what Johnson did to the black cultural productions that preceded him: interpret them!

If you ask me what we do after the song ends, my response is simple. We fight like hell for justice, dignity, and love! During the civil unrest following the tragic death of Freddie Gray in Baltimore in 2015, my wife, Lazetta, and I took our daughter, Karis, who at the time was in elementary school, to a civil disobedience and social protest training led by the well-known black activist Reverend Osagyefo Sekou. Reverend Sekou began the training session that evening with a prayer that might make humanists like you smile. He essentially said, "God, if there is a God, we appreciate any help you can offer. But if there is no God, then *we* are all we got."

PINN: Yes, but we both know more than this happens when black Christians interpret atheists like Johnson. Johnson's disbelief is dismissed from the story. And we are left to assume that only those who believe in God have the moral and ethical insight necessary to sustain the dreams of a community. Too often, there is a reduction of black sensibilities to Christian expression.

This hostile takeover by Christian sensibilities is more than interpretation. It's a theological co-optation that reduces complexity by assuming that theological vision can't be appreciated simply for the implied cultural creativity it might entail. Johnson celebrates through this song what he celebrates through *God's Trombones*—black people's cultural expressivity. We might call it the poetic transformation of language that frees it to speak concerns and perspectives not originally intended. Unlike Johnson, we lose the ability to express wonder and awe regarding the crafting of worlds of possibility without undergirding them with theological claims.

BRAXTON: Cogent observations, brother! I second the motion. Black liberation and broader human flourishing are not advanced by Christian imperialism.

It's important to analyze black engagements with the Bible with the same respect and sophistication used when analyzing other black intellectual enterprises (e.g., black literature, black performing arts, black jurisprudence). Many strands of black biblical interpretation have not fostered escapism but hard-nosed, existential encounters with theodicy. In other words, many black people have engaged the Bible not to justify suffering but to interrogate it—and interrogate the God who allows it—with irreverent questions and righteous resistance.

PINN: You'll have to point me to examples of this engagement by black theists that don't imply or explicitly state a redemptive suffering model.

BRAXTON: Many womanist scholars are "black theists." As they engage the Bible and the ethical dilemmas surrounding suffering, they reject a redemptive suffering model. Also, by honoring the complex history of black biblical interpretation, we learn that some "everyday" black readers of the Bible raised theodicy questions before black scholars such as William R. Jones voiced them. Many black Christians have attempted to use their "third eye" when reading the Bible, mindful that the Bible might present versions of a God who doesn't like black people.

PINN: There's a bit of slippage here. I'm not speaking about a lack of questioning, but rather a difference in terms of answers. What Jones finds when asking these questions is worlds away from what black theists find. The question of theodicy is important, but even more telling are the answers provided. Black theists offer answers dominated by a redemptive suffering orientation.

BRAXTON: Many black people grapple with the Bible because they might conjure from their readings of it a liberating God who accompanies black people as we fend off the tyrannical versions of God in the Bible. The presence of many black Christian denominations and traditions is evidence of the black resistance of the God whom white slave owners proclaimed from their Bibles.

PINN: I wouldn't disagree with you concerning what black theists seek, but I would disagree about what they find. Black theists typically appeal to faith rather than determining what can be said about God in light of the historical nature of our experience. Your claim—"the presence of many black Christian denominations and traditions is evidence of the black resistance of the God whom white slave owners proclaimed from their Bibles"—isn't historically accurate, although I understand why you say it.

These denominations are the result of theological disagreements human in nature. The development of three major black Baptist conventions has nothing to do with antiblack racism on the part of slave owners and their Bible. It was internal theological and political disagreement.

You turn theological-political arguments into divine involvement. What is the evidence that God has anything to do with the development of denominations? Does God have a favorite denomination? What of competing claims by black denominations? Where is God in those disagreements? Here is my concern: I sense within many theistic conversations epistemological slippage—attributing to God human decisions and conclusions.

BRAXTON: There's more historical warrant to my claim than you're admitting. When I speak about "black Christian denominations," I'm talking about archetypal moments when black Christians demonstrated their agency and broke away informally (in brush arbors beyond the oversight of slave masters) and formally to begin their own denominations. As you know, one of the classic examples occurred in 1787.

PINN: It's a leap of imagination on our part to describe what occurred within brush arbors and assume that events within these secret meetings only influenced the later development of black churches. What about the diverse religious-cultural sensibilities that enslaved Africans brought with them?

BRAXTON: In referencing brush arbor meetings, I am presuming the diverse religious-cultural sensibilities that enslaved Africans brought with them. Undoubtedly, these sensibilities influenced forms of Christianity that eventuated in what we now call black Christianity, and they were manifest in many other ways as African-derived religions took hold in the Americas.

White racism prevented Richard Allen, Absalom Jones, and William White from praying peacefully in St. George's Methodist Episcopal Church in Philadelphia. Consequently, these eighteenth-century black religious leaders left that church both physically and philosophically to protest racism. In the wonderful book about black church history that you cowrote with your mother, *Fortress Introduction to Black Church History*, you discuss how this seminal event in 1787 eventually led to the creation of the African Methodist Episcopal Church.

PINN: True, and thanks for referencing the book. Writing it with my mother was a special moment. But the call for independence that motivated their departure in 1787—only after this most graphic offense—didn't prevent Richard Allen from denying women the right to preach. We have to be mindful of the limited sense of freedom their protest was meant to enact.

BRAXTON: I agree. There was a limited sense of freedom in their protest. I'll discuss that more fully in a moment.

Furthermore, I am referring to how African cultural and religious traditions survived the Middle Passage. These traditions motivated some black Christians to protest white racism, and they also influenced how Christianity would develop in North America. So, some of the originating energy that resulted in distinct forms of black Christianity is rooted in attempts to reconstruct racist forms of Christianity through African-derived customs and perspectives.

PINN: Here's the co-optation problem. Why speak of these African sensibilities as motivating black Christians? Were these practices only the backdrop for black churches? Why don't we emphasize a more complex religious geography for black communities? This unnecessary reduction hampers the ability to fully appreciate the various ways that black people have named, thought about, and responded to moral evil.

BRAXTON: You're right about the need for a "more complex religious geography." I've argued the same for many years.

I want to return to your earlier claim about "epistemological slippage." The slippage is not in my argument but in how you are perceiving my argument. You're creating a "straw man" and offering general protestations against how black Christians discuss the origins of their denominations.

Undoubtedly, some black Christians may conflate theological-political arguments with divine involvement. That's not *my* claim. I'm emphasizing the *human* agency of black people as they have employed their cultural and theological beliefs to counteract corrosive forms of religion, whether the corrosive agent was racism, sexism, or heterosexism.

PINN: I respectfully disagree. Yes, you often talk in personal terms, but then there are the generalizations that grow from that personal engagement. I'm not convinced the qualifier of "some" you often employ produces the restriction you intend—particularly when you then move to the "human agency of black people as they have employed." We're both using personal experience to frame and discuss group activity and "the human agency of black people." The difference might be how we understand and ground that qualifier: "human."

BRAXTON: Okay, that might, indeed, be the difference. As we move forward, I'll benefit from further insights on how you're understanding the "human" and how you think it differs from my understanding.

So, let's return to the example of the African Methodist Episcopal Church in its earliest days in the eighteenth and nineteenth centuries. This denomination emerges, in some regard, as a protest against white racism. Yet emancipatory movements are often beset with countervailing forces that restrict the broadest application of emancipation. Thus, Jarena Lee, a gifted preacher, emerges in the AME Church in the early nineteenth century. However, patriarchal perspectives prohibit Richard Allen from fully embracing her ministerial gifts.

The irony, of course, is in plain view. A movement that sought to tear down white racism was upholding the walls of black sexism. Undaunted by this glaring irony, Jarena Lee engages in savvy inner-biblical interpretation. She employs the Bible as a critique against biblically sanctioned sexism. Lee employed human agency to interpret her life in terms of God whom she believed had sanctioned her to improve the lives of others. Moreover, when the religious community to which she belonged prohibited the free exercise of her gifts, she further employed her agency to craftily use the Bible against the Bible for the sake of liberation.

PINN: Jarena Lee (and many others whose names we have forgotten) read the Bible against the Bible. When I say *against* the Bible, I'm highlighting interpretations that resist oppression and the stranglehold of tradition on our thinking. Her engagement with the Bible emphasized her experience and needs explicitly in light of her circumstances. I have no problem with such a move. I simply wonder about the energy that goes into that move instead of simply relying more on our own stories.

BRAXTON: I endorse your call for radical interrogation of biblical traditions. I also believe there are more examples of this interrogation within the Bible, and within the history of black engagements with the Bible, than you acknowledge.

Also, I'm calling for a "both/and" approach concerning reliance on our contemporary stories and the stories found in classic texts like the Bible. I, of course, welcome your assessment of these comments, before I press forward to define other key terms of engagement.

PINN: Yes, black theists have interrogated the Bible. My concern and critique relate to the conclusions drawn that largely suggest redemptive suffering—a concept that works against the social needs of black people.

The interrogation of black theists is premised upon assumptions that go unquestioned, but these assumptions should be acknowledged and addressed: (1) God is good and concerned with black people, (2) history is teleological—or purpose-driven—in nature, (3) tradition trumps history, and (4) the Bible has answers responsive to the contemporary moment, as opposed to the Bible suggesting moral and ethical frameworks that might work but might not.

BRAXTON: The Bible undoubtedly promotes problematic perspectives on theodicy. Yet the Bible also offers meaningful resources for forceful critiques: critiques of problematic religious practices, narrow theological traditions, and even critiques of God. For me, the Bible is less a grand defense of God and instead more a summons for us to place what we hold most dear—including for theists our beliefs about God—on the witness stand to test if our beliefs and traditions can withstand scrutiny and emerge stronger on the other side.

PINN: I agree with you concerning critique, but I'm calling for more than that. The critique takes place in a way that assumes the larger integrity of the theological system (e.g., "our beliefs about God"). I'm calling that into question and suggesting our history is a better gauge than borrowed pronouncements concerning the workings of God.

BRAXTON: As we proceed, it might be helpful to clarify what each of us means by terms such as "God" or "evil." The term "God" for me has metaphysical "content." I believe there is a creative and complicated Spirit with whom we can connect. Because of the possibility of connecting with this Spirit, theologians metaphorically refer to God as a "person."

Let me move from abstract principle to tangible practice. Prayer—a ritual for countless people—is rooted in the belief that people who pray are communing with the sacred "Other" or sacred "Others."

According to biblical books such as the Psalms and Job, prayer often involves more than quiet contemplation (although it certainly can be that). Prayer also is more than an exercise in polished language or liturgical correctness. Prayer is an honest partnership with divine presence where the deep in us reaches out to the deep in God. In that deep, ruggedly honest, sometimes guttural dialogue, all parties involved might be transformed. Through presence and relationship, both humans and God are subject to change.

PINN: Okay, there is a range of definitions for God, but for black Christians, the moral and ethical intent—regardless of how God is described—remains consistent and points toward the "good." My concern is that this is often over against history. I agree, lots of folks pray, and this ritual has to be nuanced, but I'm more inclined to the type of prayer noted by Frederick Douglass: praying with his legs.

BRAXTON: I pray frequently—not so much as an expression of "piety" but as an acknowledgment of partnership. I'm not asking the Spirit or sacred forces such as the ancestors to relieve me of my moral responsibility to discern and do what is good and just. I'm seeking presence and guidance to enhance my capacity for the daunting discipline to do better and be better, even if the "rewards" for such actions appear few and fleeting. Permit me to explain myself with an extended metaphor.

I hired recently a fantastic physical trainer. He is an expert in his craft and knows countless exercise routines and muscle stretches to move the body to wellness and optimal fitness. In addition to his keen grasp of physiology, he also understands psychology. He talked with me about one of the most significant contributions that a trainer provides, namely presence.

My trainer never did the exercises for me. He was quite willing to do the exercises with me. The energy that emerged in mutual engagement and struggle motivated me to explore the expansive capacities of my muscles. Often, without the trainer, I might have prematurely claimed "muscle failure" when in reality I was experiencing "mental failure." His presence galvanized me to merge my mind and my muscles in ways that increased, for example, my cardiovascular fitness. In short, presence and partnership made my heart stronger.

My trainer also benefited, and the benefit for him extended beyond the fee that I paid him. Without question, my trainer was athletically superior to me. Yet when it came to racquetball, we were more evenly matched. Grit and my court experience closed the gap in athletic talent between us. My trainer is an award-winning athlete with an infinitely small amount of body fat. Yet I, a washed-up athlete carrying some middle-age luggage in my midsection, routinely stretched him and won our racquetball matches. It might be said that our competitive engagements made his heart stronger too.

PINN: I hear what you're saying, but there is an ontological distinction between your trainer and the category of "God." One doesn't assume a metaphysical distinction between the trained and the trainer that would enable extra-ordinary input into the human condition. One doesn't assume that the trainer represents what Camus would call a "Grand Unity." The function of the category of "God" is distinct.

Despite nuance in terms of its meaning, "God," for those who claim belief in God, is a category of distinction and dissimilarity. Even if it is understood as somehow speaking to human capacity, it is a capacity not currently held—a potential—that speaks to distinction. This distinction sets up expectations in terms of theodicy that result in compromise and ethical failure, if not deception. But I've interrupted. Please continue, Brad.

BRAXTON: Not an interruption at all. It's an invitation for us to clarify further some of our frameworks. Philosophical traditions such as those represented by Camus have a long and respected intellectual history and demand serious engagement. As a quick autobiographical aside, I first encountered thinkers like Camus when I took an undergraduate course on existentialism at the University of Virginia with the celebrated black professor of religion and literature Nathan Scott. To read Camus's *The Plague,* for example, under the tutelage of a black genius like Nathan Scott was a life-changing experience.

PINN: Camus, as you know, is one of my favorite thinkers. I put him in intellectual relationship with figures like Du Bois, Nella Larsen, and Richard Wright. Camus is an underappreciated resource for the study of black religion, and I'd be interested to hear your takeaway from his writings.

BRAXTON: Irrespective of my appreciation for the existentialist tradition, my thinking about God and metaphysics is more conversant with African cosmology. As you know, in African cosmology, there are ontological distinctions between God, gods/spirits, humans, animals, and the larger environment. The ability for one realm of existence to influence another realm is not hindered by these ontological distinctions. Disruption and chaos occur when dimensions of existence don't properly interact with one another. Yet interdependence and engagement are possible, and even necessary, irrespective of ontological distinctions within an African cosmological framework.

PINN: It depends on the cosmological system. There isn't necessarily an ontological distinction between God and gods. In some cases, African creation narratives suggest that the gods are associated with natural forces; in others, they are of the same substance as the high God.

I sense in your distinction some carryover from a Christian cosmology. Also, the cosmological interaction that you label as "engagement" is often material bargaining between cosmological forces. There is familiarity and challenge in these "engagements" that isn't replicated in black church thinking.

BRAXTON: The existentialist tradition that seems to fund some of your comments accentuates, in my estimation, rupture over relationality and individualism over community. Forgive me if my characterization of existentialism is morphing into caricature. Yet when I think of how some scholars portray existentialism, I call to mind the individual hero who suffers misfortune and thus protests against a hostile or indifferent universe, with little expectation of response from the universe.

Based on our philosophical frameworks, you and I probably have different working assumptions about, and answers to, fundamental questions such as: Are humans primarily alone in the universe, or are we part of a larger cosmology of interrelated beings and forces? Before I return to my thoughts on prayer, do you want to say more about existentialism or other operative frameworks for you in light of my invocation of African cosmology?

PINN: I would label my position moralism rather than existentialism. Drawing on thinkers like Camus, I think about moralism as a process of critique—a pointing out of hypocrisy and inconsistencies, and a noting of suffering and pain—without offering final solutions. This is one of the differences between the moralism of Camus and the existentialism of someone like Sartre. Existentialists are more certain with respect to their claims and tend, as you say, to be concerned with a restrictive sense of agency and purpose. The moralist is uncomfortable with ultimate claims that don't recognize our shortcomings. Concerning the human alone in the universe, I think this is the case. It's an unjustified arrogance to assume that in this grand universe there is no other life. However, based on current knowledge, we just don't know.

However, I question your assumption concerning the posture and tone of moralism. For nontheists like me, radical individualism isn't the approach. There is a sense of wonder and awe: wonder over the nature of nature and awe over the humility in recognizing that we are individuals within the context of a grand, complex, and diverse world community.

One of the differences might be the sense of accountability and responsibility this recognition entails. For nontheists, we are fully and solely accountable for nurturing this web of life because there are no divine forces at work. There are no bargains to be had with divine forces and no sources of external interference.

I appreciate your critique, but I think there's misrepresentation at work. You mention Camus—and I assume he is the basis for your comments here. However, he wasn't an existentialist. Rather he was a moralist. You are blending two approaches to existential conditions. Camus understood the importance of the individual *within* the context of community (think, for example, about *The Plague*—a text familiar to both of us).

That is certainly a good way—the individual in community—to frame his critique of the existentialists' position (Sartre et al.) regarding World War II developments and the brutality of the gulags (i.e., brutal Russian labor camps and prisons). There are the absurd heroes for Camus, such as Sisyphus, as you hint. But is that any different than the Christian appeal to Jesus or Martin Luther King Jr.? Does that appeal to particular figures for moral and ethical guidance make Christians radical individualists? Yet one could argue that the Christian doctrine of personal salvation is a bigger threat to community intent than Camus's moralism and his brand of humanism.

BRAXTON: Thanks for the nuance and correction. Very insightful. Permit me to also provide some nuance. "Personal salvation" is more a mantra of conservative Christianity than an accurate depiction of the Bible's communally oriented vision of the world's transformation.

PINN: Returning to your reference of an African framework, to what extent is an African cosmology at work? Think of the actions and mindset of the *lwa* (divinities in the African-based religion of Vodou practiced in places such as Haiti and Louisiana)? How is the divine—the sense of moral and ethical possibilities engendered—at work? There are substantive distinctions between a West African cosmology and black Christianity. How are these distinctions addressed? West African cosmology has an appreciation for the earth that isn't demonstrated in Christian circles. How should this be addressed? In short, what elements of an African cosmology are in play? And which African cosmology do you have in mind?

BRAXTON: I'm not arguing for a one-to-one correspondence between various West African cosmologies and the cosmologies in various forms of black Christianity. Neither would it be appropriate to argue for a radical disjunction between these cosmologies either. I'm thinking here about the cosmological fluidity that Zora Neale Hurston chronicles so provocatively in her book *The Sanctified Church*. She highlights how black religious people, especially in the southern portion of the United States during the early twentieth century, were improvising and thus creating hybrid religious practices informed by African, African diasporic, American, and Christian frameworks.

Many of these practices reflected a deep appreciation for the earth and nature. During my childhood, I recall the hushed awe that regularly fell upon my family's house in Virginia in the 1970s and '80s when a thunderstorm arose. Alongside our Christian beliefs, there was a powerful indigenous reverence for the beauty and sheer power of nature. My father had both African American and Native American ancestry. Also, the severance of some forms of black Christianity from a greater appreciation of the earth may be more a function of urbanization, which removes communities increasingly from daily interactions with the natural environment.

PINN: My concern is conflation—the failure to maintain the creative tension between traditions that Zora Neale Hurston maintained. Concerning a lessened appreciation for the earth, urbanization doesn't fully account for this shift. A more fundamental source supported by scripture is that humans are outside or above nature. For example, the Bible speaks of a type of "control" over nature—a sense of the natural environment as there for human use.

BRAXTON: Some scholars interpret Genesis 1:26–28 differently than you suggest. In that text, God grants to humanity "dominion" over the creation. However, dominion can be construed here as reverential care for and stewardship of the environment, instead of exploitation of the environment.

I highlight, for example, Trinity United Church of Christ in Chicago. Under the leadership of Jeremiah Wright and Otis Moss III, this congregation has fashioned a form of Christianity deeply anchored in African-derived practices and frameworks. Accordingly, this congregation is advancing an urban development agenda, Imani Village, that is ecologically sensitive. To your point, more black churches and other religious communities should devote attention and resources to critical environmental issues.

PINN: I appreciate Trinity Church and applaud its long-standing commitment to justice. But don't we have to ask about the integrity of African-based sensibilities? Are they merely ways to enhance certain dimensions of Christian thought and practice? We need to maintain the complexity of the religious landscape—how we think about the nature and significance of African-based religious sensibilities and practices. How do we avoid rendering them "exotic" within our communities?

BRAXTON: Your concern about making African-based beliefs and practices "exotic" is valid. A more complex historiography might be one antidote for this dilemma.

For example, in 2019, there were various "1619 projects" and commemorations of the four-hundredth anniversary of the arrival of enslaved Africans in the US. According to some historical accounts, these commemorations may have "misperceived" history by ignoring the black people enslaved in the Spanish colony of Florida nearly a century before 1619. Nevertheless, these 1619 commemorative events were well-intentioned, raised public consciousness in important ways, and fostered solidarity among many groups.

Yet moments like these can unintentionally define black people and black culture in terms of slavery's pathology. On the contrary, we could employ a pan-African approach to trace African distinctives and developments of those distinctives across the continent and in the diaspora rather than organizing our historical and cultural study by the pathology of Europe's transatlantic slavery.

PINN: I wouldn't disagree with you, but I wonder about the purpose of reclamation. What do we seek to gain through this *re-membering?* And how do we appreciate the "unknowable" dimensions of our cultural history and connections? As we *re-member,* don't we need to guard against a tendency to romanticize our cultural history and highlight only those elements we find useful for our current arguments?

BRAXTON: As a scholar of black Christian preaching, I study this prac-tice for what it may, or may not, teach me about cultural connections to African-influenced rhetoric. In other words, I'm more interested in the descriptor "black preaching" than the descriptor "Christian preaching."

I endorse your cautionary note about a "romantic" remembering of the past. We should remain open to the explosive power of disruptive forms of remembering; forms of remembering that challenge—and decon-struct—venerated versions of history. The recounting of history is certainly not "objective." Like any cultural practice, history can become a tool for propaganda and demagoguery, which lionizes groups already in power and further stigmatizes marginalized groups.

You rightly suggested earlier that the Book of Job is a touchstone text for theodicy. Before discussing Job, I want to further engage Genesis. In my estimation, the creation *stories* in Genesis, as well as a classic African American improvisation on it, provide fascinating insights on both the character of God and the nature of evil. Notice my use of the plural when talking about the creation *stories* in Genesis. Without plunging into exe-getical intricacies, I want to focus on an often ignored feature in Genesis. The creation story in Genesis is actually two stories written by two different authors in two different time periods, and these two stories are placed side by side: Genesis 1:1–2:4a and Genesis 2:4b–3:24.

While there are meaningful differences between these creation stories, a unifying element is that they are *stories.* We misread many ancient traditions if we think ancient narratives are naive efforts to avoid intractable philo-sophical challenges. Stories are sturdy structures for serious philosophical work. This is why individuals, families, tribes, and nations have been telling stories for millennia.

PINN: Yes, I agree; they are stories. And this "tamer" understanding of them should allow us the freedom to move beyond them—to privilege the stories that speak directly to our lives. That is to say, what is the rationale for assuming the Bible is more informative on these issues than our own stories—more than Zora Neale Hurston, James Baldwin, Richard Wright, Alice Walker, and so on?

BRAXTON: I want to return to one of these stories in Genesis. We've covered some of this ground in a previous conversation in this book, but it's important to mention other things in light of theodicy.

Many people are familiar with Genesis's depiction of God who "speaks" to create light, the land, the seas, the animals, and eventually humans. A more complex picture emerges if we pay equal attention to the "formless void" and the "darkness" covering "the face of the deep" in the Bible's first creation story (Genesis 1:2). There is a creative God, *and* preexistent, unruly waters exist alongside God. Those unruly waters symbolize chaos and evil. We don't have to wait until some serpent crawls into the Garden of Eden to tempt Adam and Eve for evil to make its debut (Genesis 3). Evil has always been present. Genesis 1:2 suggests that evil is as timeless as God.

In the second creation story (Genesis 2:4b–25), the writer offers subtle wordplays that depict God as a "sculptor" who is passionately involved in creating humanity. God forms the human (the Hebrew word is *adam*) from the dust of the ground (the Hebrew word is *adamah*). To provide partnership for the human creature, God then further differentiates the human creature into complementary genders: man (the Hebrew word is *ish*) and woman (the Hebrew word is *ishah*). Thus, creation moves along to foster partnerships. God is in partnership with the human and then senses the importance of fostering partnership within humanity by creating facets or genders within humanity.

So, creation is not about the raw, unrivaled power of God. Evil exists and is a formidable rival to God. Furthermore, creation is about the potential and beauty of partnerships.

PINN: Shouldn't we assess the character of God based on our historical experience, as opposed to ancient narratives? What's the rationale for transporting scripture's depiction of the divine into our world? We seem to refine a doctrine of God without an explicit willingness to reimagine and deconstruct it.

My concern isn't with a doctrine of God within creation accounts; I'm concerned with God in relationship to the inflicting of misery and pain.

Again, the Book of Job presents a particular narration of God's relationship to humanity that begs the question of theodicy.

BRAXTON: Whether we're talking about Genesis or Job, the Bible is grappling with not only the consequences of evil but also the causation of evil. Is evil a preexistent force just as eternal as God is? Or are evil and the suffering associated with it the machinations of a sadistic "experiment" between God and this satanic figure in the Book of Job? Who is this satanic figure with whom God conspires? From where does this satanic figure come, and what are the powers of this satanic figure with respect to God's powers? While it often employs mythological language, the Bible pursues questions about the nature of God, the nature of creation, and the relationship between evil and theodicy.

PINN: But there's a distinction. Early in Genesis, humans are blamed for their suffering; it is the result of human misdeed—ongoing disregard for God's will. However, in the case of Job, suffering is the result of divine hubris. Should we wrestle with this distinction? What do we make of this difference in the relationship between a doctrine of God and theological anthropology? My questions are meant to problematize the assumption of linear development in the Bible—of a consistent narrative with a constant understanding of human and divine character.

BRAXTON: Permit me to return to some thoughts about the nature of God and creation. In my estimation, one of the most spectacular interpretations of Genesis occurs in James Weldon Johnson's poetic sermon "The Creation" in *God's Trombones*. As noted earlier, in the second creation story in the Bible, God creates in large measure to address the human need for partnership. Johnson, however, does what fearless poets and preachers often do. He turns traditions upside down, hoping that the shaking will enable us to perceive new realities. He makes two bold moves worthy of comment.

First, Johnson insists that creation is a consequence of the need *within God* not within humanity. To address God's loneliness, God engages in a final act of creation: the creation of humanity. In chronicling that final act, Johnson makes his second bold move. He likens God to a black woman. While the use of "mammy" reflects the tortured racial dynamics and linguistics of the Jim Crow period in American history, the use of black female imagery for God is nonetheless noteworthy:

> *This great God,*
> *Like a mammy bending over her baby,*
> *Kneeled down in the dust*
> *Toiling over a lump of clay*
> *Till he shaped it in his own image;*
>
> *Then into it he blew the breath of life,*
> *And man became a living soul.*
> *Amen.*

I'm interested in Johnson's God. Not the immutable God of orthodox theology who has no need. I'm interested in a God who is responsive to change and who has need. In other words, what if God needs us as much as we need God in order for God to be the best version of God?

PINN: I have issues with the creation accounts, but that is a separate issue that doesn't satisfy my concerns regarding the explicit quieting that Job encounters when asking about his suffering. At best, there is self-absorption on God's part since God's perfection has to be acknowledged regardless of the harm caused to those who adore God. Moral evil becomes a mechanism of divine self-validation. The Book of Job depicts humans as less than the freethinking valuable beings presented in Genesis. But perhaps you're moving to a justification that explains what I find missing.

BRAXTON: What if we evaluated our thinking about God, creativity, evil, and justice according to this criterion: Do our theological musings and social practices motivate or frustrate the thriving of black women? Even before we get to Job, Genesis—and Johnson's black poetic rhapsody on it—provide grist for our mill as we grind out truths about theodicy.

As you mentioned earlier, I'm more than willing to "assess the character of God based on historical experience" as well as grapple with insights about God and humanity from our culturally nuanced interpretations of ancient narratives. The movement between ancient and contemporary narratives is not inherently dichotomous.

So let me now speak about the ancient narrative in the Book of Job. There is nuance in its treatment of the thorny issue of theodicy. As some Hebrew Bible scholars have demonstrated, there is the "prose of Job" and the "poetry of Job." In the prose section (i.e., basically Job 1–2 and 42:7–17), there is the ancient fable of a righteous man who suffers ineffable losses. Eventually God restores to Job twofold what Job had lost, and Job lives a long and contented life.

Amid this rather tame and prosaic fable, there are chapters of torrid poetry that contain Job's heroic and irreverent complaints to and critiques of God. One of my favorites occurs in Job 7:11. As if shaking his finger in God's face and refusing to be comforted by pious platitudes, Job shouts at God: "Therefore, I will not restrain my mouth; I will speak in the anguish of my spirit; I will complain in the bitterness of my soul." I disagree with your depiction of this Job as "subdued."

Tony, this might be the message when the poetry of Job is given as much weight as the prose of Job: if the Bible depicts Job arguing with God, then maybe the Bible is urging us to argue with God and the Bible. In my book *Preaching Paul*, I insist that we take the Bible most seriously when we audaciously argue with it—and often passionately disagree with it.

PINN: I wouldn't consider Job's action as an argument—certainly not in light of other instances of vigorous debate in the Bible. Job seems more troubled by his inquisition, less certain of his right to ask the question. But more to the point, God's response suggests a distinction that tames Job's right to recount his misery.

I appreciate your thoughts, Brad. However, what you present leaves me dissatisfied. You seem to assume a certain integrity to the biblical text—a certain orientation regarding its moral and ethical aims. But this is a matter of perspective, one that disadvantages those who suffer most. For example, Job's children, Job's wife, the other forms of life for which Job was accountable, are given no real consideration. This further speaks to a hierarchy of importance that minimizes the suffering of some.

So I go to your point: What if we read and interrogate the Bible from the perspective of black women? Well, as the insightful theologian Delores Williams makes clear, in doing so we don't get a very good answer to the dilemma of theodicy. You'll recall her *Sisters in the Wilderness*, in which moral evil—disproportionate suffering—isn't resolved through the redemptive model I hear reflected in your commentary. We are left with the problem.

BRAXTON: I disagree with your assessment of my appeals to the Bible. I'm not arguing for a particular orientation to the Bible's moral and ethical claims. Actually, I'm underscoring the contestations within the Bible itself about key themes such as the nature of God and the origin of evil. If anything, I'm calling into question pious presumptions about the integrity of biblical texts. By questioning the Bible, I intend to clear the ground for the kind of vigorous debates and critiques that you and I believe are necessary when addressing a complicated issue such as theodicy.

PINN: I appreciate you wanting to indicate a distinction, but I'm not seeing it. There are contestations within the Bible, but these fall in line with a particular logic that isn't questioned. A doctrine of God remains consistent and what is argued is an evolving human recognition of the fine points of this doctrine. I sense your desire for critique, and I applaud it, but there remain certain underlying assumptions concerning the moral-ethical orientation and intent of the biblical narrative that I want to challenge.

I bring up redemptive suffering repeatedly because—from early examples of African American engagement with the Bible (including Job) to more contemporary discussions—it is the dominant response. And this isn't a response that runs contrary to the biblical narrative. It is essential to it, culminating in the Christ event (the death of Jesus). This centering of suffering runs contrary to efforts toward sustained struggle against injustice. How does one hold white supremacy fully accountable if there is an underlying narrative indicating that suffering (moral evil) has benefit?

While I appreciate your reflection on scripture and its ongoing utility, I am not hearing anything that satisfies regarding this entanglement with theodicy. In part, an adequate response requires a different point of critique. Rather than seeking to theorize moral evil, the integrity of the sufferer should be assumed, and God should be cross-examined and judged. The discussion of moral evil—theodicy—typically involves an effort to correct human perception of suffering as opposed to wrestling with the utility of the God concept to promote a proper sense of well-being.

As you know, God for me is a symbol, a trope. And the question is this: Has this trope outlived its usefulness? If we prioritize the well-being of life on earth, does this God symbol encourage us to name suffering and combat it as already and always a problem? Or do we need another symbol, another anchoring "device" better equipped to help us address the misery marking our current moment? I think we need a new symbol in order to better address and struggle against moral evil in the world.

BRAXTON: You rightly critique the prevalence of redemptive suffering in black Christianity. Redemptive suffering is a major theme in the Bible, and it is also a way to read the story of Jesus in the New Testament. However, re-demptive suffering is not the only way that biblical writers, broader Christian traditions, and certain black Christian traditions read Jesus, especially Jesus's suffering and death. For example, in the homiletical tradition in certain strands of black Christianity, there are compelling political interpretations of Jesus's suffering and death.

These political interpretations advocate for solidarity with economically vulnerable people, who are the culture's crucified. These interpretations also implore wealthy and middle-class people to stop constructing "crosses" or social and economic systems upon which vulnerable people are "executed," while the economically well-to-do maintain their standard of living.

PINN: I wouldn't say it's the only narrative regarding suffering available in the Bible. My concern is the manner in which it dominates black Christian thought. Yes, there are alternate readings of the Christ event, but they don't rule out redemptive suffering: the process of exchange Jesus represents is saturated with the redemptive nature of suffering. You can't have salvation without it.

I wouldn't make a distinction between redemptive suffering interpre-tations and political interpretations. Henry McNeal Turner had a political interpretation that maintained redemptive suffering. The same for Reverdy C. Ransom, Martin Luther King Jr., and the list goes on. What they offered, and you highlight with your statement, is a critique of white supremacy's takeover of the biblical narrative. This offering, however, doesn't challenge the embedded redemptive suffering model. All that it alters is who is cru-cified, but the merit of suffering remains; it's simply a question of who is redeemed. The crucified is a scapegoat that doesn't rule out the redemptive suffering model but rather simply shifts the weight of the narrative.

BRAXTON: I disagree. By linking Jesus's death to socio-economic struggle, some black Christian interpreters forcefully reject an apolitical atonement theology. They discard the belief that Jesus's blood cleanses the "souls" of individuals, while the collective "dirty laundry" of comfortable "cross makers" remains unwashed. To talk in a political way about the death of Jesus is to wrestle with the messy and costly realities of political resistance to systematic domination. When preachers offer apolitical sermons about the cross, they participate in further crucifixions. The cross for some black Christian ministers and scholars is *not* a legitimization of passive suffering.

PINN: But do these sermons and lectures rule out redemptive suffering? My concern is that your turn to politics covers redemptive suffering rather than challenging it. The political model still assumes the old biblical model. I'm not suggesting the "otherworldly" model as constitutive of redemptive suffering. That's a misread. As liberation theologians across contexts demonstrate, a person can be politically minded and still beholden to the model of redemptive suffering.

BRAXTON: The political model doesn't assume the "old biblical model" by which you apparently mean that Jesus's suffering and death are "necessary" to save us from our "sins." My political interpretation finds *no* dignity or deliverance in suffering. Instead, my interpretation struggles to re-create a world where the mechanisms that perpetuate suffering are mitigated, if not eliminated.

Also, let me be abundantly clear. I am no fan of the redemptive suffering model. I am not glibly glorifying suffering as if it is either an end unto itself or some means to a greater end. I am *not* advocating a "Christ cult of domination" that believes that enduring oppression somehow brings one closer to God.

Nor am I suggesting that struggle and suffering have a divine origin and purpose. Some suffering results from unwise personal choices, some suffering emanates from a persistent evil that plagues the systems of this world and that is enabled by human complicity in those systems, some suffering occurs because of genetic predispositions in our bodies at birth or due to natural disasters (and these disasters may be exacerbated by human complicity in environmental degradation), and the origins of some forms of suffering are still shrouded in the fog of inexplicable mystery.

PINN: It isn't about being closer to God per se; it's about a belief that suffering brings about transformation in various forms. Avoiding excessive theological nuance here, I want to argue collective suffering is always wrong—always. And we make progress, to the degree we make any progress, despite suffering. I am talking only about collective/communal moral evil and suffering. I fear there has been a disconnect in that I read some of your response as oriented toward individual suffering and well-being.

BRAXTON: My responses are as concerned about the communal as much as the individual. Your interrogation of the concept of God in light of persistent suffering doesn't bother me a bit, nor does it make me blink. If the trope of God no longer works for you or your communities, you must discard it. And as a member of the broader body politic interested in human flourishing and diverse ways to promote it, I'm eager to listen to and learn from you as you discard an unserviceable moral trope and create new ones.

By the same token, what responsibilities do you, and the communities you represent, have to demonstrate patience and openness as other communities hold on to and renegotiate the meaning of God in service of human flourishing? There are large segments of the black community who join you in a desire to promote widespread human flourishing. Yet for them, God and the Bible remain powerful, if at times problematic, tropes.

PINN: I appreciate your comments, and I'm not demanding a difference in how theists think. I'm simply noting an element of useful conversation about consistency between thought and deed, between texts and our history.

Siloed conversations among the like-minded are the problem. We are pushing against that, but such a push is unusual. We must continuously challenge a sense of comfort within our worlds that allows retreat rather than confrontation. We must respect the positions we bring to this conversation. Yet having these worlds into which we can retreat doesn't constitute an answer. I'm not suggesting you're saying, "Okay, do your thing and I'll do mine." Rather I'm highlighting the need for discomfort as a marker of engagement and openness to exchange. We are modeling that, and I want to emphasize its importance.

BRAXTON: Absolutely! I'm glad that we're dismantling "siloed conversations among the like-minded." Some pedagogical scholars identify the valuable role that discomfort and disequilibrium play in fostering learning and long-term growth.

For example, Delores Williams motivated a generation of justice-seeking scholars not by jettisoning God and the Bible but by engaging in an audacious rereading of biblical tropes in light of contemporary circumstances. Hagar, the African woman in Genesis, becomes the prototypical womanist theologian in Williams's creative remix. Despite the oppression foisted upon Hagar by Abraham and Sarah, Hagar demonstrates audacity and tenacity by being the first person in scripture to name God (Genesis 16:7–14).

PINN: Williams's work is outstanding, but what you are pointing to is an internal critique involving arranging oneself within a general theological framework. This isn't the same as challenging the framework. However, what you and I are engaged in is external critique based on distinct positions. The former—the internal critique—doesn't suggest a model for the latter—external critique.

I understand that many are theistic in orientation and labor in the world in light of that position. We need to find ways for that community and the nontheist community to forge solidarity on shared issues. But that can't come at the expense of recognizing and discussing our significant differences.

BRAXTON: I'm ready to take the trip with you, Tony, toward new tropes and symbols. At the same time, I recall those words of Jesus when he suggested that wise scribes bring forth treasures that are new *and* old (Matthew 13:52). So, as we quest after new tropes, might some blessings still be found in the old ones as well?

PINN: This is exciting, Brad. And I want to answer your question with a question: Doesn't that depend on the task? And doesn't it depend on how those tropes are presented and used? Sure, we will bring into play some old tropes, but what I'm calling for is a use of those tropes that assesses their value based on human history and our existential condition(s). In a word, friend, I want those tropes to bend to the will and weight of our history and condition.

BRAXTON: I renew here my earlier call for the importance of history and humility. I want to always caution against any hubristic notion that our present critiques and reconfigurations are "novel," categorically different, or more rigorous from what other communities have done across history. I don't want us to become prisoners of the moment.

For example, early Christian communities assessed the utility of existing tropes within Judaism and also created new tropes based on their understanding of history and existential conditions. So, let me respond to your questions above with further questions: Isn't it possible for theists to both appreciate human history and possess a sense of divine presence and partnership? Similarly, isn't it possible for nontheists to both appreciate human history and possess a sense of awe and ethical commitment that does not presume divine presence and partnership? Thus, a rigorous engagement with history is neither categorically frustrated by theism nor categorically facilitated by humanism.

PINN: I agree with you concerning the need for humility and an appreciation for history. You ask if theists and nontheists can both appreciate and critique sources, both appreciate history and have a sense of wonder. Of course, yes. However, I wonder—ha-ha, maybe I should have used a different word—how often either of these groups maintains such a balance. What tools do we use to maintain that balance? Is it revelation? Reason? Utility?

Also, the challenge isn't an appreciation of human history, it's the manner that we *use* that history. I'm not arguing that Christians have a problem with history. Rather I'm saying we have to give careful attention to what we understand as constituting "our" history and how we draw from it to produce contemporary structures for engagement. This is a challenge for theists and nontheists.

Within the context of individual belief and practice there is no issue. People should be free to believe what they want to believe and use whatever source material they desire. The question for me is what texts and tools define the workings of the public arena. This raises other concerns for me: What is the priority for our communities? Against what do we measure our claims and practices? What does our sense of moral evil prevent us from doing, and what does it encourage us to undertake? What does it authorize us to say, and what does it disallow?

BRAXTON: In a public arena genuinely interested in healthy dissent and democratic possibilities, shouldn't there be room for arguments via revelation, reason, utility, and other persuasive modes? The key word for me in the previous sentence is "arguments." No perspectives or approaches are inherently privileged or ruled in or out of bounds. Instead, perspectives or approaches receive public affirmation or castigation not as a result of the brute force of the state or other forms of coercion but through the power of persuasion.

PINN: I agree with you in theory, but we know those are not the terms of public engagement in a country that has denied "truth" and "facts" for the sake of social hierarchy. (This isn't limited to the years that Donald Trump was president.) We need a strong sense of suspicion—not as a hermeneutic but as a more general posture or mood toward engagement in the world.

BRAXTON: Of course, political practicalities and social hierarchies complicate the situation. Yet we should never minimize the importance of persuasion that seeks to inform and transform the moral imagination.

Consider, for example, pressing resource allocation issues, especially considering the COVID-19 pandemic and ongoing struggles for racial justice and for inclusive belonging in national and global spheres. Resources, which entail a wide variety of personal and institutional assets, are always needed to meet objectives and achieve goals. The current economic climate has intensified concerns about resources and challenged many institutions' assumption that their survival is self-evident.

Since the academic institutions that employ educators like us are affected by larger economic forces, prudence dictates that we pay attention to economic trends and forecasts. Theologians have much to learn from economists. Yet mission-driven institutions such as schools and universities should not simply capitulate to "bottom-line" economics. Moral frameworks can enrich the conversation, encouraging us to utilize more effectively the resources at hand, even as we develop new resources. In this regard, theologians have something to offer economists. Indeed, a distinguished economist once told me so.

PINN: I appreciate your argument in general, but I'm not certain of the target for your critique—or "encouragement." Institutions of "higher" learning certainly need to reassess themselves (including resource allocation and endowments) in light of various modes of disregard and injustice from which they have actively and passively benefited. But this doesn't change the tone and practice of public engagement on the issues you highlight.

To some degree, these institutions still work based on a claim to the importance of truth and facts, while the public arena (always suspicious of these institutions) has rejected "truth" and "facts" as mediating realities for public life. Yes, I agree that moral frameworks can be of great value. But which moral frameworks, and how are they impressed upon public debate?

Also, as you know, I wonder about the role of religion within public life and the context of these public debates. I hold this view not simply for personal reasons but in light of the growing population of US citizens living and thinking outside religious communities. And these groups—the "nones"—have significant political potential, but the framing of religiously inflected morality will have no appeal for them.

BRAXTON: I celebrate the growth of the "nones." As discussed previously, the "nones" are adding needed texture and diversity into public dialogue about social and political possibilities.

Your last sentence above, however, leaves me a bit puzzled. The appeal or lack thereof of various frameworks for one group or another cannot be the predicate for a lively and diverse public arena. If a preexistent "affinity for" certain ideas and approaches is the ultimate motivation, then we might simply reinscribe the very balkanization we are trying to dismantle. I am advocating for an ethic of public engagement that both seeks to persuade and is open to being persuaded in the name of building communities that are more diverse and equitable.

Let me return now to the intriguing engagement my students and I had with a renowned economist. Several years ago, I taught a graduate school course that explored the impact of culture on Christian preaching. In one seminar session, we discussed socio-economic class and the role of preaching in the alleviation of poverty.

We interviewed via conference call Peter Henry, a distinguished economist who was teaching at Stanford University at the time. As it pertains to the fairer allocation of resources, he indicated that the morally relevant question is: How do we change assumptions about what is possible? Changing assumptions, he rightly said, is a role for theologians.

Transforming people's imagination and engaging in moral persuasion about resource allocation fall squarely in the domain of theology or moral philosophy. Thus, in these challenging economic times, how might religious scholars like us employ the wealth of wisdom contained in religious and moral frameworks to ignite more equitable dialogue in the public arena about our collective resource base? Resource allocation is not just about income and politics—it also involves imagination and persuasion.

PINN: I appreciate the intent in your statements, but I wonder about relying so heavily on theologians and philosophers for this assessment and this moral vision. I say this in part because many scholars have lost the ability to communicate with the public. Despite its assets, advanced scholarly training also comes with a liability: it renders many scholars unable to connect in practical ways with the public. Don't we need a greater range of participants in the framing of our moral and ethical commitments?

Should it really be left to such a small group—a group that suffers from some of the very problems that undergird the turn to them? Don't we need a vocabulary and grammar for public engagement that aren't simply drawn from the thinking of (privileged) academics but rather from the collective communication of a larger group?

BRAXTON: Yes, we absolutely need a "vocabulary and grammar for public engagement" that invites diverse groups to constantly refine that vocabulary and grammar. Trained scholars such as you and I have a role to play. Yet as you rightly indicate, our role should not be outsized.

Along these lines, while establishing The Open Church, I have had the privilege of teaching at Southern Methodist University, Harvard Divinity School, and Georgetown University. These university appointments have been invigorating. Nevertheless, the work of establishing The Open Church has been as intellectually demanding, if not more so, than my university assignments precisely because The Open Church is unapologetically situated in the grassroots and concerned with "the folk."

Grassroots wisdom is often more profound than ivory tower knowledge. When engaging in serious dialogue about complex topics like theodicy, I remember wise words from Mariah Taylor, a matriarch in my home church in Virginia. She emphatically exhorted me in my early undergraduate years at UVA, "Don't get educated away from your people."

Tony, irrespective of our similarities and differences on these topics, a deep concern for all people, and more specifically black people, animates our dialogue. We must continue to grapple with this question: How can we create a world where suffering is mitigated and justice and joy are accentuated?

WHAT ABOUT BLACK DEATH?

Tony,

In the days leading up to this month's writing session with you, there was discomfort in my body—a kind of queasiness in my gut. Knowing that we were tackling a topic as difficult as black death, my mind must have sent some shock waves to my body. My initial comments are attached. I hope my reflections do justice to the magnitude of the topic. Writing from a place of "dis-ease" might compel me, and us, to be ruggedly honest about the brutalities of black death.

Best,
Brad

> Brad—
>
> "Busy work" is done, and I have some time to catch my breath. So here we go. The sun is shining bright, the birds are singing, and the sound of my computer keys adds yet another layer to the morning. Thanks for this fantastic start! Motivated by and appreciative of your insights. I think this topic will require a lot from us.
>
> Cheers,
> Tony

．　　．　　．

BRAD R. BRAXTON: As writers, Tony, we regularly face the "how" question with any writing assignment. How should we begin the paragraph, the chapter, the book? How should we frame the story we want to tell or the issues we will examine? The "how" question looms larger than life when exploring the topic of black death. The topic is so complex, evocative, and visceral. How should we narrate the gnarly narrative of the history and ongoing tendency for black people to experience violent, premature, unexplained, and unpunished death?

ANTHONY B. PINN: I agree with you. Yet this death *is* explained. The long history of antiblack racism and the many forms of "control" and "subjuga-tion" name and explain why black people face the death you are bringing into question. But please, go on.

BRAXTON: You're right. According to the "logic" of antiblack racism, which valorizes whiteness as superior, black death "makes sense" as a way of en-suring white domination. By using the term "unexplained" above, I was hinting at the deeper absurdity of antiblack racism.

The perpetration of systematic homicide, and even genocide, to establish an entire cultural system based on racial phenotypes violates deeper "laws" of human dignity and decency. So at the sociological level, black death is understandable even if utterly lamentable. At the existential level, this im-position of death upon black people still causes me to shake my head and ask: Why do cultural differences trigger such vile responses in certain people?

PINN: But we know the answer—race follows racism. The gains (e.g., eco-nomic, political, and social) made through the disadvantaging of certain populations require a justification: race. So differences don't trigger these "vile" responses; they serve to sanction the "rightness" of that death-dealing treatment.

BRAXTON: For now, let me leave that larger question of "why?" and return to the more targeted question of "*how?*" How should we approach the topic of black death? Unfortunately, there are so many examples and entryways into the topic across the long history of black people in the United States. So as we mourn and remember the victims of black death, this is how I want to begin . . . Breonna Taylor.

In the spirit of tenacious love, righteous remembrance, and fierce resistance, we must continue to say her name. Breonna Taylor. In *fact,* I never
met this twenty-six-year-old black woman who was born in Grand Rapids,
Michigan, and lived in Louisville, Kentucky. In *truth,* I am acquainted
with her.

In a way that rings true to me, I know Breonna Taylor. As the son of
a black woman, the husband of a black woman, and the father of a black
woman, I know her . . . Breonna Taylor. Consequently, I must say her name,
and I invite us all to do likewise.

Like all of us, Breonna Taylor was creative and complex. She had hopes
for the future, even though she had experienced many low valleys. She had
family and friends who loved her and made her the best version of herself.
She also had proclivities and relationships that complicated, and at times
compromised, her efforts to live her best life.

In a photo collage in Breonna's scrapbook, there was a childhood picture
of her holding a teddy bear, and the teddy bear was holding a heart with
the words "I Love You." Concerning love, Breonna loved her work as a
healthcare professional so much that she often showed up twenty minutes
early to work, even though the financial compensation at her job might not
have incentivized that level of passion. She also apparently loved hot sauce
so much that she topped her pancakes with it.

It is important to recount some facts of her life, lest we miss invaluable
truths in the ongoing struggle to ensure that black lives matter and to
grapple with the brutalities of black death. Breonna Taylor is not a statistic
or a "problem" to be solved. She is a sister, who in life and death, has many
stories to tell us if we could be quiet and still enough to listen to, and learn
from, them.

Occasionally, "facts" and "truth" dwell in the same domicile. On other
occasions, truth breaks beyond the gravitational pull of facts to give us a
larger view of our individual and collective experiences and the universal
neighborhood in which we all live. Accordingly, in a balanced curriculum
that unites head and heart, science and spirituality are allies, not enemies.
They enable us to navigate the delicate tension between facts and truth.

PINN: I don't understand what you mean here: "Science and spirituality
are allies, not enemies." Science and spirituality are tools for use in our
desire to "know," but this doesn't require collapsing their differences and

antagonisms. They see and name the world differently; they understand and present embodiment differently, highlighting different dimensions of being. Consequently, they offer different forms of resolution. I wonder if we do them and ourselves a disservice by collapsing their differences.

For example, I agree with you that there is something familiar about Breonna Taylor. But do we (as black men) deny dimensions of her unique "touch" on the world by suggesting we know her? If we dig, what is familiar about her? Yes, black men also face death-dealing circumstances, but there are dimensions to the suffering she endured that are foreign to us in that we are shielded from them through our maleness. What do we gain by collapsing those differences? What is lost?

The losses outweigh the gains when we flatten the complexities of black life—thus reducing ourselves—and fail to fully appreciate the impact of intersectionality. To say we know Breonna Taylor is a layered proposition that reduces the complexity of her life, her person, and her experience of the world as a black woman. What about her complex experience can two black men know?

A claim "to know" Taylor also potentially reduces the cause of her death to race (and perhaps class). But is that enough? We have to develop patterns of solidarity that recognize the shared dimensions of our encounter with the world without ignoring our differences. Blackness—as Black Lives Matter teaches us—is complex and isn't reducible to race. Isn't it, then, a more powerful statement for us to stand against her murder despite much of her experience being foreign to the two of us? Otherwise, you and I could be guilty of a mode of "cheap grace"—requiring everything to be reduced to the familiar in order to engage?

BRAXTON: Your response to my fleeting allusion to "science and spirituality" seems excessive. I wasn't suggesting that we collapse the methodological differences between these modes of exploration. By referring to them as potential "allies," I was in turn acknowledging their different approaches.

Also, by harnessing (not erasing) these differences, we might reach a more "balanced" or comprehensive understanding of vexing dilemmas such as black death. Why is it necessary to describe the differences between science and spirituality in "antagonistic" terms? What moral and social good might emerge in the quest to eradicate black death if practitioners within the fields of science and spirituality conferred more with each other in a spirit of humility and curiosity?

PINN: I see what you're trying to accomplish here, but I'm not certain it works. It isn't that science and spirituality are antagonistic, but rather that they have viewed the world and our relationship to the world differently. They frame possibility in different ways—using different modalities of "evidence."

To the extent that science and spirituality "see" the problem differently, I'm not certain how much could be achieved. For example, there is a clarity of language and method in science, but is that the case for spirituality? What, for instance, is spirituality? We often move too quickly to commonality, as if rigorous difference and disagreement must be eradicated. This is one instance where difference and disagreement are fundamental.

BRAXTON: I don't want to stray too far afield and lose our focus on Breonna Taylor. Yet now more than ever, science and spirituality need to partner with one another as we seek to combat another disturbing demonstration of black death, namely the disproportionate suffering and death in black communities during the COVID-19 pandemic. I'm heartened by the creative alliances that have emerged between scientists and religious leaders as we're addressing the understandable "vaccine hesitancy" in black communities and galvanize black people to receive the COVID-19 vaccine as an antidote against black death.

PINN: There's some slippage here. You name spirituality and then move to religious leaders as if religion and spirituality are synonymous. I agree that churches using their networks and opening space provided some aid with respect to COVID-19 testing and vaccine distribution.

In terms of spirituality, I'm left to wonder what you mean by it. Again, you seem to blend religion and spirituality, when there are distinctions to be made. To say religious organizations have partnered with science and federal/state/local organizations isn't the same as saying there is a needed alliance between science and spirituality. What I see here is a much more pragmatic connection between science and spirituality that doesn't require deep agreement.

BRAXTON: I disagree. The straightforward call for a stronger, more positive partnership between science and spirituality can—and in various instances does—work. I renew my critique by saying again that your protestation feels forced and anachronistic. It almost feels as if you are dragging us to a previous century when either spirituality or science was arrogantly fighting to express its dominance as the singular interpretive framework for engaging the world.

PINN: To be clear, I didn't say the partnership doesn't work. I'm arguing that it isn't a necessary alliance. I'm questioning what comes across in your statement as a *required* alliance—as if advances can't take place unless religious or spiritual organizations and personalities are involved. Also, it remains unclear to me what you mean by spirituality over religion.

BRAXTON: As I suggested in a previous conversation, science and spirituality were responsible for many types of abuse in previous decades and centuries. Each of these disciplinary perspectives hopefully learned from these tragedies and adopted a more humble posture. The physiological, psychological, emotional, and existential dimensions of human life and death (especially when death's arrival is premature and unjustified) are too thick for any one explanatory or knowledge-producing system to claim dominance in providing frameworks, posing questions, and providing responses to those questions.

PINN: You call science and spirituality "disciplinary perspectives," but is that accurate? Science requires the rules of evidence and verifiability. Is that the case for spirituality or religiosity? They have very different approaches, often contradictory in nature.

BRAXTON: I'm simply advocating for a multidisciplinary approach to the topic of black death. There's no hidden agenda to erase important distinctions between these diverse approaches. Neither am I ignoring the canons and questions of science.

PINN: Is it really accurate to call spirituality a disciplinary approach? It gives spirituality a certain "reasonableness" that cuts against its perception of the world and our relationship to it. Spirituality seeks to fill in the "gaps" left by science.

BRAXTON: Spirituality is, indeed, a discipline. First, as previously discussed, the word "discipline" (similar to the word "disciple") comes from a Latin word for "student" (*discipulus*). Spirituality involves diverse practices, perspectives, and philosophies that can be, and for millennia have been, taught and learned formally and informally. Conversations with practitioners of spirituality—from Buddhist lamas to Benedictine monks—have enhanced my appreciation for the role of intellectual rigor, emotional fortitude, intuition, embodied knowing (e.g., "mother wit"), and keen attention to detail and process in the cultivation of various forms of spirituality.

These attributes of spirituality explain why some of the great centers of learning in world civilization—from Timbuktu to Harvard—have roots in spirituality. Spirituality, at least as I am approaching it, is not a willy-nilly, intellectually vacuous endeavor. On the contrary, it can be a sophisticated enterprise that pursues knowledge and wisdom through different modes, including the cognitive, the emotive, the volitional, the intuitive, the aesthetic, and the kinesthetic dimensions of life.

Second, spirituality is also an academic discipline where trained scholars engage in description, codification, analysis, critique, and refinement of bodies of knowledge and practice. Furthermore, our grappling with black death would be more robust if we afforded the same respect to the canons and questions of spirituality that we afford to science. It is not a zero-sum methodological game. Various disciplines and approaches should be honest about their strengths and weaknesses and humble enough to consider what can be learned from the strengths and weaknesses of other disciplines. Consequently, we could benefit considerably from the cumulative knowledge and wisdom that emerge when multiple disciplines confer.

PINN: I've not denied a spiritual perspective on death. Rather, I've argued against the assumption of a necessary agreement on the nature and meaning of black death between science and spirituality. Through this discussion of science and spirituality, we've moved away from my initial argument concerning the nature and meaning of black death. Black death involves cultural codes (such as the value of whiteness) and responses to the safeguarding of those codes, and that isn't terrain fully articulated in scientific or spiritual terms.

BRAXTON: This science-spirituality excursus might, indeed, be a detour. Yet on occasions, detours enable us to appreciate some terrain of a topic that might otherwise go unnoticed. I won't linger too much longer. Yet I hope you will permit me to speak briefly to your query about definitions.

Spirituality is derived from the Latin word *spiritus,* which means "wind," "breath," or more figuratively the "breath of life." Spirituality is a way of being and thinking that attempts to place one's life and the lives of others in a larger interpretive framework in order to ascertain the meaning of life. To have a "spiritus" is to be alive, and spirituality is a way of being and thinking that asks poignant existential questions: From where does this breath come? For what purposes am I alive? And where (if anywhere) might this breath take me?

I understand spirituality in an expansive way that can potentially create opportunities for greater understanding and mutual enrichment among diverse religious, spiritual, and ethical traditions. This expansive definition can also foster more meaningful dialogue between science and spirituality. My allusion to religious leaders was not meant to suggest that religion and spirituality are inherently synonymous. Similarly, depending on the cultural tradition under consideration, religion and spirituality may be deeply congruent and contingent upon one another.

In the so-called terminology debate between "religion" and "spirituality," it's problematic to always assume that "religion" is the inferior or suspect term that needs defending or that "spirituality" is the preferred term. Had I anticipated that my passing reference to science and spirituality would elicit the response it did from you, I would have been more intentional in defining my terms. In my understanding of black Christianity, religion and spirituality exist in an interdependent relationship where they mutually enrich each other. So for the record, I consider myself to be both religious *and* spiritual, with each term possessing strengths and weaknesses.

PINN: I get your point, but I've not suggested that religion is "inferior or suspect." Rather, I'm arguing that religion and spirituality aren't the same. A distinction, therefore, is needed. It's a distinction that allows for the statement of one being both religious and spiritual.

BRAXTON: Although you didn't identify religion as "inferior or suspect," many people do. Thus, it was important to articulate my perspective on this more fully. With respect to how religion and spirituality might partner with science, permit me to reflect on an event.

I was honored to participate in a Facebook Live interdisciplinary conversation among scientists, educators, and religious leaders as we sought to empower black communities to embrace the COVID-19 vaccine. Sisters Together and Reaching (STAR), a Baltimore faith-based organization led by black clergywoman Debra Hickman, assembled scientists and educators from leading research universities in Maryland and several clergy connected with congregations in Baltimore. I was invited because of my pastoral role at The Open Church of Maryland.

Anthony Fauci, the renowned public health expert on COVID-19, was the guest presenter at the event, and there was an amicable and informative exchange between science and spirituality in the forum. The large viewership for the program indicates a growing public desire, especially amid the pandemic, for science and spirituality to talk with each other and not at each other.

PINN: The event you describe is impressive, and I applaud the sharing of space and networking between constituencies. But you make too much of a link between science and spirituality. There are distinctions between them that need to be noted and maintained. These distinctions don't prevent an embrace of both, neither do they prevent conversation between adherents to each. Yet it isn't a necessary conversation.

Again, I resist the assumption that such a "meeting of the minds" is required, or by definition, beneficial. Neither science nor spirituality of necessity understands the cultural underpinning of antiblack racism and black death. Anti-black racism isn't a biological (or scientific) arrangement nor does it necessarily relate to spirituality. This cultural code is constituted by a different grammar and vocabulary equally foreign to science and spirituality.

BRAXTON: You make too little of the relationship between science and spirituality, especially as it pertains to black death. For instance, I applaud the educators and journalists who are explaining the social history underneath the hesitancy about the COVID-19 vaccine in certain communities of color. A considerable amount of this hesitancy is rooted in a pathological relationship between science and spirituality that contributed to black death.

PINN: Science and spirituality serve to justify and reenforce patterns of thought and conduct, but they don't create those patterns of thought and conduct.

BRAXTON: This warped relationship enabled science to operate with a system of values or a "spirituality" that viewed black life as inferior or sub-human. According to the dictates of that "spirituality," black death never rose to the level of great moral concern precisely because black life was not an issue about which science was concerned. Hence, black bodies, when they were "alive," could be fodder for inhumane medical experimentation. Furthermore, even in death, black bodies were subjected to indignity and indecency by science.

PINN: We seem to disagree on the ordering of circumstances. I believe racism gives rise to race, and you seem to suggest the opposite.

BRAXTON: No, I'm not suggesting that. The pithy phrase "racism gives rise to race" is helpful because it reminds us that "race" is a social construction designed to preserve inequitable power dynamics. Yet like most aphorisms, the phrase also obscures or downplays other issues.

When defining race as a social construction, we are overturning centuries of scholarship that wrongly asserted that race is an "essential" characteristic of human groups rooted in genetic differences. We now know that genetically there are virtually no differences between and among distinct "racial" groups. Yet there are obviously phenotypical or physiological differences between and among these groups (e.g., skin color, facial features, hair texture). Cultures around the world have established elaborate and oppressive hierarchies based on these differences.

By labeling race a social construction (which it is), do we, however, unwittingly ignore the role of physiology and embodiment in fostering fear and the desire to dominate in groups of people? So even if we rightly acknowledge that "racism gives rise to race," are there not still deep, primordial questions of why genetically insignificant differences can trigger in people the desire to oppress one another? Science and spirituality have played, for better or worse, roles in chronicling various forms of difference and the values we attach to those differences. In the effort to understand and counteract black death, might there be some significant moral advancement and public good that could emerge if we forged a more positive partnership between the two disciplines?

PINN: That relationship wouldn't solve the problem because both science and spirituality respond to and justify racism, they don't create it. Society would simply create other ways of justifying antiblack racism and black death. Think about it: advances in science and spirituality have not decreased the culture of antiblack racism and black death.

BRAXTON: I disagree. Science and spirituality don't simply respond to or justify racism. Warped versions of these disciplines, along with other cultural practices and perspectives, have created racism and race. You seem keen on acknowledging the social construction of racism and race, while simultaneously downplaying key aspects of culture, like science and spirituality in the creation of racism and race. Perhaps, I'm misreading you here.

Furthermore, it's hyperbole to suggest that advances in science and spirituality haven't lessened antiblack racism and black death. Some progress has been made, and more progress might occur if science—with its commitment to precision—and spirituality—with its commitment to justice and compassion—spent more time in constructive dialogue.

Bias, in any form, is pernicious because it is often implicit and unspoken. Consequently, male bias, for example, can unwittingly creep into our most well-intentioned acts of solidarity with women and gender nonconforming people as they resist oppression and death. Vigilance is always needed to ensure that our positive intentions as allies do not result in negative impact.

Mindful of the tendency of males to co-opt the story, I initiated the discussion of black death by calling attention to the love story between Breonna Taylor and her mother. That love story, like any human relationship, was unique. Those of us who stand outside that relationship will never fully understand the rupture created in that particular relationship by that particular death.

PINN: Yet an undeniable danger exists here. In claiming a type of "knowing"—even as a poetic move—you risk collapsing the distinction of experience that is vital. You and I don't know what it means to be a black woman in a racist, sexist, and classist world. What do we really know of "the love story between Breonna Taylor and her mother" that doesn't involve us reading ourselves into that story? And do our solidarity and engagement really require us to even poetically attempt to fill this gap? Is our solidarity really premised on our ability to place ourselves in Taylor's circumstances?

BRAXTON: By saying that I "know" Breonna Taylor, I was not lording my maleness over her story. Rather, I was trying to respectfully situate my maleness in the ecosystem of my relationships with women who are integral in my life—and by extension create solidarity rooted in empathy. Patricia Hill Collins suggests that empathy begins by paying attention to the personal details and societal forces shaping the lives of others.

PINN: The challenge here is that there may not be a difference between "lording maleness" and "situating maleness." We as males aren't in a position to suggest the difference. Our relationships with the women in our lives tell us nothing, really, about the nature, content, and meaning of our relationship to women outside our immediate experience.

BRAXTON: I, of course, could never know the depth of the relationship between Breonna Taylor and her mother, Tamika Palmer. I, nevertheless, am fortunate to witness daily, even if I don't understand it fully, the amazing relationship between my wife, Lazetta Rainey Braxton, and our teenage daughter, Karis Jendayi Braxton. It is so educative to respectfully eavesdrop on their conversations and interactions, as they discuss their similarities and differences, their likes and dislikes, and fascinating topics ranging from music to hair care to body image and body positivity among black women.

PINN: But you view (and interpret) this through your maleness; to that extent, you observe but you can't "know." This is the same as white people saying that they learn a great deal and note similarities when they see or hear black people talk about their relationships and their worth. Is their whiteness not a barrier in that context? Isn't our maleness a barrier already and always?

BRAXTON: The depth and complexity of their love are profound, and I gain inspiring perspectives on the beauty of black life and love from them. Lessons on black life and black love from my wife and daughter also open vistas on the despair of black death as I ponder the rupture that would occur if our daughter were prematurely caught in the jaws of death. Solidarity requires both an honoring of difference and empathetic thinking enabled by analogy.

PINN: But again, what do we know of the story of Breonna and her mother? Don't we do them a disservice by assuming that the little the media has provided tells us what there is to know about the complexities of Breonna's relationship with her mother? Doesn't such an assumption truncate the layered nature of their relationship? Don't we better appreciate the depth of their connection by saying we don't know?

BRAXTON: At a philosophical level, I appreciate your questions, yet you're missing the pragmatic goal I'm striving for, namely empathy and coalition building.

Empathetic imagination involves respectfully engaging the stories of others, while relentlessly refusing to co-opt those stories or collapse important distinctions in identity markers and cultural traditions. This kind of imagination enables people to have honest cross-cultural dialogue and build transformative cross-cultural coalitions involving many identity markers including, but not limited to, gender, race, sexual identity, class status, religious/ethical affiliations, and nationality. These thick coalitions can become sites of empowerment, healing, and resistance to domination.

PINN: Engaging the stories of others as *they* tell them, but is this the case here? Have the family and friends of Breonna Taylor really told their story outside the limited context of this particular tragedy? Can we know their story only in light of how it is reflected through her murder?

BRAXTON: Undoubtedly, any of our identities can be a "barrier" (to use your earlier term). Yet when we analyze our identities, and especially interrogate any dominant identities we possess in the name of equity and justice, our identities can also be tools for building *bridges*, thereby connecting diverse people in allyship in the struggle against black death.

PINN: Yes. Bridges between experiences of distinction but not sources of "sameness."

BRAXTON: Having engaged briefly how the story of two women in my life provide touchstones for my thinking about black life and death, I want to return to Breonna Taylor's story. What stories is she telling us today? The absence of justice through no criminal charges against her murderers is absurd. Colored flesh continues to be dispensable in ways that white flesh is not.

PINN: Is it absurd? Really? Or is it consistent with the basic framework and logic of the nation? Policing wasn't developed to protect us, but rather to protect the white population from us. Isn't this killing in line with that purpose?

The situation isn't absurd. It is morally and ethically problematic from the perspective of black life, but that is a different statement. The question is: Should we expect a different outcome from the same system designed to render us docile? The answer to that question informs the target of activism—reformation or radical reconstruction.

To take it a bit further, in light of the nature of the United States, blackness is equated with death. Whiteness requires a strong relationship between the two. To be white is to be somewhat safe from contamination by either blackness or death. To be white is to assume there are regulations, rights, and structures to safeguard against the challenge of blackness and death. How does one think about black life within that context?

BRAXTON: I use the word "absurd" here similarly to how I used the word "unexplained" earlier. Her death is congruent with the logic of white domination. On this, you and I agree. Thus, I said unequivocally that colored flesh is dispensable per the logic of white supremacy. Yet other logics of human decency and dignity exist—or should exist. By those higher standards, the impunity afforded to those Louisville police officers is absurd.

In the case of Breonna Taylor, death did not apprehend her while she was running from police in the streets. Death, aided and abetted by certain Louisville police officers, invaded the sanctity of her home in the middle of the night, without even the decency of knocking on the door. Breonna Taylor had no criminal record, and there were no drugs found on the premises. She, however, was "guilty" of sleeping while black, and this was enough for police officers to puncture her body with up to eight bullets. "Innocent until proven guilty": this is one of America's *white lies* covered in the *red blood* of way too many *black people*.

PINN: What story is Taylor telling us? Well, the message seems loud and clear. There is no safe space for bodies identified as black. The very existence of these bodies is both a social necessity and a social threat. I want to pause and recognize an important distinction related to the impact and social meaning of blackness—it is deadly when it marks a body (Taylor), and its absence produces opportunities framed in terms of white privilege. We shouldn't lose sight of that.

BRAXTON: You're right. We shouldn't forget this distinction. We'll never know how much good Breonna Taylor might have done if she had been afforded more time. Instead of dying in explainable ways from an exhausted body that had lived many decades, Breonna Taylor was prematurely exterminated in an inexplicable way as the sun was still rising in her life and upon her possibilities.

How do we respectfully examine black death? Perhaps one way is to honor the beautiful, complex story of one recently fallen sister and acknowledge the ache in our souls for the eclipse of positive possibilities that her absence makes so very present. By saying her name—Breonna Taylor—we are commemorating concomitantly the dignity of her life and the indignity of her death.

PINN: On a somber note, let me say again—a lesson we learn is the already and always linking of blackness and death in a world defined by white privilege.

BRAXTON: There are so many painful dimensions of black death, yet some of the most acute aspects for me include the insidious, institutional ways that premature death robs the black community and the broader human community of positive possibilities. Black death also serves as a tangible reminder that even if the Declaration of Independence was penned in black ink, it certainly did not have black people in mind.

PINN: Just a quick interruption: this founding document had black people in mind but as objects necessary for the construction of a society that safeguarded white privilege. It didn't have black people in mind as subjects or citizens; it is built on and guided by our presence as a necessary means for white people to fight off the threat of certain forms of demise.

BRAXTON: On this point, you and I are singing from the same sheet of music, and the tune is unfortunately a funeral dirge. The "truths" of "life, liberty, and the pursuit of happiness" are constantly falsified by the "facts" of the centuries-long assaults on black bodies, black spirits, and black communities in this country. Again, the relationship between "truth" and "facts" is a complicated one. Unfortunately, the brute facts of violence against black people reveal how paltry and insincere our professed "truths" and "values" really are.

PINN: There is a thickness here that we shouldn't miss—a framing of blackness and black bodies that isn't limited to the physical but also shapes and forms what is meant by the social world and its operation. There are ways in which blackness is totalizing—informing both the material and conceptual birth of the nation. This reality raises important questions concerning the ontology we assume.

Does this construction of blackness really afford us opportunity to speak about black people using ontology? Are we (human) beings from the vantage point of the social world? The demise of black people you convincingly highlight would suggest the answer is no. What do we do with that? What does it mean to protest under this understanding? What does it mean to mourn? To lament? To be melancholic?

BRAXTON: Thank you for inviting us to consider more explicitly ontology and the construction of blackness. As we wade into these deep waters, it's important to think about black people as subjects toiling mightily for life and not simply as passive objects upon whom death falls. Let me expound a bit more.

PINN: Following the lead of a range of thinkers, I argue that the subjectivity of black people is the open question—not the conclusion. But please continue.

BRAXTON: West African societies had (and still have) a robust appreciation for ethnic or tribal diversity. This diversity involved the veneration of different ethnic deities, even though many African ethnic groups still believed in the one Great God who created the universe. In order to frustrate communication and quell the threat of slave revolts, slave traders often mixed

West African ethnic groups. Consequently, some ethnic customs and beliefs faded during the time of slavery in the United States, including the beliefs in certain lesser ethnic deities.

While the deities of various West African ethnic groups may have "died" in the Middle Passage of transatlantic slavery, certain pan-African understandings of spirit/God and of important values emerged among many of the enslaved. These pan-African understandings placed the survival of black people atop the spiritual and moral agenda. Hence, these enslaved people no longer identified themselves according to their ethnic heritage but rather by their "racial" heritage (e.g., black physical features and an amalgamation of cultural beliefs and practices from the African continent).

Thus, in a white supremacist culture, "race" was a social construction for the perpetuation of white privilege. For many enslaved black people, "race" became a social construction to facilitate the survival of black people. This historical process partly explains why "race" is a cherished, albeit complex, concept for many black people.

PINN: The historical record makes it difficult for us to know how our ancestors wrestled with these epistemological and existential issues as a matter of thought. We know what they did physically to survive, but how they thought themselves out of this ontological arrangement is somewhat unknown to us.

Also, it's too strong a statement to speak of the death of the African gods. This claim has been refuted in compelling ways over the decades. It might be more accurate to speak in terms of alternations of energy—new formulations of vertical and horizontal encounters that are shaped by and responsive to the new environment. This enables a more fluid sense of metaphysical and material engagements.

BRAXTON: Thanks for refining my language concerning the African gods. I was trying to acknowledge the fluidity to which you allude by using quotation marks when noting that certain African deities "died." Your comments bring into sharper relief the complexities of this long and complicated process of cultural adaptation and transformation.

Furthermore, your earlier question is apt: "Are we (human) beings from the vantage point of the social world?" A fulsome response to the question should consider not only how white people have answered the question, but it also should provide a robust inventory of the ways that black people—as ontological subjects and agents of resistance and innovation—have responded to the question.

PINN: We know how many white people have shaped and responded to that question. But go ahead, please make your point.

BRAXTON: While white supremacist culture constructed "race" as an instrument of death, black people have utilized "race" and "blackness" as mechanisms to fend off death and affirm black humanity. The affirmation of black humanity often required, and continues to require, deep and sustained lamentation. On other occasions, the affirmation manifested itself in celebration, or at least, the imagining of more positive possibilities.

PINN: I would say "blackness" is a category of death (on a variety of levels), as Orlando Patterson, among others, names it. It seems to me you conflate race and blackness when I'm not certain that's a necessary or productive move.

BRAXTON: Perhaps I am conflating race and blackness; if so, I'm not sure that's a problematic move.

PINN: How can it not be a problem—particularly when "blackness" here seems to constitute (in a somewhat restricted sense) African American?

BRAXTON: I find it interesting that you emphasize blackness as a category of death (from the vantage point of white supremacy) without in the same breath acknowledging the positive aspects of the construction of blackness (from the vantage point of black people and black possibilities).

PINN: Throughout our conversation, I've pointed out the subversive efforts of marginalized folks to reconstitute themselves. However, seeking to find something useful in blackness as it is used to constitute death is, for me, akin to redemptive suffering. As you know, that's a problem for me.

BRAXTON: I, like you, have spent many years pondering dimensions of blackness at the corporeal and ontological levels. Many books and essays have been written, and can be written, on that topic alone. Accordingly, blackness for me continues to involve a complex amalgamation of physiology, social construction, and ideological commitments. Thus, blackness is not only a category of death, but it is also a constructive instrument for the affirmation of black life. Some of the earliest and most sophisticated grappling with black death and black life occurs in the black spirituals.

PINN: One could easily add the blues here, a form of musical expression just as old and just as telling (but without the theological assumptions). Unlike the spirituals, the blues destabilize religious claims and mark a path in the world defined not by divine proclamation but by human experience. The blues celebrate embodiment and measure a worthwhile affective response to the world through what these bodies give to and take from the world.

BRAXTON: In response to your earlier question about melancholy, I think of the haunting lyrics in one spiritual: "Sometimes I feel like a motherless child, a long way from home." In that one phrase, this spiritual mournfully examines how suffering and black death foist upon black people both a rupture in intimate human relationships and a disorienting exile from the safety of home.

PINN: I'll say it again: we also can place ditties, seculars, and the blues in this category of early expression. They seem to offer an interrogation of blackness in a hostile world without the leaps of faith offered by the spirituals. It's also important to recognize that much of what we have regarding the spirituals involves later refinements.

BRAXTON: Yes, there are various "early" aesthetic responses to black death and black life, all of which have something to offer us. Considering your affinity for the blues, I wanted to highlight the spirituals, fully expecting you to match my invocation of the spirituals with an invocation of the blues.

We find another compelling example of mourning and melancholy in the words of the spiritual "Lord, how come me here . . . I wish I never was born." In the distinctive idiom of black folk expression, the first line of this spiritual immediately poses the ultimate existential question: If my existence is laden with so much sorrow and suffering, wouldn't nonexistence be a better option?

PINN: Here's the question for me: Is it really a matter of mourning or melancholy? How do black Americans lament or mourn what they have never encountered? Isn't mourning and melancholy dependent on an earlier arrangement or circumstance lost? Some of what is at work here is a "wish"—a theological "wish."

BRAXTON: Deep-seated mourning and melancholy are undoubtedly in the spirituals. The rupture, for example, of transatlantic slavery did not eradicate the deep memory of African humanity, cultures, and freedom prior to the rupture. This memory was passed on to succeeding generations by the elders, the ancestors, and the spirits. So even those generations who only knew the horrors of American slavery could draw from cultural reservoirs whose tributaries connected them with the African continent.

PINN: You might be romanticizing the situation. As we know, memory and the fine points of that experience "beyond" are lost over time. I want to emphasize the development of uniquely "black American" cultural expressions that grow from the unique horrors of antiblack racism in the context of American dehumanization. Also, it's important to demonstrate how these new cultural expressions draw from a range of sources and influences, signifying in the process cultural ownership and imaginative application.

BRAXTON: Furthermore, beyond the transmission of cultural memory, there was the unassailable experience of humanity that black people had as subjects who possessed a spirit which communed with the sacred spirits. The scholar M. Jacqui Alexander ruminates beautifully on how African cosmologies and sacred energy provided enslaved black people a sense of their incontrovertible humanity, despite the grotesquery of enslavement.

So in my exploration of mourning in the spirituals, I am also acknowledging the "prior knowing" of humanity/subjectivity that black people experienced. Thus, the dehumanizing *sociology* of American slavery may not have been the only determinant of black mourning or black musings on existence and freedom. A resilient African *cosmology* may have also funded understandings of an inherent humanity which could not be eradicated despite slavery's grotesquery.

PINN: The privileging of Christianity, for example, limits a more expansive embrace of origins and influences. For example, black folktales and folk wisdom might better present the diversity of expression rather than the spirituals which, as they come to us, involve alterations and don't reflect their initial creation. There is a tendency to reduce the complexity of thought and expression to one organizational framework, and this does us a disservice. Why not maintain the complexity and competing orientations and perspectives? What is presented is often too straightforward and too "neat."

BRAXTON: I am exploring the spirituals as one of many responses to black death. My exploration is not intended to suppress the diversity or complexity of responses.

Our dialogue calls to mind an emerging intellectual discourse that some scholars call "sonic politics." Sonic politics encompasses not just what the lyrics of a song say, but also how the production and reception of sound open space and create meaning in the social, political, and theological realms.

Kathleen Battle's inimitable 1990 rendition of the spiritual "Lord, How Come Me Here?" (archived on YouTube) offers a compelling example of sonic politics. One of the premier vocalists of our time, she uses the full range of her vocal gifts to bring to life poignant lyrics that wrestle with black death:

Lord, how come me here? . . . I wish I never was born.
They treat me so mean here, Lord. . . . I wish I never was born.
They sold my children away, Lord. . . . I wish I never was born.

As Battle sings, her voice soars to a vocal summit, while also possessing an eerie vibrato emanating from her gut. In that one sonic moment, her soaring pitch and the purposeful trilling of her voice interpret the acute psychic pain and physical trembling that countless mothers and children felt as black death violently separated them.

The spirituals also highlight the agency of black people in creating alternative worlds where black humanity and dignity were affirmed. In her lucid exposition of the connection between the spirituals and other African-derived religions in the Americas, Rachel Elizabeth Harding, a scholar who studies indigenous spiritual traditions, explores how black people sang spirituals to invoke spirit and bend lethal oppression toward more life-affirming possibilities.

PINN: You're requiring the spirituals to carry too heavy a burden. Again, let's be mindful of how the spirituals have been altered and refined. If the language is coded, how can we be so certain that we (twenty-first-century black people) are "reading" them correctly? Perhaps Du Bois is correct, and they are sorrow songs. Do we really "know" the workings and arrangements of the spirituals? To the degree that they develop in "hush arbor" gatherings, the spirituals may be as foreign to us as they were/are to white people.

Aren't we reading into the spirituals, making them do the work we need? What of the black folk wisdom and tales that run contrary to the claims of the spirituals? An overemphasis on the spirituals truncates black cultural responses to circumstances and reduces the grammar and vocabulary of engagement to black Christianity and its theological conversation. So much of our ancestors' complexity is lost.

BRAXTON: We aren't reading too much into the spirituals. The autobiographies in the slave narratives and the folklore tradition curated so ably by anthropologists such as Zora Neale Hurston corroborate these ways of interpreting the spirituals.

PINN: Here's the problem: limited sources and limited conversation partners. Available scholarship also provides accounts that run contrary to the spirituals. Scholarship on the cultural lives of African Americans don't reduce this discussion to the spirituals. In these resources, humanism, atheism, and African-derived sensibilities, for example, are expressed. The complexity can't be reduced to the spirituals and the world forged through the spirituals.

Also, we have few autobiographical accounts from enslaved Africans, and many of the later narratives assume full disclosure on the part of the formerly enslaved. These narratives emphasize traditions and practices that run contrary to the world of the spirituals. Hurston may provide a certain reading of the spirituals that you confirm, *but* her scholarship isn't limited to that world of the spirituals. Where do these other practices and perspectives fit?

BRAXTON: There are undoubtedly aspects of that past that we can't retrieve or that remain vague. Yet as black people increasingly chronicle formal and informal family histories and genealogies, we are reminded afresh of how close we still are to people and events connected to American slavery. This might make "retrieval" of certain aspects of the past more reliable than we might otherwise think. For instance, I, like many others, have great-grandparents who were born as enslaved people. These oral histories often run more readily through our family trees than we acknowledge.

Let me return briefly to my earlier comments about "sonic politics" and invoke another example from Kathleen Battle's vocal artistry. I'm also enthralled by her 1990 rendition of the spiritual "Over My Head" (archived on YouTube). Once again Battle utilizes her exceptional vocal skills to interpret the tenacious effort of black people to find or create a world of life, love, and vitality. As she sings the lyrics, there is a lively tone in her voice, which conveys the life-affirming spirit in black people, which refuses to surrender to death: "Over my head, I hear music in the air. . . . There must be a God somewhere."

PINN: This, my friend, is a faith claim. A beautiful and haunting faith claim. But is it nothing more than that, and so it doesn't capture an adequate conclusion to black death?

BRAXTON: Tony, since you're a humanist, and I'm a Christian, we have vastly different opinions on the theological conclusion of that line in the spiritual ("There must be a God somewhere."). Nevertheless, the lyrics in the spiritual (and Battle's performance of it) point to the belief of many black people, amid black death, that there are more songs on life's playlist than funeral dirges. Another kind of music—a soundtrack of life and dignity—is also playing.

So, you're correct. The last line in that spiritual is a faith claim. If faith is the tenacious openness to positive possibilities, I'll gladly embrace, and employ, faith as an instrument to fend off death and foster life.

PINN: I will simply balance those spiritual assertions with the more humanistic leanings of the blues.

BRAXTON: In your voluminous writings, you have grappled in deep ways with black ontology. Thus, I'm curious to learn from your musings on these matters.

PINN: I've come to conclude that black ontology is an open question—not a conclusion. In light of history, for example, can we speak of black being? In light of white supremacy and the ongoing dilemma of death, what does it mean to speak of black being? There's a great challenge in Afropessimism that we must consider.

BRAXTON: We must, indeed, grapple with Afropessimism. And we should attend with equal vigor to the possibilities of Afro-futurism.

PINN: My concern is that we've not grappled with Afropessimism's critique. We've moved quickly to the projection of future.

BRAXTON: Our exploration of ontology, lamentation, and alternative worlds prompts me to reflect on the recent anniversary of the death of Trayvon Martin—a tragic episode that began catalyzing the Black Lives Matter movement. Also, we learned that no police officers were charged in the death of Daniel Prude, an African American man in Rochester, New York. A mere ten days after Breonna Taylor was shot in Louisville, Kentucky, Daniel Prude was apprehended by police in Rochester, New York, as he suffered effects of mental illness. Police officers used restraint tactics that resulted in a loss of oxygen to his brain, and a week later, he died.

Black death—and the antiblackness sentiments that precede and precipitate it—expose many paradoxes. Letitia James, a black, high-ranking official in the criminal justice system, was candid enough to tell afresh an age-old, unvarnished truth and admit the paradox in black and white: because of the afterlife of slavery, our so-called system of justice tends to ignore or incriminate black victims of violence while exonerating individuals who visit the violence upon black people.

PINN: This isn't a paradox. Rather it is the intended working of our sociopolitical system. It is this "democratic experiment" at work.

BRAXTON: The painful paradoxes of black death exist beyond black people's encounters with law enforcement and the criminal justice system. In wrestling with diverse dimensions of black death, we must constantly valorize black people's audacious efforts to fend off the encroachments of black death. In other words, in this gnarly narrative about pathological systems of violence and indignity foisted upon black people, death is not the only actor. Black people are complex, resourceful protagonists in this story, who engage in routine and sometimes heroic acts of resistance.

PINN: Yes, this is precisely the point: the relationship of blackness to death isn't simply a matter of (police) policy. It is the very logic of the social world we inhabit. It *is* the United States. Again, what does it mean to protest, to struggle, to fight, to be abolitionists under such circumstances?

Black death exposes the social world in that the social world depends on black death to safeguard and justify white life. One requires the other. Death isn't an "actor"—sole or one of many. Rather, it is the logic of the social world and the framing for the social world—undergirding the arrangements of whiteness in and of the world. Death is the United States.

We certainly must acknowledge black people's resistance, while also giving attention to the persistence of the problem. Again, we can't move quickly to the projection of a future. We see in the history of this nation the persistence of injustice. Resistance has pointed out the toxic nature of US society, and it has forced the system to reconstitute itself, but it hasn't deeply damaged the system. The question is how we forge moral imagination and ethics in light of this persistent death.

BRAXTON: Your statement that "death is the United States" makes sense on many levels, especially as it pertains to what is "required" socially to perpetuate white supremacy. But does your provocative statement give a full accounting of the valiantly "seditious acts" of otherwise marginalized and brutalized Americans who conspired, and are conspiring, to make "America" a social reality that connotes life and the embracing of radical inclusion?

PINN: Yes, it does. Struggle and resistance speak to the nature of the system. Death is the United States, but we struggle against it. Our struggle doesn't destroy this realization: death is the United States. Our struggle simply recognizes this reality and pushes against it. Yet the United States remains what it is.

BRAXTON: When I read your last comment, my mind immediately went to Langston Hughes's poem "I, Too," where the reader is reminded that American identity has always been larger than the narrow definitions offered by white supremacy. In the physiological and ideological struggle to subvert black death, isn't there continued value in contesting what "America" means, even as we acknowledge how death-laden many constructions of "America" have actually been?

PINN: True, but I read Hughes in relationship to Richard Wright—and through that, one gains a very different sense of our ability to be "American."

BRAXTON: The appeal to Langston Hughes also calls to mind an invitation from the scholar Christina Sharpe. To appreciate more fully black resistance to black death, Sharpe encourages us to plumb the depths of "black expressive culture" including the works of poets, novelists, performance artists, and visual artists.

PINN: Yes, *but* we have to be mindful of the multiple applications of what Sharpe names "the wake" in her book *In the Wake*—and the relationship of blackness to death suggested. This forces a wrestling with the very language and conceptual frameworks we use to speak about black people, to perform blackness, and to seek change.

BRAXTON: In this moment in US and global history, a serious examination of the complexities of black death and the resilience of black people amid these lethal onslaughts is timely. This examination can provide the moral pillars, the political will, and the aesthetic expressions necessary to build a "beloved community," where there are fewer premature visits to the cemetery. As we, in the words of the poet Lucille Clifton, stand on the bridge between "starshine [possibility] and clay [pain]," we must lament the times when death snuffed out black life. We also must vigilantly celebrate every time that death *failed*, because in that failure, black life received a respite, no matter how ephemeral that respite might be.

PINN: I appreciate your tenacious commitment to black personhood, but I wonder about the underlying optimism. We have very different orientations in this matter. You continue to allude to "future"—to the possibility of a different arrangement of life. And I tend to think in terms of the inability to detangle blackness and death using the vocabulary and grammar of life produced in a context committed to and developed for the preservation of whiteness. We are left with the question: What do we make of black death in a world that demands it?

BRAXTON: This is my response to your question: We passionately resist the demands in our world for black death with a defiant black life, and in so doing, we continue creating other worlds. This defiance can take many forms (protest, lamentation, innovation, black joy, and black love). I may recant many things, but I refuse to recant my fierce commitment to the future.

PINN: We must first come to an understanding of what black life is in a world framed by black death. Is it simply opposition? What is life—white or black—in a world defined by death? Rather than the future, I emphasize a struggle with the present.

We should fight against the injustice that captures our current existential context without slipping into what "might" be. How can we know the portrait of a just world when there has never been one? We do this work through negation: we know what a just world can't contain. This, again, requires more rigorous attention to the present and the past.

BRAXTON: Your poignant sentiments are greatly appreciated. Every time you rightly sound cautionary notes from Afropessimism, I will balance them with visionary notes from Afro-futurism.

PINN: But which more accurately describes the nature of our social world and our circumstances? Concerning the answer to that question, we will continue to disagree.

HOPE AND TALK OF THE FUTURE

Tony,

Thanks for your patience. My reflections are attached. I anticipate another engaging exchange this month. I have a hunch that we are going to have fun with this topic. The pandemic has made the dreary days of late fall even bleaker than usual. So an infusion of fun and positivity are most welcome.

Best,
Brad

> Brother Brad—
>
> The semester never ends—and I'm feeling a certain way about that! (I think you know what I mean. Ha-ha.) But perhaps this feeling is intensified by the time confined to the house? Anyway, I apologize for the delay in getting this to you. Much appreciation for your insights and perspective here.
>
> Cheers,
> Tony

■ ■ ■

BRAD R. BRAXTON: In the summer of 2020, you and I collaborated in an online seminar about hope and black religions sponsored by the Smithsonian Center for Folklife and Cultural Heritage. I'm eager to renew and deepen our reflections concerning hope and how we might talk responsibly about the future.

ANTHONY B. PINN: That was an important conversation. If memory serves, it significantly shaped ideas for this book.

BRAXTON: Permit me to begin with these reflections. Once during the Christmas season, James and Bettye Forbes, who are dear friends, treated my wife, Lazetta, our daughter, Karis, and me to the Christmas Spectacular show at Radio City Music Hall in New York City. As we entered the hall, we received cardboard and plastic 3-D glasses. At a point in the show, we put on our 3-D glasses and watched the video images on the gigantic movie screen on the stage. The screen simulated a sleigh ride through New York City. The 3-D glasses enhanced our viewing experience by adding depth to the length and width of the images on the screen. With the addition of another dimension, our viewing experience was more immersive.

I am interested in understandings of hope that have depth and texture. Our country has experienced seismic shifts in the wake of the COVID-19 pandemic, ceaseless episodes of antiblack violence, and the 2020 presidential election. Some people were stunned that even after four years of President Trump's demagoguery, he won over seventy million votes from our fellow citizens. As a staunch progressive, I am in no way surprised by the election results, both in 2016 and 2020. Like you, I am a student of the ebbs and flows of the history of the United States—a nation whose bizarre deeds often contravene its lofty creeds. Consequently, nothing about the United States surprises me.

What does surprise me is the way that some of us have allowed this period in history to create in us a deep despair. If the contrary winds of one or two presidential elections cause those of us concerned about justice and inclusion to despair to the point of inaction, then our hope might have been too insubstantial in the first place, or at least, our hope was not grounded by a serious reading of American history.

PINN: I see your point, but I wouldn't necessarily label the affective response to the hatred, antiblack racism, and other modes of disregard in the Trump era as "despair." We could easily call this response a deep recognition that there is no early point of community and civility to which we should simply return. This being the case, I would call it a vested realism as opposed to despair. It's a recognition that Trump didn't initiate anything; rather, he played on long-standing social codes and encouraged others to make public what typically were, as a friend once said, private responses to difference.

BRAXTON: Your observations about Trump are spot-on. His election and absurd behavior during his presidency authorized covert xenophobia to unmask itself again and overt xenophobia to gain further traction.

Your insights about Trump also enable me to clarify my comment about despair. I have sensed this despair more in white friends and colleagues who are committed to restorative justice than in black people. Many of these white people believed, to employ Martin Luther King's words, that "the arc of the moral universe is long, but it bends toward justice." What some of these white people failed to remember is that there are countervailing forces in the universe, or certainly in the body politic, that are constantly contorting that arc to benefit already privileged groups.

PINN: I agree and add that the disregard, often violent, is as old as the country. It isn't as if Trump ushered in the mechanisms of racial hatred, greed, and xenophobia; he is simply the most recent embodiment of these toxic principles.

Also, it's difficult to assess allies in the current moment. I can't forget that Trump received over seventy million votes—many coming from white evangelicals, *but* white people in general voted for him in high numbers. This signals the ongoing logic of white privilege as the underlying ground rule for collective life in the United States. I don't see this changing simply through a different occupant in the White House.

BRAXTON: Subscribing to a simplistic myth of linear progress, some white allies construed the election of Barack Obama as an indelible sign that our country was ready to end its lengthy entanglement with white supremacy and other forms of identity-based oppression. This partly explains why some people started spouting the ridiculous claim that Obama's election heralded a post-racial age in the United States. The Trump presidency shattered the linear myth of progress for some people, thereby causing their despair.

PINN: Didn't many black voters share this optimism as well? Didn't liberals across racial lines see Obama's election as a break with old (and problematic) patterns of disregard?

BRAXTON: Many black people shared this optimism, but in the black communities where I spent most of my time, the optimism was tempered. This tempered optimism could be described in grammatical terms.

Obama's victory in 2008 heralded a cause for rejoicing, both in terms of the policies his administration might enact and the symbolic power of the White House being occupied for the first time by a black First Family. So many black people used both an exclamation point *and* ellipses to depict their state of mind after the 2008 election. In other words, many black people in effect said: "Obama won the presidency! . . ." Many black people happily marked this historic moment with an exclamation point *and* cautiously followed that phrase with big bold ellipses (ellipses are those punctuation marks indicating either an omission of content or an incomplete and unfolding thought).

Some black people worried that Obama's election would usher in a "sense of arrival" and "satisfaction" among many distinct groups who might let their guard down and become politically complacent. Others worried if the Obama administration would have the political courage to accentuate, not modulate, more strident demands for social accountability and radical reconstruction of how the United States treats marginalized groups.

PINN: Good point! I hear what you're saying, and you aren't disagreeing with my statement. There was an optimism—with certain assumptions that cut across racial lines. Millennials from diverse backgrounds saw in Obama a certain promise that made hope reasonable.

BRAXTON: During the 2008 election, Obama could have explained to the nation how Reverend Jeremiah Wright, Obama's pastor at the time, was expressing righteous indignation about America's injustices through a long-standing moral tradition of black prophetic preaching. One of Wright's sermons titled "The Audacity to Hope" inspired the theme of the "audacity of hope" for Obama's 2008 campaign.

With his razor-sharp mind and silver tongue, Obama could have carefully connected the audacity to hope, especially in black communities, to the audacity to express rage at the circumstances that hinder hope. Obama's reticence about justifiable expressions of black rage, as exemplified in some of Wright's fiery sermons, tethered the optimism of many black people to a political realism about how whiteness impacts national politics.

PINN: There seems to be a discernible theological gap between Wright and Obama. Wright represents the "radical" edge of black theology within the church context, whereas Obama's theological-ethical orientation is a more staid social gospel model (i.e., rectifying social problems rather than revolutionizing the social systems producing those problems).

BRAXTON: Let me return briefly to the myth of progress among white people. When I worked at the Smithsonian National Museum of African American History and Culture, I frequently took groups on tours. During the tours, I highlighted how the museum's artifacts and exhibits moved between the poles of "grotesque inhumanity" (reflected in the torment inflicted upon black people) and "indomitable hope" (reflected in black people's relentless quest for a better today in spite of the brutalities of yesteryear or yesterday).

During a post-tour seminar at the museum with a group of racially diverse seminary students, some white students were lamenting racial injustice in the United States and its intensification during the Trump administration. Certain white students empathetically inquired how the black students were feeling as they experienced the xenophobia in the current political climate.

A black student then made a poignant observation: this moment in US history and the trip through the museum highlighted the tenacity and realism of black communities. Although many black people did not support Trump's election in 2016, they were not surprised by it. According to this black student, the despair that many white people felt at Trump's election was a manifestation of the fragile hope of many white progressives, one that had not been toughened by the repeated disappointments of the American dream mutating into an American nightmare.

PINN: I'm glad you brought this up. I'd say that the response of the white students is a performance of invisibility. The white students, apparently disconnected from the injustice presented by the museum, forced black students to be hyper visible. White students made it an issue of affective response to racial pain as opposed to wrestling with their participation—passive or active—in a system of disregard that privileges them. The problem, instead, is perceived as "out there" with its cartography determined by the feelings that black people have about unjust circumstances, as opposed to marking it through the display of privilege represented by their whiteness.

While I understand what the black student was saying, I'm not convinced that black people weren't surprised. Many black people assumed that there were limits to the public display of hatred in the nation—certain terms of public engagement that would be maintained. Liberal white people weren't alone in assuming the existence of a moral compass guiding the nation (even if that moral compass was a standard to measure the nation's failures). Yes, black people are continuously denied, but doesn't the fact that black people keep trying in a country that proves itself unwilling (if not unable) to include us speak to a similar optimism or naivete? We need to pay more attention to an appropriate realism.

BRAXTON: Naivete bewitched some black people momentarily during the opening decades of this century, but that was not how I experienced the responses of many black people during this time. As noted earlier, many of us never suffered amnesia about the limitations that white fear and white supremacy impose on the reconstruction of America toward radical inclusion and justice.

I also have invited many white friends and colleagues to examine more candidly the contours and contents of hope, especially the kind of hope that knows how to respond to profound disappointment and, in your words, disregard. Historians and political scientists can debate whether the 2016 and 2020 elections were a referendum on Obama's agenda of hope. But as a theologian, I believe that hope must and will survive our polls and politics.

PINN: I understand the motivation for this statement, but what in the history of black people in the social world of the US justifies or sanctions this hope? Is it a hope grounded in material evidence? How does this hope sanction itself within the parameters of human history? I also wonder about the "substance" of hope in the rhetoric of the Obama era. What is the nature of that hope? What are its signs?

BRAXTON: Concerning the sanction for hope, I call to mind the work and words of Samuel DeWitt Proctor, the educator and religious sage who mentored many civil rights leaders and advised Presidents John F. Kennedy and Lyndon B. Johnson. Proctor mused often on the power of hope to widen the boundaries of the soul and the society. He spoke about the importance of the subjunctive mood in fostering hope during his childhood in Virginia during the Jim Crow era.

The subjunctive is the grammatical mood for imagining possibilities. So hope, in some religious traditions, might be construed as an overall perspective on life that brings *what is* (the indicative mood) into conversation with *what may be* (the subjunctive mood). To your point, the "indicative mood" of US history is filled with countless examples of the victimization of and violence toward black people. Hope does not ignore or whitewash (pun fully intended) this history. It looks squarely in the face of history, while also imagining a different and better story and social arrangement that rectify the injustices of history.

PINN: I appreciate your comments, but I'm still left with a question: What "authorizes" this hope? What in the movement of history suggests such a stance is grounded? It isn't clear to me how this hope "looks squarely in the face of history," as you put it, and still assumes the viability of transformation. What some people call "hope" in this context is better described as "faith." I say this because faith has a lower bar regarding evidence.

BRAXTON: We may not gain much ground by parsing too closely the differences between "faith" and "hope." In a frequently quoted passage in Hebrews 11:1, the New Testament writer doesn't distinguish between "faith" and "hope" with philosophical accuracy but suggests in a broad-brush way that faith and hope are related.

The text reads: "Now faith is the substance of things hoped for, the conviction of things not seen." Biblical commentators have spent thousands of years and thousands of pages trying to delineate the nuances between faith and hope in this verse, and I won't burden us with that tedious history of interpretation. In short, this verse and the broader corpus of Christian scripture suggest that faith includes confident actions based on a deep belief that one's positive expectations (i.e., hope) will eventually come to fruition.

PINN: I disagree with your first point. There is a need for parsing the differences as closely as possible because there are moral and ethical implications and requirements associated with each. And this is a vital distinction: faith might have a more significant limitation in that it isn't a concept that necessarily functions well within a "secular" context. This, however, is not the case with hope. There are a host of consequences to this distinction that shouldn't be lost.

BRAXTON: To move from more abstract language to more picturesque language, I have often depicted faith this way. Faith is when our inner being stands on tiptoe in anticipation of positive transformation. An everyday example of faith occurred for me once in the kitchen when our daughter, Karis, was a toddler.

Karis loves grapes, and we kept the grapes in a container on a counter slightly beyond her reach. As a toddler, Karis began to realize the value of standing on her tiptoes. By standing on her tiptoes, she was able to reach and enjoy the fruit placed on the counter. By standing on her tiptoes, she experienced what would be out of reach had she stood flat-footed on the floor. In this illustration, faith is the active posture of standing on tiptoe and reaching, and hope is the steadfast expectation that nourishment is available or can be produced.

I don't want to strain the metaphor too far. Yet I wonder if a lack of hope causes some people to remain emotionally flat-footed on the floor of doubt, constrained by limited human perception. The diminishment of expectations about what is positive and possible can subsequently diminish the intensity of our stretching and reaching for what is positive and possible.

PINN: Not at all. There are too many examples of black thinkers and activists who work based on the present without a deep regard for the future. Think in terms of Du Bois and his reworking of the concept: "a hope not hopeless but unhopeful." Think in terms of his *Souls of Black Folk* in which every effort to justify "future" for black people is met with failure.

Your assumption only works if one assumes the necessity of hope, that is to say, assumes a singular orientation as plausible. One can appreciate the absurd—and be what Albert Camus calls an absurd "hero": deny hope and push against injustice by seeking moments of positivity. Foucault refers to this as "spaces for the practice of freedom." But, as Foucault notes, those spaces collapse, and we continue to struggle.

BRAXTON: Hope is *audacious*. While confronting the brutal facts of history, hope refuses to capitulate to those brutal facts. This imaginative reconstruction then empowers people to tangibly build new and more equitable social arrangements, or at least lay the foundation for them.

So hope is more than dogged determination that is resigned to push on. It is a portrait of a reimagined world that energizes us to make that world a reality. We work passionately for that better reality because we realize that the subjunctive mood or "what may be" is not guaranteed to be positive without our steadfast effort.

There is transcendent spiritual energy—moving through history yet not bound by it—that seeks to foster harmony and goodness. In the midst of our successes and failures concerning justice and inclusion, this Spirit nudges us in the present, if we are open to those nudges, to imagine greater possibilities in the future. This Spirit then partners with us, again if we are willing, to implement those possibilities. I subscribe to metaphysical beliefs that engage human history and expand beyond that history to larger "worlds" beyond this world.

Our principled differences about these metaphysical realities cause us, I suspect, to interpret what counts for "evidence" very differently. Notwithstanding the differences in our philosophical/metaphysical frameworks, I'm intrigued by your somewhat bleak reading of history. It almost seems as if you believe there has been little, if any, progress toward justice.

PINN: Rather than hope, perhaps we should talk in terms of perseverance or persistence as the determination to push against injustice despite the ongoing conditions of disregard. Something about this language of perseverance, for me, better grounds the commitment and better situates the activity within the arena of history lived.

BRAXTON: My musings on hope call to mind the initial meeting between President Obama and President-elect Trump after the 2016 presidential election. I appreciated how President Obama ensured that a black bust of Martin Luther King Jr. peered over the shoulder of President-elect Trump as the two met in the White House in January 2017 for the transition of power. Prophets should always peer over the shoulders of politicians to signal to the despondent and downtrodden that hope will prevail.

PINN: I get and appreciate the symbolic value of the bust of MLK. However, does it have more than symbolic value? Does it really suggest a standard by which Trump would have to measure himself? Nothing about his presidency would suggest that the critique of prophets had power. For instance, think about the number of evangelicals who have invested in Trump with the same moral authority associated with MLK.

BRAXTON: For some people who resisted Trump's demagoguery in the name of hope, symbols of hope from the past provided inspiration. Yet for such symbols to have substantive social power in the present, groups such as evangelical Christians would have had to place more hope in the power of the positive principles of Christianity (justice, peace, and inclusion) and less hope in their proximity to presidential power.

PINN: This demonstrates the link between evangelicalism in the US and the racial politics of the US. They are connected—one offering theological rationales for the other. Evangelicalism offers spiritual rewards for those practicing divisive racial politics. Evangelicalism also allows purveyors of divisive racial politics a cosmic justification that ignores history.

BRAXTON: The links between evangelicalism and racial politics should be rigorously examined. Unfortunately, many evangelicals valued proximity to presidential power more than a principled critique of misused power. Their misguided hope enabled the Trump administration to inflict significant trauma on many already traumatized communities. This is precisely why we need diverse groups of people coming together to reconstruct hope so that hope can help us reconstruct a more inclusive society.

Yet even when despair and destruction tried to push hope off the scene, hope continued to hang around, waiting in the wings. Hope—the quality to go on in spite of it all—must take center stage now.

PINN: This is interesting, hope as "the quality to go on in spite of it all." However, couldn't that just as easily be called "persistence"? This going on in spite of requires the assumption of future or resolution that hope entails. This going on is persistence, or perhaps, perseverance. But what makes it hope? There are connotations to hope, as certainly you've gathered, that bother me.

BRAXTON: Hope is more than persistence, even as important as persistence is. Hope is a future-oriented disposition that imagines and subsequently seeks to facilitate better alternatives.

PINN: Yet persistence isn't without vision and doesn't exclude the possibility of imagination; persistence instead grounds all this in human history.

BRAXTON: Given the scope of our problems, a paltry, superficial hope will not do. It is time now to add depth to our discussion of hope. We must place spiritual spectacles on our "third eye" so that we apprehend the deeper dimensions of hope. In spiritual matters, it's the "third eye" that really matters. Regardless of the ability or inability of our physical eyes to provide sight, each of us has a "third eye" that provides us with moral insight and prophetic foresight.

PINN: I have some difficulties with your assertions. You speak in terms of what we must do, but what sanctions or authorizes that approach? It is what we must do in order to . . . ? The word "must" has surfaced in religious rhetoric for centuries of black church life, but what has it generated? It is a "must" that brings about what? And what is "paltry, superficial hope"? My fear is that your approach demands more than can be delivered.

BRAXTON: I appreciate your suspicion about religious rhetoric utilizing the word "must." Undoubtedly, many black Christians have used that language in a heavy-handed way. There are many ways of thinking about hope. Some of the ways are complementary and others contradictory. I was simply suggesting that we might benefit from making discussions of hope as robust as possible.

Let me return to my opening metaphor in the prompt. If we peer at hope through spiritual spectacles, there are at least three dimensions of hope: an *internal* dimension, an *external* dimension, and an *eternal* dimension.

When I speak of the internal dimension of hope, I mean the deep truths inside of us that we can hold on to no matter how barren the land or broken the situation. When I think of internal hope, I remember Mariah Taylor, the spiritual matriarch of my home church in Virginia, who would always say to me, "Son, just keep on keeping on." The black spiritual elders had a profound relationship with internal hope.

PINN: I'm not fully understanding what you mean by the "internal" dimension. It seems to speak to the concept of human dignity or what MLK called "somebodyness." Yet I'm not certain what it has to do with hope. Can you help me with this?

BRAXTON: You're on target. The internal dimension is rooted in an abiding sense of self-worth and love of one's community and one's people. If you love yourself, your community, your people, then you will find it hard to accept social values and political circumstances that constantly demean your inherent worth. Consequently, you begin to (re)imagine alternative values and circumstances that correspond with your estimation of yourself.

In addition to internal hope, we also should have *external* hope. By external hope, I mean the aspirations that we have for the world beyond our narrow confines. I cite one external hope that I have for our nation. I hope that we will increase, not abandon, our efforts to address, for example, intertwined enemies such as racism and poverty. Instead of patting ourselves on the back, we should put our hands increasingly on the plow until everyone, regardless of color and economic status, can reap the American harvest.

PINN: I appreciate what you're saying, but it begs the question for me—the question I've asked often: What sanctions or justifies this hope? Upon what is it built, other than more hope?

BRAXTON: As alluded to earlier, what sanctions hope for me (beyond an explicit theological claim I will discuss momentarily) is the connection among the past, present, and future. Here, I might push back on you.

The hope of black people in the past did much more than simply build more hope. This hope built tangible infrastructure and institutions that substantially improved the lives of black people and enriched the United States and the world. For example, after the Civil War, members of black churches, with the assistance of white Christian missionaries, established and supported colleges and training institutes. Without the tireless and hope-filled support of many black church folk, there would have been no Howard and Hampton, no Morehouse and Morgan State, no Spelman and Shaw.

PINN: I disagree with some of your claims. You've talked about hope in terms of imagination beyond current circumstances, but here you provide examples that are grounded in these circumstances. I don't see at work what you label "imagination" in these examples.

While I appreciate and applaud these historical black institutions of higher learning, let's not assume that the white people and black people involved in their development had the same mission in mind. Think, for example, of the differences of opinion about black education and progress even between black leaders like W. E. B. Du Bois and Booker T. Washington. Are both Du Bois and Washington exercising hope tied to imagination that is transformative—as you've suggested?

We also have the benefit of hindsight. Did these institutions transform our circumstances? While they may have made possible an Obama, they didn't make impossible a Trump. From our position in the twenty-first century, is this hope justified in light of what we know about the long centuries of disregard that continue to shape the death-dealing nature of antiblack racism *as* the United States? In short, I'm calling for a more explicit link between hope and history. The expansive reach of what you label hope is a problem for me. It seems totalizing in terms of black imagination.

BRAXTON: Let me amplify my point. After helping to establish these educational institutions, many day-laboring black people tenaciously clung to hope in order to support the next generation having a better present and future. I call to mind those audacious black church sisters, mothers, and missionaries who paid tuition for black students by washing and ironing, sowing and frying. These church women tied money up in handkerchiefs, in knots that only they could untie, and stored them under mattresses for safekeeping. And when young persons needed money to further their education, church sisters would lovingly untie and empty those handkerchiefs, persuaded that the change *in the handkerchiefs* would result in a big change *in the world.*

Advocates for justice and inclusion are not the only ones who employ imagination. Proponents of injustice and inhumanity are equally invested in the power of imagination, not to promote goodness but rather to sow discord and inflict harm. There are many horrible examples of how imagination was used as a weapon of warfare against humanity. Yet history also offers many compelling examples of how imagination has been used as an instrument to uplift humanity.

Things are as well for us as they are, Tony, because somebody invested in hope on our behalf, even though they knew they would never meet us. Similarly, I want things to be better for us and others, even though I may never meet some of those others. I invest in hope for those who come after me, just as those who came before me invested in hope on my behalf.

Concerning the role of hope in sponsoring forward progress, a black president and a black vice president are important milestones on the journey to racial and economic justice, though justice is still being denied to many people, especially people of color and economically vulnerable people in our country.

PINN: Doesn't this speak against hope? Or we might have different ways of defining hope because all you say about hope—and I appreciate your remarks—can be captured through perseverance or persistence: the determination to keep pressing despite the tenacious nature of disregard. This persistence is a push against injustice that isn't outcome-driven nor does it measure the importance of our effort based on what it achieves. Instead, persistence finds value in the very act of resistance.

BRAXTON: Evidence of injustice doesn't invalidate hope. Rather it highlights the tenacity of those forces that seek to impede hope.

PINN: From what you've said, hope seems like another way of naming "yearning" or "desire"—neither of those is premised upon an evaluation of the evidence or a deep look into what circumstances warrant.

BRAXTON: I'm happy to include words such as "yearning" or "desire" in my lexicon. I, however, disagree that my depiction of hope ignores the evidence. In actuality, the social reconstructions that hope often posits and seeks to produce emerge precisely because the evidence has been lived, evaluated, and found severely inadequate and in need of major overhaul.

Finally, concerning my three dimensions of hope (this is where you and I differ most significantly), I have an *eternal* hope. With all due respect, my ultimate hope was never grounded, for example, in Obama's presidency. Barack Obama is a brilliant and morally centered man. But in the words of the Bible (Psalm 146:3), he is a "prince"—a world leader who is constrained by faults, failures, and finitude like us all.

So when I speak of an eternal hope, I am not promoting otherworldly escapism. Rather I am acknowledging a deep-seated openness to partnership with dimensions of spiritual power that can embolden us as we struggle against vicious demonstrations of unjust power. My eternal hope enables me to declare that the brutality of "now" cannot swallow the beauty of the "not yet."

PINN: What you describe seems to be a matter of faith—hope grounded in faith. But that involves a circular logic in which the desire or yearning for better justifies the yearning for better. The appeal to scripture, while I understand why you make it, doesn't resolve the issue for me. Rather it points us back to the issue of theodicy. This raises a concern: What is the relationship between hope and theodicy? The history of African Americans might just as easily suggest the "not yet" is actually a "never."

BRAXTON: On the one hand, your use of the word "never" is instructive. You are exhorting us to honestly read the complicated history of African Americans.

On the other hand, your use of "never" seems problematic. There is a considerable space between acknowledging formidable foes and ceding the battle prematurely to those foes. The forces that seek to frustrate hope and hope's positive alternatives are real and rugged. Yet I want to narrate the ongoing story such that sentences conclude with another word: "possibilities."

PINN: I appreciate your position, but you're misreading me. I say "the history of African Americans might just as easily suggest the 'not yet' is actually a 'never.'" I'm not using "never" or arguing for it. I'm simply saying the historical evidence makes it a viable question that has to be addressed and not assumed away. "Ceding the battle" isn't what I'm suggesting—far from it.

My turn to persistence or perseverance offers precisely the opposite of this type of surrender. Persistence is a mindful fight that isn't outcome driven, rather it is akin to what is meant by liberation or transformation that occurs in the process of struggle itself. Again, I question the underlying assumption that there is hope *or* surrender, just as I question the steep optimism I hear in your argument.

BRAXTON: You once spoke to me about moving away from outcome-based strategies, and I appreciate you renewing that important theme. While I'm intrigued by your assertions, your rhetoric raises concerns for me. In explaining your ethic of perseverance, you speak about a "mindful fight." The fight is mindful of what? Futility or at best the prospect of negligible progress? At what point does perseverance cease to be heroic and simply become "fatalism in motion"?

PINN: I don't speak in terms of "futility" because that is framed by outcome-driven thinking. An ethic of perseverance is mindful of the persistent nature of injustice—its long (and only slightly disrupted) history. Perseverance is always heroic, to the extent it pushes against normative modes of thinking about activism; it is always heroic because it resists injustice . . . always. The "fatalism in motion" notion only holds *if* one assumes an outcome-driven orientation or philosophy. By denying that framing, the impact of such a question is lost.

BRAXTON: To your point, we should avoid easy binaries. Maybe the goal is to find the right balance. When there is too much hope, we run the risk of utopian thinking. When there is too little hope, we run the risk of nihilistic thinking.

PINN: This risk is viable only if one assumes outcome-driven strategies. It isn't a required connection. Also, there are several ways to frame nihilism, which could simply entail a rejection of a certain logic of life, not a surrender to circumstances.

BRAXTON: Don't we need some semblance of hoped-for outcomes to invigorate the fight with larger purpose and direction? I understand the importance of not fixating on outcomes, yet I would not want to leave the impression that the articulation of hoped-for outcomes is inherently problematic. I value the importance of negation, of resolutely saying "No" to the forces of injustice.

The repeated "No" to injustice is crucial, but I wonder if "No" by itself has the capacity to carry us all the way to where we want to be. "No" keeps us appropriately tied to past and present pain. And "Yes" elevates us to imaginatively consider present and future possibilities. Thus, I receive your words about my "steep optimism" as a compliment, not a critique. At its best, hope is steep. It elevates us to rigorously and joyfully consider heretofore unimagined opportunities.

PINN: Your question regarding getting where we want to go betrays an orientation, or posture, that assumes outcome-driven strategies as normative. Such isn't my thinking—and isn't the thinking for many like me.

Hence, getting where we want to go isn't the concern. Do we really know what "freedom" or "liberated life" looks like—in a way that really allows us to aim for it? Rather than getting where we want to go, the orientation I'm suggesting involves pushing against where we are.

WHAT DO WE LEARN FROM BLACK LIVES MATTER?

Tony,

How are you faring, brother? I hope you were not impacted too badly by the ice storms and power outages.

Best,
Brad

> Brad—
>
> Greetings. We'll complain about the cold . . . until the heat hits. I have to say, it has been hard working with a winter coat and gloves on! But now we're good—no damage, and power and water are back. Thanks.
>
> Cheers,
> Tony

■   ■   ■

ANTHONY B. PINN: The election of President Obama authorized a certain type of hope—a hope that the nation could actually acknowledge and correct its long-standing antiblack patterns of thought and practice. A black man was in the White House. However, it is also during his presidency that the need for Black Lives Matter (BLM) emerges.

BRAD R. BRAXTON: A type of hope was, indeed, wafting through the air after Obama's election in 2008. Many people from diverse cultural backgrounds felt immense pride and a significant sense of accomplishment when the Obamas walked on to that stage in Chicago's Grant Park where President-elect Obama gave his victory speech on November 4, 2008. The picture of a soon-to-be black First Family was a remarkable sight.

While the symbolism and optics of the moment were profound, the moment also affirmed the importance of grassroots mobilizing. Through a delicate mixture of old-school organizing and new-school social media, of corporate money and small-dollar donors, the "Obama coalition" assembled diverse groups that propelled him to victory. In hindsight, the hope in that moment reflected a soaring aspiration for a new and better direction for racial dynamics in the United States. Also, many of us were longing for a political and social cohesiveness rooted in intercultural collaboration.

PINN: This is all true. Obama's speech at the 2004 Democratic National Convention prompted his rapid rise to prominence. In the speech, he linked the possibility of his historic candidacy to the basic democratic vision within the United States. Yet during his climb, he frequently avoided strong critique of US injustice. For example, he distanced himself from Reverend Jeremiah Wright in his "A More Perfect Union" speech in March 2008. Obama promoted a type of hope that softened the hard realities of antiblack racism being endemic to the US's self-understanding as a nation.

BRAXTON: Undoubtedly, some versions of hope during Obama's candidacy and earliest days in office were untethered to social realism. This led to outlandish assertions that the United States had entered a post-racial era. As we have discussed, many of us never associated hope with amnesia. When I speak of amnesia, I am referring to how some people wanted one election in the early twenty-first century to counteract centuries of assaults on the bodies and dreams of marginalized people in the United States, especially black people.

PINN: We have covered some of this, but I still wonder if hope is the proper grammar for our posture toward the world when considering the "long centuries," as Richard Wright called them, of injustice and demise. What anchors this hope? This sense of hope requires a "taming" of the past—a subduing of the history of the United States that doesn't make racial disregard and other forms of violence a part of the nation's very character and content.

BRAXTON: As we set the context in which BLM emerged, we should avoid another form of amnesia. We should not forget the sociopolitical environment during Obama's ascendency to the White House. Formidable forces sought to neutralize the promise and audacity of hope.

First, the aftershocks of the 9/11 terrorist attacks were still vibrating in the American imagination during Obama's rise to power. Influenced by the neoconservative military hawks who played decisive roles in his administration, President George W. Bush led the US into wars in both Afghanistan and Iraq. The US waged these wars not only to avenge the 9/11 attacks but also supposedly to carry the torch of democracy to other parts of the world.

A deep-seated hatred of "colored" people already existed in certain segments of the US population. The Islamophobia, which was intensified by the 9/11 attacks and these wars, fueled that hatred and further promoted a public narrative that America's "way of life" was under attack by "dark people" who held different and dangerous beliefs. Misguided notions of American exceptionalism caused some people to downplay or ignore past and present manifestations of white nationalism.

PINN: I get your point and don't disagree. However, aren't we talking about different modes of racialized disregard? I'm not certain that antiblack racism and Islamophobia are the same. I wonder if we soften our outrage against disregard by linking them too closely.

For example, don't we have to think about the "Middle East" as a geography of the slave trade and antiblackness? The African slave trade moved both west and east. What does this realization mean with respect to a shared sense of disregard? Are religion and race identical markers of difference? Isn't religion more fluidlike and not bound to the cultural codes of embodiment?

Don't get me wrong. Islamophobia is a critical issue to address. This isn't an attempt to narrow the meaning of injustice. I'm suggesting that there's no need to equate them; it's important to build bridges of solidarity that amplify our understanding of and struggle against the weblike nature of oppression.

BRAXTON: After the 9/11 terrorist attacks, many people in the US were not making those subtle distinctions. There was a basic link between the horrific treatment of black and Indigenous People in the US and the deep disdain that many Americans felt toward Islamic communities in the US and worldwide. This link—plain and simple—was xenophobia, or fear of the other. In cultural contexts where whiteness and Christianity are key markers of "normativity," blackness and religious diversity represented by Islam, for example, generate considerable, albeit unjustified, fear in certain groups that are easily swayed by stereotypes and caricatures.

Several months after 9/11, I delivered the keynote address for the 2002 Martin Luther King Jr. citywide celebration in Winston-Salem, North Carolina. In the speech, I insisted that the roots of American "democracy" have been irrigated for centuries by the blood of oppressed people in the US and around the world. Furthermore, America's wealth was created violently through *terrorizing* whole groups of people.

I became the target for several days after the speech in the editorial section of the *Winston-Salem Journal,* the city's major newspaper. Guest editorial writers excoriated me for professing such deeply "unpatriotic" views in the speech. In one especially bitter editorial, the guest writer, assuming himself to be a respectable, patriotic American, raised this question, "Braxton, are you with us?" When reading the editorial, I smiled and said to myself, "It depends on how you define 'us.'"

PINN: I understand and appreciate your points, but I'm thinking in terms of the relationship of Islam to enslavement and antiblackness as akin to what we have found in the West in relationship to Christianity and slavery. The system of slavery moved both west and east across the African continent—both movements guided by a certain model of antiblackness. BLM is exposing some of the worst disregard for black humanity within religious traditions such as Christianity and Islam. Consequently, BLM can help us forge a grammar of humanity that isn't warped by narrow theological claims of authority.

BRAXTON: Yes, the creation of more liberatory grammars is happening in BLM. I am benefiting, for example, from the work of Taurean J. Webb, a millennial BLM scholar and activist. Webb is exploring solidarity politics rooted in black radical thought that connects racial justice efforts in the

US with Palestinian struggles for justice. To forge a stronger coalition for transnational justice between black people and Palestinian people, Webb uses womanist, queer, and postcolonial analyses to interrogate the "Exodus motif" in the Hebrew Bible/Christian scriptures.

The Exodus motif privileges the actions and aspirations of Israel, while ignoring the injustices suffered by Palestinians. In the Exodus narrative, ancient Jews are liberated from enslavement and then kill indigenous Canaanite (or Arab) communities in ancient Palestine. Similarly, the Exodus motif continues to work in current American foreign policy. By challenging cherished cultural and religious tropes, BLM is opening spaces for innovative, transnational partnerships and for critiques of the US's domestic and foreign policies that render white, Jewish, and Christian identity as normative and beyond reproach.

PINN: These are good points. Reading the Bible from the "margins" in a more general sense (that extends beyond frameworks of tradition) also fosters a rethinking of the general salvific narrative.

BRAXTON: BLM is exploring connections between the US's militarized aggression against enemies on foreign soil and its militarized aggression toward black people who are often perceived to be enemies on domestic soil. There may be a stronger relationship than we realize between the US's militarized foreign policy as evidenced in the wars in Afghanistan and Iraq and the US's militarized domestic policing as evidenced in the surveilling, incarcerating, and killing of black people in seeming war zones in some US cities.

PINN: This is certainly, in part, what BLM is calling for. Yet writings like Alicia Garza's "Herstory," which recounts the origins of BLM, reveal that this movement is more than a critique of militarized aggression. It also is addressing a fundamental disregard for black humanity in a more general sense—black humanity understood in more complex and overlapping ways than was the case with the civil rights movement which set its sights on racism (and, only later, capitalism and class).

As you mention policing, I'm reminded of the general state of suspicion under which black people live, a state that renders embodied blackness out of "place." Policing is one response to blackness as suspicious and hyper visible. Whether we are talking about policing or foreign policy, there are artificial boundaries marking "place" or nation/state to justify power and behaviors generated in relationship to that power. Based on the workings of white supremacy, there is an assumption that blackness marks black people as marginal to the workings of the nation, with the exception of us as labor, cultural target, and cautionary tale.

BRAXTON: I totally agree. Since black bodies are often deemed "suspicious," we are surveilled more frequently and accosted by mechanisms of hegemony—from aggressive policing in neighborhoods to inequitable protocols and practices in organizations and social spaces. Similarly, an unapologetic embrace of our blackness, as a philosophical stance and epistemological commitment, is often interpreted as a threat to white ways of knowing and being.

Two insights in Garza's excellent article are especially apropos. Garza rightly criticizes dominant social groups' attempts at allyship when those groups place their cultural perspectives and concerns at the center of the conversation. She also acknowledges how progressive groups are often interested in "unity without struggle." In many of my intercultural experiences, these two themes have manifested themselves.

PINN: That's a good point. White progressives often fail to adequately interrogate their privilege because they measure it against the most graphic examples of racial hate and disregard. This approach fails to recognize how privilege works to curtail expansive diversity, preferring instead shades of the same.

Privilege is often a colorblind—hence toxic—mode of engagement with difference. White privilege also involves a denial of history—a kind of convenient forgetting—which allows those who hold it to pretend it was earned rather than having emerged as a residue of antiblack racism. So when thinking about the plight of the marginalized and disadvantaged, white privilege quickly turns to arguments of culture and morals and defines black people's plight as a matter of moral failure and cultural shortcoming as opposed to what is really at play: racism that harms certain populations for the benefit of white people.

BRAXTON: I offer a fleeting example about my intercultural engagement with certain white progressives. From 2008 to 2009, I served as the senior minister of New York City's historic Riverside Church, one of the nation's flagship progressive Christian congregations. I was honored to succeed my mentor and friend, James Forbes Jr., who was the first African American to hold that post; I was the second. Contrary to sensationalized media reports, I willingly resigned that pastorate not because of financial compensation issues or even a difference in theological principles. (It is laughable that some detractors at Riverside Church labeled me a "fundamentalist.")

PINN: How true! You're on point. There isn't a space or place free from social logics that impact black life. The church may be a "safe" space in *some* ways for *some* people. It's "safe" for some, not because people leave their troubling philosophies and biases at the door, but because there is a soft agreement not to mention them in "polite" (read: ritualized) conversation and practice. But there are some situations where this politeness takes a back seat to social codes and practices.

BRAXTON: During my candidacy for the position at Riverside, the issue of "blackness" being "out of place" surfaced in a major way. In the final weeks of the year-long search process, a prominent white member in the congregation "discovered" that I had written a scholarly book advancing a black, liberationist reading of Christian scripture (my book *No Longer Slaves*, which was used in divinity school and seminary courses across the country). However, in this white person's mind, my unapologetic embrace of blackness was "out of place" and categorically made me "unfit" and too "narrow" to be the pastor of a demographically diverse congregation such as The Riverside Church. If I had written a book advancing Eurocentrism, this member would have likely lauded me as a "broad" and "cosmopolitan" thinker. LOL!

PINN: This is liberalism. One can easily read it as a polite maintenance of the status quo—a type of "be different but don't make me uncomfortable in the process"!

BRAXTON: Permit me to return to the larger cultural factors during the Obama presidency and emergence of BLM. In addition to the aftermath of 9/11, the Great Recession was a second factor that mitigated hope and set the stage for the emergence of BLM. In the early 2000s, Wall

Street financiers created financial products like bonds backed by residential homes. When housing prices plummeted in 2006, these risky moves from Wall Street caused countless bank accounts on Main Street to evaporate. Subsequently, financial markets experienced their greatest crisis since the Great Depression.

Black communities, which experienced disproportionate rates of unemployment, suffered the worst of the Great Recession. A black president in the United States was an important milestone on the journey to racial justice. However, the Great Recession was a sobering reminder of how assertively justice was still being denied to people of color, especially black people, in the US.

PINN: Did we really need a reminder of, as you wisely frame it, "how assertively justice was still being denied to people of color"? Wasn't the evidence hard to ignore, although it was interpreted through a haze of moral arguments that blamed the victims? Obama's election also prompted an unfounded posture of "relief"—the assumption that physical representation was the same as a commitment to transformation, or that Obama was something other than a politician.

BRAXTON: Wealth disparities have existed among racial groups within the US for centuries. By exacerbating the already pronounced wealth gap between white people and black people, the Great Recession further destabilized social and economic networks in black communities. The destabilization left those communities more vulnerable to the lethal effects of the COVID-19 pandemic. The disproportionate impact of the pandemic on communities of color is not a matter of biology but, rather, sociology.

PINN: I agree that it can be mapped sociologically—given a quantitative reading. However, it's more intrinsic than that—if sociology is understood as a "second-order" enterprise that describes circumstances after the fact. The disproportionate impact could be described in class terms, but it is at its root ontological in nature: a failure to recognize fully the humanity of the marginalized, especially black and brown peoples. Some might call them "people of color," but that language is troubling for me to the extent that it maintains the assumption of whiteness as normative. If that language is to be used, I prefer "people of despised colors."

BRAXTON: Whew! "People of despised colors" . . . you're walking heavy, Pinn! Public health leaders know that the promotion of wellness or the spread of disease and death are significantly influenced by "social determinants"—a complex matrix of environmental, cultural, and personal factors that impact health outcomes.

PINN: I appreciate this reminder, but was there a forgetting of these issues? Or was there a denial of their significance? While what you say is true, I can't forget that it is with the murder of Michael Brown that BLM emerges as a slogan and movement. What was it about a certain presentation of black disregard that motivated this call for recognition?

BRAXTON: Even prior to the death of Michael Brown, it was the death of Trayvon Martin and the acquittal of his killer, George Zimmerman, that prompted Alicia Garza, Patrisse Cullors, and Ayo Tometi (formerly known as Opal Tometi) to create the social media hashtag Black Lives Matter. In Trayvon Martin's death, the so-called stand-your-ground law was very much at issue. In this approach to "justice," persons may be authorized to exercise deadly force if they feel an imminent threat.

Living in New York City, I frequently remind my progressive New York friends that the most committed proponent of "birtherism" (i.e., attempts to delegitimize Barack Obama) was a New York businessman who came straight out of Queens: Donald John Trump. By installing Trump as the standard-bearer of the Republican Party in 2016 and nearly reelecting him for a second term in 2020, white power brokers repeatedly sent the message: the delegitimization of black people is a price they are more than willing to pay if it means the perseveration of their political and cultural power.

PINN: Yet we knew this. I'm mindful of Ta-Nehisi Coates's framing of Donald Trump as the "first white president," whereby Coates names whiteness as the fundamental authorization of power and place. Trump simply provides a graphic presentation of white supremacy and white privilege. He expresses explicitly what many people in this country feel and believe, and he does so without the cover of political nuance.

BRAXTON: We, of course, knew this with our rational minds. But don't we err if we act as if racism is an utterly rational phenomenon? If racial justice were simply a matter of rationality and logic, we could achieve it with more education. Yet ironically, European and American universities, those factories of knowledge supposedly running on the wheels of rationality, have often been bastions of racism. Racism persists not simply at the cognitive level but also through other emotive mechanisms such as denial, fear, and repression.

PINN: Unquestionably, higher education in the United States has a core (unspoken) mission: the development of citizens compliant with the dynamics of social norms—citizens who "fit" in. Vitriolic responses to BLM and other challenges to white privilege reveal the implicit demand to "fit" in.

BRAXTON: In addition to factors that mitigated hope during the Obama years, we should highlight a key factor that accentuated hope and provided scaffolding upon which BLM built. During the last twenty years, our country has made noteworthy progress toward embracing the moral and civic equality of LGBTQ people and renouncing sexism and heterosexism. I celebrate these feats while also avoiding any sense of triumphalism.

More progress could have occurred and needs to occur. Public hostility and retrenchment are ever-present realities. Yet the inspiring visibility of more LGBTQ people and women in American public life and the vital social movements to ensure their wellness are crucial steps to a more robust democracy. Black people who identify as women, as girls, and as LGBTQ people often are the most acute victims of unjust public policies and harmful social practices. So fostering a climate where they are valued is a meaningful step toward affirming that black lives do, indeed, matter.

PINN: You frame your discussion in terms of "factors that mitigated hope during the Obama years." However, your observation is a challenge to "hope" as the proper grammar of collective effort. I'll go back to something with which we've already wrestled: What does it mean to hope in light of continued disregard? What justifies hope when the centuries provide ongoing violent dismissal? What grounds this hope? This, for me, is missing. As I hear you, hope seems an ungrounded conclusion and an unquestioned assumption.

BRAXTON: I wonder if your diminishment of the "grammar of hope" is somewhat out of step with the ongoing maturation of BLM. For instance,

Alicia Garza and others have poetically named a multidimensional initiative emerging from BLM the "Black Futures Lab." This project, which aims to foster deep and lasting black political, economic, and cultural empowerment, seems rooted in *hope,* imagination, and innovation. In our earlier discussion on hope, I mentioned my commitment to the subjunctive mood—the grammatical mood of possibility. Thankfully, some key leaders in BLM are retrieving and remixing the grammar of hope to narrate new stories about black *futures.*

PINN: It might be out of step, but I don't embrace all the perspectives and opinions of BLM. Instead of hope, BLM seems grounded in what I have called the persistence of possibility. By this, I'm emphasizing how BLM's critique of civil rights strategies tempers hope as we have often meant it. How could this not be when BLM is challenging modes of disregard that are layered and dependent? BLM seems to work by negation: they know what a productive society *can't* contain.

Additionally, you seem to be layering civil rights orientations onto BLM—reading them through a particular grammar and vocabulary that are more rightly reflective of the civil rights movement. For example, you apply "hope" as an interpretative device; it isn't found explicitly in commentary from Garza. Also, since BLM is a "leader-full" movement, the framing of its mission by one figure doesn't capture all plausible (or operative) strategies and perspectives. This would include perspectives on future and hope.

BRAXTON: Taking cues from BLM, we don't have to reconcile these differences to be allies in the effort to dethrone antiblackness and other oppressive practices and philosophies. Furthermore, BLM's decentralized and "leader-full" approach is commendable and cuts both ways concerning our diverse perspectives on hope. For some leaders in BLM, hope is no longer a viable concept and could be considered detrimental to revolutionary progress. For other leaders in BLM, hope remains a valuable instrument for orchestrating revolutionary progress or, riffing on your language, facilitating "persistent possibilities."

Your comments prompt another thought about the diverse coalitions within BLM. Many BLM leaders are members of the LGBTQ community. The heterosexism in many black churches cuts churches off from the wisdom and incisive critiques of these powerful leaders. For more than twenty years,

I have proudly affiliated myself with black Christian communities that assert that LGBTQ equality is a human right and an ethical and theological mandate. Accordingly, LGBTQ equality is a fundamental commitment at The Open Church.

PINN: I'm not certain this embrace of BLM—including its critique—is so common in black churches. Arguably, you and your church are exceptions that prove the rule. Does the existence and work of progressive congregations effectively counter the thousands of churches that promote biblically sanctioned disregard?

BRAXTON: On behalf of The Open Church, I appreciate your gracious affirmation. In the earliest days of The Open Church, the congregation read Howard Thurman's *Footprints of a Dream,* a book recounting the radically inclusive ministry of the Church for the Fellowship of All Peoples in San Francisco in the mid-twentieth century. Thurman's book really inspired us.

Similarly, I hope that years from now people will continue reading this book that you and I are writing. Maybe readers across more than one generation might be inspired by the principles of The Open Church espoused here and by the example you and I are trying to set—the example of the respectful embrace of deep differences for the sake of building more inclusive alternatives.

Irrespective of the hope that many of us had during the Obama years, multifaceted assaults upon black lives and black dignity were prevalent prior to and during the Obama presidency. Also, efforts to foster a more fulsome understanding of justice and coalition building were also emerging. While assaults on black life remain a constant facet of public life, I am heartened by the fearless ways that BLM is resisting injustice and affirming the beauty and significance of black lives.

PINN: BLM draws from, but also extends beyond, the mid-twentieth century's civil rights movement. It is harnessing the energy and insights of a wildly diverse group without losing sight of differences within the group. BLM maintained a theme of the civil rights movement, namely that racial injustice is a moral and public issue that expands beyond the behavior of individuals and is supported by expansive structures and practices of disregard.

Like the earlier movement, BLM recognized a need to target moral and ethical assumptions through the presentation of black bodies in public spaces—shocking the nation into a moment of discomfort and confrontation with its legacy of racialized violence. In both movements, black bodies brutalized and black lives taken mark the imaginaries and existential arrangements of life. In both cases, to be black is recognized as being—potentially and too often—a death sentence.

Both movements aimed to alter the grammar and vocabulary of engagement as well as a rethinking of public space to confront and abolish injustice. Furthermore, both movements understood the need for multigenerational involvement: a recognition that injustice premised on a demonizing of difference isn't restricted to the dynamics of a particular historical moment or generation.

BRAXTON: Your summary of similarities between the two movements is compelling. I appreciate how you frame the comparison. Your language rightly avoids depicting these movements in an adversarial or confrontational manner. It calls to mind a loving affirmation that my father once offered me. He said, "Brad, I expect you to see farther and more clearly than I do because you are standing on my shoulders."

PINN: That's a powerful statement!

BRAXTON: We should appreciate and analyze the distinctions of BLM. Yet the words "Black Lives Matter" are a different naming and framing for an age-old struggle waged by many freedom fighters across the centuries.

PINN: It's more than "a different naming and framing for an age-old struggle." BLM outlines injustice more broadly than any other single movement, and, by extension, it has a more expansive demand for justice—including communities rarely named, let alone championed.

BRAXTON: BLM's skill in building thick coalitions across diverse identities and issues is noteworthy. This capacity is an extension of important impulses that emerged in the latter days of the civil rights movement. There were attempts, which had mixed results, to incorporate the concerns and tactics of diverse groups such as SNCC (Student Nonviolent Coordinating Committee) and the Black Panthers. The civil rights movement also endeavored to assemble a diverse coalition of white people in Appalachia, black people in Chicago and Detroit, and the concerns from global communities in Africa and Asia who also were victimized by US economic exploitation and militarism.

BLM nimbly uses social media to create cohesion amid its decentralized approach. As BLM enhances its work, it will be interesting to gauge how effectively it holds these diverse coalitions together, especially when the national and international attention span is not squarely focused on racial justice as it was in 2013–2015 or 2020.

PINN: This shifting focus on racial justice is helpful for BLM's larger agenda because it opens space for attention to other forms of injustice. It also helps us avoid the old mistake of "get black together first" (i.e., black groups addressing racial injustice while downplaying other forms of injustice).

BRAXTON: Both the civil rights movement and BLM had a reverent understanding of the significance of public spectacles of injustice. While the activists in both movements were engaged in meaningful efforts of social transformation before these spectacles, their respective movements seized the public imagination in more poignant ways through these public spectacles. In the civil rights movement, the lynching of Emmett Till in 1955, or police attacks with fire hoses and dogs against Birmingham protesters in 1963, or the carnage of Bloody Sunday at the Edmund Pettus Bridge in 1965 became catalytic moments in that movement.

In a similar way, the death of Trayvon Martin in 2012; the acquittal of his killer, George Zimmerman, in 2013; and the police-related deaths of Michael Brown and Eric Garner in 2014 and Breonna Taylor and George Floyd in 2020 galvanized freedom fighters who were already committed, and these events awakened others who previously were sidelined by apathy. I use the word "reverent" above because both movements never "exploited" these horrific tragedies in a vulgar or voyeuristic way. Instead, both movements understood that to compel America to address its deep-seated pathologies, the nation had to painfully gaze at the grotesque consequences of those pathologies.

PINN: Agreed. Black death has always exposed the antiblack nature of social life in the United States, while urging the liberation-minded to resist the normalization of black death. Amid these tensions, white supremacy seeks to position black bodies as objects for the advancement of white privilege. The civil rights movement and BLM present black bodies in resistance to the status quo.

BRAXTON: Permit me to highlight a similarity that was not in your initial list. Like the civil rights movement, BLM is smartly collaborating with key cultural influencers including artists and athletes. Cultural forms such as art, entertainment, and sports can popularize and contextualize abstract theories about freedom and justice. The list of cultural influencers in each movement is extensive.

PINN: I agree and add that BLM more explicitly uses the arts and athletics in ways that make them more than footnotes to the movement.

BRAXTON: A fulsome account of the civil rights movement must include artistic and athletic geniuses such as Nikki Giovanni and James Baldwin in literature; Aretha Franklin and Harry Belafonte in music; and Wilma Rudolph and Muhammad Ali in athletics. Similarly, a fulsome account of BLM must include names such as Brittney Cooper and Darnell Moore in literature; Beyoncé and Kendrick Lamar in music; and Serena Williams and LeBron James in athletics.

PINN: But there is a difference. Many of the artists you name in the civil rights movement were already known nationally and internationally for their mastery of expression. The civil rights movement didn't "make them." However (and no disrespect intended), BLM created visibility for some of the artists you name. For example, Moore's brilliant book comes after his involvement. Also, it isn't clear that Lamar is reflecting on BLM in particular, but rather his profound lyrics would be relevant and significant during any liberation movement. His lyrics aren't necessarily shaped by the demands of BLM.

These differences are noteworthy. We typically think of the mid-twentieth-century civil rights movement as tied to (and drawn from) the black church tradition, despite the hard work of so many who claimed no allegiance to theism of any kind. BLM holds together competing faith claims. Black churches, for the most part, are unwilling to recognize, let alone embrace, nontheistic stances as legitimate. BLM, however, understands and appreciates the "truth" of faith claims for somewhat pragmatic reasons: these claims work for those who embrace them. And—this is crucial—the aggregation of distinctive faith claims and worldviews *doesn't* hinder protest.

Theists and nontheists claim the new movement. The civil rights movement—at least the figures who received significant attention—embraced a hierarchical structure drawn on the organizational logic of black churches (with the minister in charge). BLM, however, is more decentralized without the same rigid model of leadership and criteria for authority. Of course, those brave, powerful three women (and others) called us to order and began the thinking and organizing that would result in BLM; yet BLM extends beyond them and moves in ways that are more geographically specific.

BRAXTON: Just a word about Kendrick Lamar's lyrics. Lamar's song "Alright" has become for many in BLM what freedom songs like "We Shall Overcome" were for the civil rights movement. As I understand it, Lamar's 2014 trip to South Africa was a major impetus for this song and his brilliant and evolving artistry. He witnessed there both economic poverty and the amazing resiliency of black people. So this song is evidence of the importance of thinking about BLM in a more global and interconnected way. In my earlier comments, I attempted to make these larger connections by tracing links between racism and Islamophobia and US militarism in the "Middle East" and militant policing in black neighborhoods, for example, in West Baltimore where I have done ministry across the decades.

Also, the opening lines of "Alright" are a remix of Sofia's words in Alice Walker's *The Color Purple*, where Sofia says, "All my life I had to fight." Alice Walker is, of course, a progenitor and matriarch of the womanist movement, another key movement influencing BLM. Thus, socially conscious black art from one generation of freedom fighters connects with, and contributes to, socially conscious black art in the current generation. May the cycle continue!

I largely agree with your account of the differences between these movements. Yet there appears to be a perceptible shift in your tone. Your evolving analysis seems more "oppositional" rather than "evolutionary." Upon a first reading of your last comments, it seemed like BLM emerged as a direct response to black churches rather than a direct response to the ongoing onslaught against black people. BLM in your account sounds like the stark corrective to all that was wrong with "the church-influenced" civil rights movement. I may be misreading you; yet I wonder if we can appreciate the differences in a more nuanced way.

PINN: I don't see your point about a lack of nuance. I'm talking about BLM's organizational and ideological distinction. I use the counterpoint of an approach affiliated with the black church to provide clarity regarding BLM.

I don't want to give the impression that BLM emerged as a direct response to black churches. Its agenda and style of leadership developed in opposition to the limits of the black church's race agenda. The relationship is both "oppositional" and "evolutionary." I'm questioning your assumption that what is "oppositional" can't also be "evolutionary." Isn't it a matter of perspective?

BRAXTON: I'm glad that we are exploring this issue further. Your explanation is helpful. I concur with your critiques of problematic aspects of black churches. Still occasionally, your brushstrokes seem quite broad in these critiques.

I have served as the senior pastor of three churches. The formal and informal power dynamics in all three congregations were more fluid and intricate than you suggest. The dynamics involved more than the minister being "in charge." Undoubtedly, autocratic leaders and leadership styles exist in black churches and existed in the civil rights movement. Nevertheless, our account of the power dynamics within the civil rights movement should give as thick a description of those dynamics as possible.

PINN: Are you suggesting that the circumstances in these three churches represent a general trend in church leadership? Most churches maintain the hierarchical dominance of the minister—the fundamental authority of the pastor. How do the doctrinal creeds, church bylaws, and other documents guiding most black churches suggest a shift in how leadership is understood? Once again, your approach and experiences in your three churches serve as exceptions to the rule.

BRAXTON: Let's take for example the issue of decentralized power and authority. In assessments of the civil rights movement, do we occasionally fail to tease out the differences between "historiography" (our ideologies and frameworks for telling history) and "history" (culturally nuanced depictions of complex personal and social events)? In many humanities fields, the historiography is fueled by a "big male heroes" approach. On the contrary, disruptive storytelling can reveal the errors and omissions in such approaches.

For instance, I appreciate the disruptive storytelling in Rosetta Ross's book *Witnessing and Testifying: Black Women, Religion, and Civil Rights.* Motivated by an inclusive "historiography," she recounts a more fulsome and accurate "history" of the civil rights movement. In this history, the people-centered leadership of Ella Baker and the student-centered leadership of Diane Nash are as important to the civil rights movement as the more celebrated episodes involving the "big male" heroes of the movement.

PINN: I'm not clear on how your discussion challenges my argument concerning power and authority within the civil rights movement. Ross's book also shows how black women as agents of change are downplayed. How much public attention does Martin Luther King Jr. give to figures such as Fannie Lou Hamer?

You're failing to note the way that Baker and others were marginalized within a movement that assumed male leadership. This speaks to the power dynamics I highlight. I'm not debating the importance of these female leaders—on that we agree—but rather on the power and authority exercised by men in the movement over against women. You offer a reading "under" the power structures. I'm emphasizing how the power structure requires by its very nature attention to this "under" reading.

BRAXTON: Perhaps I'm continuing to mishear you. Your insights seemingly support my distinction between "historiography" and "history." Of course, patriarchy and sexism were appalling aspects of the civil rights movement. Accordingly, I'm not minimizing how oppressive forces sought to marginalize leaders such as Baker, Nash, or Hamer. On the contrary, I'm emphasizing how wonderfully significant and brilliant these female leaders were in the face of not only white racism but also the insidious dynamics of black sexism within the movement.

PINN: The "appalling" sexism in the civil rights movement warped the potential of the movement and justified larger patterns of gender bias guiding

US social norms. It also created an unproductive tension between racial justice and an embrace of other dimensions of social activism.

BRAXTON: You're right. The inability to sustain a multipronged offensive against various forms of injustice was a significant shortcoming of the civil rights movement.

I applaud how BLM is creating a larger canopy that valorizes diverse religious and ethical worldviews and gender and sexual identities. BLM is both benefiting from and contributing to courageous work that is slowly decentering, if not fully dethroning, sexism and heterosexism. The civil rights movement could not fully embrace the worldviews or humanity of an atheist like Lorraine Hansberry or a gay man like James Baldwin. Nevertheless, that movement was elastic enough to accommodate, and benefit from, significant contributions from these and other figures who represented diverse approaches and identities.

PINN: On this we disagree. The movement could have incorporated these perspectives in a more transforming manner since it wasn't synonymous with the black church. Your comment suggests too close an agreement between the two that makes distinction moot. The movement used figures such as Bayard Rustin, another gay man, but it didn't appreciate them.

Your comment implies that to benefit from a diverse group of figures is the same as to recognize the value of these figures. I fear your comment underestimates the impact of homophobia on the movement and blurs a useful distinction between the civil rights movement and the black church. Rustin and Baldwin could be used when convenient, but their sufferings couldn't be recognized as part of the agenda of the movement. Where is the liberative value and appreciation for diversity in that?

BRAXTON: Ironically, I began this line of inquiry because you, in my estimation, were aligning the civil rights movement too closely with the leadership styles of black churches. In your description of the differences between the civil rights movement and BLM, you remarked: "We typically think of the mid-twentieth-century civil rights movement as tied to (and drawn from) the black church tradition . . . "

The way we typically think about the civil rights movement and the way it functioned are different things. The approaches to power in the civil rights movement, whether drawn from black churches or other traditions, were not all messianic or problematic. Precisely because the civil rights movement was more expansive than black churches, perspectives from people in that movement who were marginalized in ways beyond race (e.g., women and LGBTQ people) impacted the movement, even if, tragically, their full personhood was not valued.

PINN: We disagree here. If these approaches to power exclude segments of the marginalized, they are problematic. There is little to suggest—from my vantage point—that the civil rights movement was as expansive as it could have been had it not drawn its leadership so heavily from the black church. Some who participated in the civil rights movement did so at the expense of their personal liberation. This is more than "tragic"—it is morally and ethically wrong; it participates in the demonizing of difference that the movement was meant to address.

BRAXTON: Come on, Tony. We're not really disagreeing here. We should save the term "disagreement" for when it really matters.

I, like you, find exclusionary approaches to power problematic, immoral, and unethical. I'm not trying to shield the civil rights movement, or any liberative movements, from critiques of their conflicts, hypocrisy, and practices that betray robust inclusion and freedom. We should similarly validate and investigate how power is working in BLM. The approaches to power in BLM are not all radically democratic and without challenges and flaws.

PINN: I've not indicated BLM is without flaws or problems. BLM is still young, and the demarcation of its flaws requires some hindsight. BLM, however, has a more promising ideological framework that assumes the need for reorientation and change. It has a more nuanced sense of the weblike structure of oppression. BLM's orientation more readily permits self-critique and correction.

BRAXTON: Yes, you acknowledged flaws in BLM. I wasn't suggesting otherwise. BLM is to be applauded for its more sophisticated understanding of the interlocking nature of oppression.

This is both an achievement and an acknowledgment of my father's wisdom cited earlier. We hope that each successive generation of freedom fighters will see farther and more clearly as they stand on the successes and learn from the failures of previous generations. The self-critical gaze emerging in BLM about power and resources reveals that many, if not most, liberation movements struggle with these power dynamics, especially as they mature beyond the white-hot heat of their founding moments.

PINN: I'm having a challenge following you here. Where is the connection between BLM and "many, if not most, liberation movements . . ."? This is a rather significant leap. You point to this dynamic in BLM, but the larger claim you make requires more evidence.

You're correct, but you're conflating things that should be held apart. Black churches and BLM aren't comparable. There is often an assumption that black churches and the civil rights movement are synonymous. The ability of black churches to self-correct tells us nothing about the self-reflexive nature of the civil rights movement. BLM seems more self-reflexive than the civil rights movement was. This is a noteworthy distinction between the two movements.

BRAXTON: I'm not trying to make any intricate philosophical connections here. I'm making a basic observation about humanity. As beautiful and flawed creatures, humans can unwittingly infuse problematic dynamics into liberation movements that are inconsistent with the noble principles informing these movements.

PINN: You highlight the wrong thing here. Yes, there are problems in BLM, which makes BLM like other movements. However, BLM promotes self-critique that I don't find with the civil rights movement (certainly not in real time). You highlight the problem. I highlight BLM's structuring of communication that addresses such problems.

BLM appears to have few of the black church's glaring shortcomings (and little of humanism's radical optimism and individualism). It seems more oriented to action and involvement than titles and authority. There are fewer restrictions related to who can play a role and how information and agency are formed and shared.

Whereas the civil rights movement was hard-pressed to think beyond race (and later class), BLM has a much larger sense of what it means to be "black" (i.e., marginalized and brutalized by US systems of thought and practice). Consequently, it has a more extensive sense of what a reconstituted US *cannot* entail or embrace.

BRAXTON: I appreciate the self-critique of BLM. We should not take this critical awareness for granted. Neither should we congratulate it too much. We would hope that emerging freedom movements might incorporate more inclusive strategies after nearly a half a century of analyses of the shortcomings in the civil rights movement.

Furthermore, to commend BLM for its critical awareness, must we also characterize the civil rights movement as a phenomenon lacking self-critique? This doesn't have to be zero-sum game. I am not an apologist for one movement over the other. Like you, I'm trying to provide an evenhanded assessment of strengths, weaknesses, connections, and dissimilarities in these movements.

To continue with the theme of critique, black churches undoubtedly should confess and repent for their many failings that have hindered revolutionary struggles like the civil rights movement and BLM. Yet some leaders in BLM are also acknowledging the difficulties of balancing principles and practices within this emerging freedom movement. Thus, even when progressive leaders have the benefit of hindsight and historical examples, they still struggle with power dynamics.

PINN: BLM has also learned hard lessons from the civil rights movement regarding the moral imagination of the US. BLM isn't as naive as many within the civil rights movement. There is no assumption that redemptive suffering is a useful model. Instead, redemptive suffering is interpreted as a mechanism to maintain white supremacy.

BLM activists have seen too many setbacks and too many murders (whose scenes are graphic due to the speed and sharpness of social media) to be easily convinced of repentance from a nation that continues killing black people. BLM also appreciates the value of forcing new patterns of thinking and communicating—of producing a new grammar and vocabulary for life. They discover in this work what struggle produces. Based on the benefits of hindsight and decades of rigorous theorization of disregard by diverse academic and public intellectuals, as well as ongoing examples of US hatred, BLM possesses a greater sense of what is at stake and what the US system will do to preserve itself. Said differently, BLM works based on a measured realism.

From BLM, we learn the expansive and tenacious nature of violent disregard. We, however, also learn about the power of black bodies to disrupt cycles of disregard when these bodies occupy public space and (national) time. We learn that collaboration doesn't require dismissal of differences and that our differences do not define our ability to collaborate on shared concerns. We learn the potentiality for radical struggle in a secular framework housing theists and nontheists. Also, we learn, and if nowhere else we will disagree here, the limits of "black church tradition" in the public arena because now we see more clearly its warts and inner "demons."

BRAXTON: Let me be clear. I'm not conflating any of these movements. I'm simply saying that just as black churches contributed to various freedom movements, they also have subtracted from those movements. Let's give credit where credit is due, and let's invite a confession of complicity when such confession is warranted.

Your recounting of lessons learned from BLM is eloquent, and my head nods in agreement with much of it. Yet again I wonder if your rhetoric is a bit overstated and oppositional in some cases. When you say that BLM is "more oriented to action and involvement than titles and authority," what is your point of reference for this critique? Are you suggesting that past freedom fighters were unduly preoccupied with titles and authority? Are you equally suggesting that BLM has inoculated itself from these afflictions of leadership?

PINN: It's important to remember the sentence that follows that claim: "There are fewer restrictions related to who can play a role and how information and agency are formed and shared." There is little doubt about this distinction between the two movements. BLM's leadership model prevents some of the authority issues experienced in the civil rights movement. What would you point out as arguments against this claim?

BRAXTON: Your claims about naivete in the civil rights movement seem a bit overstated. Well documented is the growing realism that began to overtake the civil rights movement as it proceeded to address the complications of deep-seated poverty and the US's lust for the exercise of military power.

PINN: But let's keep in mind the general response—both by white liberals and members of the movement—to King's turn to class and his challenge of the Vietnam War. Also, these changes within the movement occur shortly before King is murdered, so we don't have a good sense of the response to such shifts. King is murdered in Memphis before the planned march related to class and poverty occurred.

BRAXTON: Yes, the assassinations of King in April 1968 and Robert Kennedy in June 1968 traumatized the US and severely hampered the impact of the Poor People's Campaign. Prior to those assassinations, the nation was already reeling from the violence of the Vietnam War and the massive civil unrest that engulfed many cities such as Los Angeles in 1965 and hundreds of other cities including Detroit and Newark in the so-called Long, Hot Summer of 1967.

My point was simply to acknowledge how the civil rights movement was making measurable strides, amid internal and external critiques, to a deeper understanding of what Kimberlé Crenshaw would famously define in 1989 as "intersectionality"—the complex ways that people experience and mediate privilege, power, oppression, and liberation based on their overlapping identities (e.g., race, class, gender, and sexual identity). To its resounding credit, BLM has embraced and operationalized the concept of intersectionality in remarkable ways as it has used its social power to build broad and deep coalitions.

PINN: I'm not convinced that the civil rights movement offered a model of "intersectionality." There are too many social codes unnoted and unaddressed within the civil rights movement for it to constitute an approach sensitive to Crenshaw's brilliant intervention. To frame it as such would narrow and truncate the meaning of intersectionality, which is a conscious connecting of social codes and their impact. Simply look at the list you provide as an example. How many were missing from the civil rights movement? How many of those challenges shaped the thinking and doing within that movement?

BRAXTON: The civil rights movement didn't model intersectionality—that wasn't my claim. I was indicating how the civil rights movement was evolving (slower than it could have) beyond a narrow focus on race.

Also, in the span from the civil rights movement to BLM, many freedom fighters and activist groups remained keenly aware of the nation's enduring commitment to white supremacy. I cite but a few examples: the assaults on civil rights during the Reagan administration, the devastation of the crack cocaine epidemic and inequitable drug-sentencing statutes, the mass incarceration crisis that began largely under the supposedly "black-friendly" Clinton administration, and the destruction of black neighborhoods and black cultural infrastructure in the wake of urban gentrification.

BLM rightly reminded us of the need to "stay woke." Many people, however, never "went to sleep" precisely because the issues named above, alongside many other dilemmas, continued to threaten the well-being of so many marginalized communities, especially black communities.

PINN: "Staying woke" involves a level of recognized connection that previous movements—despite their profound importance—didn't achieve. BLM's grasp of the web of oppression isn't present in early work. Early efforts seem to see these modes of oppression as linear in nature: you can move from one to the next. BLM has challenged linear thinking. So being "woke" involves a higher sense of interdependency, which was less prevalent among baby boomers and Generation-Xers.

BRAXTON: Also, as noted earlier, many people appreciated Obama's rise to power, while remaining completely aware of national and international factors that challenged Pollyannish approaches to hope. Some of us understood that Obama's presidency could ironically defang some liberation efforts by creating a false sense of satisfaction and achievement in various groups.

Furthermore, on issues of black identity, there is more intellectual synergy between the movements than perhaps you admit. I am struck by how many BLM activists and theorists are returning to ancestral figures in earlier movements such as Audre Lorde, Zora Neale Hurston, James Baldwin, and Toni Morrison.

PINN: This seems like a stretch. Morrison's *The Bluest Eye* is published in 1970 and addresses colorism in a way not tackled in the civil rights movement. Maya Angelou was working with Malcolm X and planned to return from Ghana to work with his new organization before his murder.

What writings by Baldwin were being read in the civil rights movement, and what role did they play in shaping the thinking of the movement? The same question regarding Lorde: Can the master's house be dismantled using the master's tools?

BLM uses these figures to forge a grammar and vocabulary capable of holding together an expansive sense of injustice and the work needed to foster justice. Where's the attention to these figures in the civil rights movement? Beyond chronological challenges to the argument, where would you point for examples of such figures influencing the thought of the civil rights movement?

BRAXTON: I was not mounting a detailed chronological argument that situated these writers in their precise historical or sociological contexts. I identified Lorde, Hurston, Baldwin, and Morrison as "ancestral figures in earlier movements." I made the word "movements" plural on purpose to indicate that these figures may or may not have been identified directly with the civil rights movements; nonetheless, these pivotal figures were deeply committed to liberation struggles and used their considerable talents to advance these struggles.

In summoning these ancestors, I was simply noting the intriguing interplay between the "old" and the "new" as BLM culls from old-school tracks to both "remix" and write new "lyrics, beats, and rhymes." So perhaps the "new grammar and vocabulary for life" about which you speak has more ancestral fragments than we realize. Maybe the relationship of past and present liberation movements is more like a cycle or the intertwining strands of a helix than the straight line of temporal evolution.

PINN: You may have misunderstood me. I acknowledge the historical roots to the language and work of BLM. I, however, also note where BLM has advanced beyond earlier efforts.

BRAXTON: BLM's achievements are impressive and weighty, and we are learning much from this movement. Our wisdom also will grow exponentially if we remain open to further tutoring from lessons from the past. Allow me to use bibliographic citations, a key tool for us scholars, to illustrate my point. As a DEI scholar-practitioner and school administrator, I am grateful for the lessons on anti-racism from a leading contemporary scholar such as Ibram X. Kendi. And I may learn as much, if not more, about these issues, by continuing to grapple with Carter G. Woodson's *The Mis-Education of the Negro*, written nearly a century before BLM came into existence.

PINN: I agree. We shouldn't forget previous work. I've contextualized BLM in consideration of that work. I've acknowledged the links and the connections, while also noting the distinctions. But I'm not certain how this critique (gentle as it is) speaks to how I've framed BLM.

BRAXTON: Yes, I applaud your meticulous efforts in framing BLM. While our respective frameworks and methodologies differ at times, I, too, am committed to analyzing these movements deeply and describing the thick social contexts from which they have emerged.

In terms of similarities and differences between the civil rights movement and BLM, our exposition would be woefully incomplete if we did not mention, and celebrate, some late-breaking news. Amid us writing this book, BLM was nominated for a Nobel Peace Prize! This is a marvelous testimony to the global influence of this powerful and courageous revolutionary movement.

PINN: This is, indeed, good news, along with Stacey Abrams's nomination for that same prize! But the struggle continues. White supremacy gives a little to keep a lot. What does the ongoing nature of violence toward difference tell us about the nature of white supremacy? Rather than a type of outcome-driven approach that assumes "future," I prefer perpetual rebellion against injustice—an effort to see deep and humanizing value in the persistent push against injustice, despite what it does or doesn't achieve.

BRAXTON: No doubt, Tony! White supremacy is shrewd. However, there is no way that white supremacy's machinations should get the "last word" in a dialogue on BLM.

As black men committed to BLM, a movement largely facilitated by black women, we have sense enough to let a sister have the last word. So with respect and deference, we gladly invite Assata Shakur, a Black Panther and audacious freedom fighter, to send us forth with a revolutionary charge:

> It is our duty to fight for our freedom. It is our duty to win. We must love each other and support each other. We have nothing to lose but our chains.

DOES (OR SHOULD) RELIGION HAVE A PUBLIC ROLE?

Tony,

Good morning, brother! Let's do this one more time. My initial reflections are attached. Writing this book with you has been an amazing experience. I tell anyone who will listen that I have learned more about religion from Pinn in a few months than from most of the preachers I have heard throughout my entire life. Christians like me should spend more time learning from secular humanists like you. LOL.

Best,
Brad

> My brother!
>
> Can you believe we are almost done? It's been a good number of Fridays. Each Friday entailing a different way of getting at our work together, and each producing consistently enjoyable exchanges. Attached you will find our conversation with a few more thoughts on my end.
>
> Cheers,
> Tony

■ ■ ■

BRAD R. BRAXTON: What happens when piety and politics embrace?

ANTHONY B. PINN: I like that question. It acknowledges, but isn't confined to, the direct involvement of religious grammar and insights in shaping public perception of the "good." You're pointing to a structuring of how individual behavior informs collective obligation. But I'll need to hear a bit more before I can answer the question.

BRAXTON: Religion remains an important source of meaning for many people around the world, and its diversity provides a deep reservoir of cultural creativity. In the perennial quest to answer existential questions, many religious traditions support diverse and intentional encounters: between our inner and outer lives; between rigorous thoughts and passionate feelings; between who we have been, who we are now, and who we might become at our best; between comparable and competing worldviews; between our individual bodies, the body politic, and our shared environment.

PINN: Brad, what do we mean when we say "religion"? As evident from our previous discussions, we don't have the same thing in mind. You're thinking in terms of organized doctrines, creeds, ritual structures, and moral-ethical imperatives framed in relationship to "sacred texts" and other "sacred traditions." In a word, an "institutional" sense of religion undergirds your conversation. My mind has changed on this topic (away from religion as a "quest for complex subjectivity" that characterized my thinking in my book *Terror and Triumph*).

I now think of religion as a mode of exploration. Religion is a hermeneutical tool—a technique or strategy for exploring the dynamics of our engagement with the world and a way of wrestling with the interplay between occupants of the world. There is a relationship between the fundamental questions of existence and religion. Instead of religion providing answers, religion is a tool for exploring those questions. You, on the other hand, might highlight religion as a type of content (answers to those questions). However, I could be misreading you, so please say a bit more.

BRAXTON: It's important to define and refine our definitions and frameworks. "Naming" in African-derived cultures has special significance. To name (or "define") is to shape the trajectory of a person or a process.

Consequently, different emphases will emerge based on how we define religion. Yet before examining further our different understandings of religion, I want to accentuate a commonality between us.

An exciting aspect of this dialogue is the earnest attempt to learn from our principled differences—theism and humanism—on significant matters. Difference is frequently vilified, and the vilification results in personal attacks that prevent people from wrestling with challenges and critiques from those with whom we differ. Yet amid our significant differences, Tony, we share a commonality that is a useful launching pad for a dialogue on religion's public utility. We are both *black intellectuals*. I think that both terms "black" and "intellectual" have resonance for us and create a sum that is greater than the parts.

PINN: Our two worldviews—humanism and theism—represent what has been understood as a basic contradiction in the cultural world of the US. Also, blackness has been defined and projected in the US as a profound marker of distortion that undermines human status. "Black intellectual," as you highlight, marks a capacity for thought and a particular capacity for imagining a world of "possibility restricted." I say "possibility restricted" because many white people assumed that the capacity for deep thought was negligible with people of African descent. Think of David Hume on Africans, or Immanuel Kant, or countless contemporary examples suggesting that people of African descent are intellectually inferior.

In view of this racialization of thought, to be a black intellectual involves breaking free of the framing of imagination and creativity harnessed to whiteness. As an example, perhaps we need to interpret the Enlightenment through the Harlem Renaissance. And this should involve a claiming of our own categories, the development of a distinctive grammar and vocabulary that represents black presence and experience. I once heard the ethicist Katie Cannon put it this way: "We need to get white people off our eyeballs." That is so rich! We need to think our blackness and interpret the world in light of that blackness. Black intellectual pursuits involve a reimagining of robust possibilities, and this process occurs within the sociocultural geography of black life.

BRAXTON: Incisive observations! When I think of the term "intellectual," the idea of "hard, solid thinking" in Martin Luther King Jr.'s classic sermon

"A Tough Mind and a Tender Heart" comes to mind. As *intellectuals*, we live and breathe to engage in hard, solid thinking. The activities that facilitate hard, solid thinking, like reading and writing, can be laborious; yet for us, these activities are labors of love and pleasurable pursuits.

PINN: I agree and add that it's an obligation tied to who we are. Intellectual work is how we measure the world and our place in it. When I think of what we do, I'm reminded of Richard Wright. For him, language, words, and the crafting of ideas brought people to life, allowing them to do battle with the disregard and "hunger" gnawing away at individual and collective being.

BRAXTON: We also are *black* intellectuals. While we both were trained in and have spent many years teaching in predominantly white academic institutions, we actively employ frameworks, methodologies, and experiences of people of African descent. When we show up in classrooms, lecture halls, and webinars, we bring "black folk" with us figuratively, if not literally. We know that without black folk we would never have made it into those spaces in the first place. So our differences are an animating energy for this dialogue, and our shared commitment to black intellectual life also contributes significantly to the conversation.

As black intellectuals, we raise questions—seen at times as inconvenient and irreverent questions. We might have some hunches about where the questions might lead or what our initial responses to the questions might be. Nonetheless, we revel in how serious questions and rigorous repartee can create new road maps. Thus, as we investigate whether religion has (or should have) a public role, our responses will increasingly seek greater nuance. Also, in response to your previous comment, religion for me is both a "tool" for examining questions and "answers" on occasion to those questions.

PINN: The questions that "matter" to us as black intellectuals propel us beyond what is comfortable, urging us to explore unfamiliar territory. These questions aren't always well received, but that isn't the point. Black intellectuals often confuse acceptance of an idea with the value of an idea. The confusion has resulted in black intellectual life doing little to challenge and change thinking and behavior in many of our institutions and organizations. We restrict our resources and moderate perspectives toward what is "acceptable" rather than pushing boundaries and urging discomfort as the "home" of possibility.

BRAXTON: You provocatively point in your writings to the compelling aesthetics and cultural productivity of rap artists who challenge the assumption that religion necessarily belongs in public. Many of these artists also challenge the assumption that religion is inherently a social good that fosters morality and justice. As a theist, I applaud their critiques.

PINN: Much appreciated, and while I'm always happy to talk about hip-hop, I want to mention first an often ignored issue: the middle-class status of the black intellectual tradition.

Doesn't this status, and its relationship to the infrastructure and ideologies of the market, impact the "work of liberation"? We black intellectuals often operate from an act of bad faith with respect to positionality. We speak of (and claim to speak for) the most vulnerable and the most economically disadvantaged as if we do so from within that existential position. Concerning the middle-class assumptions, if not aspirations, of many in the church (e.g., Christianity's privileged tax status), isn't the church positioned to benefit from the very misery it seeks to combat?

With respect to the public engagement of the church, how is this class dilemma to be named and addressed? The church isn't based strictly on a secular model of consumption. Its theological claims and sensibilities mitigate such an orientation. However, don't black Christians need to acknowledge and respond to this dimension of the church—the "business" dimension of the church?

BRAXTON: Thanks for shining the light on the often ignored issue of class, both in terms of black intellectual life and church life. Let me offer a word first about class in black intellectual life.

bell hooks explores the invisible and insidious ways that class undermines robust coalitions across social difference. She critiques a race-based rhetoric suggesting that black people are unequivocally united in the quest to combat racism. A race-based solidarity often obscures the deep fault lines of class among black people. Unfortunately, there are many middle-class black people who are contemptuous of anyone not occupying their class status or sharing their privileged worldviews.

As a black intellectual who has benefited from middle-class status throughout my life, I think black elitism is shameful. As a scholar and teacher, I'm earnestly trying to combat classism and acknowledge my class privilege. For example, this year marks the twentieth anniversary of my first professorial appointment, which was at Wake Forest University School of Divinity. In one of my staple courses at Wake Forest—Introduction to Homiletics (the art and science of preaching)—I routinely highlighted the importance of class consciousness and class-based critiques in the practices of religious leadership. Furthermore, I'm seeking stronger alliances with people from diverse economic strata in the name of liberation and flourishing. What are your thoughts about the role of class in your life and work?

PINN: Like for many others, middle-class status came to me after my academic training. While my family did okay, finances weren't without challenges, and tough times weren't uncommon.

The challenge is twofold. First, forgetting the diverse range of relationships to financial well-being and its connotations—a type of monetary paramnesia. For instance, in any classroom where you and I teach, manifestations of economic class can differ dramatically, ranging from first-generation, working-class students to so-called legacy students, who are the offspring of economically elite alumni. This forgetfulness can distort how and what we teach, and it also can create understandings of liberation and well-being that further normalize the economic status quo.

Second, there is another type of forgetfulness that we academics often suffer. We often forget our class status and assume we talk from the vantage point of those who suffer the most. The middle-class status of some academics results in a type of anxiety and paranoia—a preoccupation with the fragile nature of our success. This is tied to the impostor syndrome that some academics face (i.e., the anxiety that we don't belong in these "elite" academic circles). My concern as a professional is to live in balance, by recognizing my advantages and trying to use them to be of assistance. I also try foster discomfort in myself and others about class-based oppression.

For example, I've tried to motivate Rice University to think beyond the boundaries of the campus in ways that open it to the city of Houston beyond areas of affluence. We can concentrate on sociocultural, economic, and political issues through sustained interaction and conversation with the larger Houston community. This involves moving beyond people in neighborhoods that reflect a more "comfortable"—read: white—engage-ment. It involves engaging the diversity of the city in ways that transform our research and teaching.

So, the center I direct—the Center for Engaged Research and Collab-orative Learning—brings community leaders to campus to teach in the regular curriculum. This disrupts shallow thinking about who is authorized to instruct; there are class dynamics at work with this hierarchy of instruc-tion. Most of all, it's important for me (and other middle-class academics) to recognize how we both fight *and* represent the problem. We've done some of this concerning the intersections of race and gender, but we need to bring class more forcefully into the deliberations.

BRAXTON: We also need a more full-throated class critique in church circles. Discrimination based on social status and class identity violates the inclusive principles that should characterize church life. In particular, the Book of James in the New Testament compels Christians to confront and correct classism. Many black churches passionately protest racial discrimination, while remaining eerily silent about class-based oppression. We must break the silence and come from the shadows of denial.

There is a moral imperative for churches to put faith back to work. Too many churches are filled with "unemployed faith": faith that ain't working, faith singing hymns while the world goes to hell, faith fussing about church bylaws while teenagers are shot in alleys and schoolyards. God is not pleased with unemployed faith. Consequently, the Book of James declares: "So faith by itself, if it has no works, is dead" (James 2:17).

The Book of James is abundantly clear: Christianity is a religion of concrete deeds, not abstract creeds. James corrects a misunderstanding about faith. Faith is supposed to be employed in acts of righteousness and love. However, some first-century Christians were living as if all they had to do was believe. Their error sounds like an ancient version of contem-porary "name and claim it" prosperity theology (i.e., the assumption that adherence to certain religious beliefs and practices will result in financial affluence and influence).

Religious belief isn't a justification for inactivity. Faith is supposed to work. Faith by itself is never enough. If faith is simply declaring dogma, shouting slogans, and confessing creeds, then faith isn't working. I say to fellow Christians frequently: "We must put our faith to work; we must find faith a job—and especially a job fighting poverty."

Jesus was concerned about economic justice. Yet some Christians preach so much about the death of Jesus that they neglect the justice principles Jesus taught during his life. The journalist Barbara Ehrenreich rightly criticizes Christianity's amnesia about the *living* Jesus.

In the name of Jesus who blessed economically vulnerable people and cursed the conditions that subjected people to economic hardship, churches should actively participate in anti-poverty campaigns. The theologian Allan Boesak suggests that economic injustice is "an assault upon the dignity of God." From Baltimore to Beijing, from Dallas to Darfur, from Harlem to Haiti, the diseases and despair caused by poverty are an attack against God since God has placed the divine image in every person regardless of income.

PINN: You make some important points. Concerning the role of class and the church, the prosperity gospel is especially intriguing. While we tend to critique the prosperity gospel in total, are there dimensions in Christianity that speak to a long-standing interest in economic security as a marker of God's grace and salvation? On one level, churches work to address issues of class, but on another, they are dependent on the very frameworks associated with classism. After all, churches are also businesses.

BRAXTON: There are Christian scriptures and traditions that associate God's blessings with economic security, as well as Christian scriptures and traditions that warn about greed and materialism. As you wisely intimated, an ethic of balance concerning material well-being is the goal. The discussion about class identity adds texture to our dialogue. Yet let's return to the larger question of religion in public life, bearing in mind these nuanced observations and unresolved issues about class.

We also should investigate problematic assumptions in certain forms of secularism in the public sphere. Some secular frameworks naively assume that they are "objective" and that religious communities are necessarily predisposed to values and behaviors that impede participation in the broader democratic processes in a freedom-loving society. Assumptions about the inherent "morality" of religion or the inherent "neutrality" of secularism lead to oversimplifications. An intellectual history of modern western civilization could be written based on the problematic assumptions and oversimplifications of both religion and secularism.

Centuries ago, theology was hailed as the "Queen of the Sciences." Thus, religious people and perspectives tended to dominate the public sphere, and religious people vilified those outside of "orthodox" religious frameworks (e.g., religiously motivated "witch hunts").

As a correction to religion's dominance, rationalists and Enlightenment thinkers sought to depose religion and instead coronated "reason" and "objectivity" as "King" and "Queen." Yet ironically, as white Enlightenment thinkers (some of whom influenced the founding of the United States) were celebrating "reason" and "objectivity," many European nations were promoting genocide and transatlantic slavery. Thus, neither religious commitment nor secular objectivity inherently made the public sphere a more just or inclusive space.

PINN: This is true. However, defining secularity is a slippery topic. One can be a theist or a nontheist and advocate for a secular public. A sense of the secular, as philosophers like Charles Taylor have noted, can simply mean an increased ability to engage public life without reliance on religious language and ideals. In short, secularity can be what the Constitution calls for: the separation of church and state. There are no inherent moral claims or jabs with this configuration of secularity, and no required sense that religion is inherently bad or nontheism inherently reasonable and better.

Furthermore, with secularization and modernization, there were efforts to modify the reach of theology and turn to the "classics" as a way of reshaping education along the lines of the "humanities." But the human within *human*ism was exclusive: the human was white and typically male. This is a problem to fix, but one that doesn't require imposition of the moral and ethical insights of religion.

By secularity we can simply mean, again as Charles Taylor suggests, a shifting context where describing and arranging life without theological assumptions and markers becomes easier and more normalized. This doesn't wipe out religion but repositions it over against the public arena. That's how I tend to think about secularity—as a shift with respect to the language and larger assumptions for defining and engaging the collective life of the nation.

BRAXTON: Thanks for outlining possible understandings of secularity. We cut our teeth as scholars while another "intellectual correction" was taking place, namely the correction of postmodernism and contextual methodologies such as black biblical scholarship and black and womanist theologies and postcolonial studies. It was considered groundbreaking, and even radical, in the 1990s to offer an academic interpretation of the Bible that privileged the distinctive cultural experiences and idioms of black people. Biblical scholarship based on the distinctive cultural experiences and idioms of white people was considered in the white academy to be "objective" and "rigorous." However, when black scholars simply wanted the opportunity to do what white scholars were doing—bring our culture with us into our scholarship—we had to receive special permission from the white academic gatekeepers, lest we black scholars be seen as somehow lessening the quality of "objective" and "rigorous" scholarship.

These frameworks and methods exposed and interrogated the overt and covert biases in appeals to "objectivity." These methods also encouraged scholars to work from, and even on behalf of, specific cultural identities (e.g., race/ethnicity, gender, class, sexual identity and orientation, geography). Like other corrections across the centuries, postmodern and contextual approaches (to which I am committed) might have unwittingly swung the pendulum too far in the other direction. This is often the nature of intellectual corrections.

PINN: For sure. Based on these theoretical shifts, we have come to critique and challenge assumptions of objectivity—to the degree that claims of objectivity hide and safeguard normative structuring of thought and action to disadvantage marginalized populations. Yet even theoretical challenges to objectivity must be challenged. For example, there have been too many assumptions in black theology concerning sexuality and identity, which over-determine who is constituted and celebrated through "blackness."

BRAXTON: The public sphere remains extremely fragmented. On the one hand, white nationalist groups are endorsing white supremacy, and on the other hand, the Black Lives Matter movement is organizing for black empowerment. It remains to be seen if contextual approaches can both highlight the inescapable influence of our cultural identities (whether positive or problematic), while also fostering diverse coalitions beyond our respective social identities that promote broader well-being. Various people in white nationalist groups and the Black Lives Matter movement appeal to religion. These competing appeals to religion define how religion is typecast in the public sphere. Religion, like many other human endeavors, is a social construction and a cultural production.

In defining religion this way, I'm neither endorsing nor dismissing the belief claims of any religious or ethical tradition. Instead, I'm highlighting the importance of *culture* as we examine the viability of religion's public role. Culture emerges as people inhabit places, engage in practices, and create tangible products and intangible productions. Thus, culture is shorthand for the processes by which individuals and communities convey and renegotiate meaning, identity, and deeply held convictions.

Like other long-standing cultural practices (e.g., teaching, medicine, law, and business), the practice of religion can become a host body for positive or parasitic energy. There exists within all cultural traditions trusted practitioners and shady quacks. All cultural traditions possess genetic predispositions that can foster healthy communal cells to develop or increase the likelihood of communal malignancy.

So the positive potential of any cultural tradition in the public sphere, including religious and secular traditions, might depend on our ability to embrace deeper understandings of culture as sites where power and meaning are constantly renegotiated. To promote healthy exchange in the public sphere, we might need to increasingly make *intercultural education* an integral "course" in the curriculum of becoming a responsible citizen in the body politic.

PINN: I understand what you're saying, but I'm a bit uncomfortable with your conclusions. While religion involves a type of culture, it isn't the same as other cultural codes and practices. Medicine and religion aren't the same with respect to the intent and impact of their workings. The "secular" and "religion" aren't equivalent structures. The "secular" is an approach that curbs the overreach of religious practices and theological language. "Religion" is a mode of conduct and thought.

It isn't simply a matter of how people use a cultural practice but the cultural practice itself. There aren't "good" and "bad" uses of religion because

Christianity, for example, supports various patterns of thinking and conduct. Christian scripture doesn't rule out behaviors we now call problematic. So I see "good" and "bad" religion as naming the same reality—with a difference just in perspective.

I have strong concerns about religion being the "language" of the public arena. Unless I'm misunderstanding you, it feels to me that you are collapsing the distinction here—that all cultural practices are the same. I, like other humanist thinkers such as Sikivu Hutchinson and Norm Allen, want to keep religion a protected, private affair. I propose the development of approaches to the public that don't privilege any particular "faith" commitment—neither theism nor atheism. I favor instead approaches that draw from a larger structuring of democracy and public exchange. The Constitution points in this direction, but we have work to do.

We need a new language and collective practice of public exchange that produces policies and practices open to a full and contradictory range of personal beliefs and postures. Yet this new language and approach would hold us all accountable and afford us all opportunity. We aren't there yet, and simply privileging any particular faith stance won't get us there. Should a faith I don't claim determine my public conversation and my private conduct? Again, we need a new grammar and vocabulary for the public arena that draws on our diversity and doesn't privilege the claims of any particular faith community. Think about the way Christian nationalists are demanding their faith be the guiding logic for all US citizens. Should our public lives, our rights, our liberties be determined by the moral codes of their brand of faith? Should women's bodies be controlled by the dictates of a faith commitment—even when it isn't a faith they claim? But I want to hear more from you, particularly related to the process of re-envisioning collective life and the intercultural education you've highlighted.

BRAXTON: The theologian Luis Rivera defines intercultural education as processes that help people understand and positively engage human and cultural diversity. Furthermore, intercultural education equips people to challenge harmful ideologies and social practices.

Returning to your earlier comments, I don't think about religion primarily as "institutional." That word for me is loaded and is often used to denigrate or dismiss religion. I know that's not what you're doing. Instead, religion for me is a matrix of cultural practices and beliefs (including traditions, texts/narratives, and rituals) that can create the kind of ethical accountability you are calling for.

Undoubtedly, communal religious practices can become authoritarian and exclusionary. Yet communal religious practices, like other communal practices, can sponsor noble and abiding commitments in both individuals and large groups. Your description of religion as a hermeneutical tool is helpful. Yet your previous understanding of religion as "complex subjectivity" is quite abstract. Please break that down a bit for me.

PINN: As I said earlier, my mind has changed. The idea of religion as "the quest for complex subjectivity" presented in *Terror and Triumph* is abstract. The goal was to point out a condition or meaning beneath competing claims. In other words, what about blackness, for example, links various traditions within black communities? So it's abstract because it's meant to be a theory of religion as opposed to a description of a religion.

I have proposed a shift in more recent work. I now believe that the quest for complex subjectivity is a psycho-ethical response to injustice. Religion—and this is even more abstract—is a technique or strategy for capturing and exploring human experience and examining the nature of our engagement and interaction with various forms of life.

BRAXTON: It's impressive to witness intellectual revision and refinement in the mind of an accomplished scholar like you: ideas and theories previously articulated are constantly renegotiated. Instead of being "settled" and "satisfied," you clearly have a growth mindset.

I'm fascinated by religion's interaction with various segments of American public life. Many pressing contemporary concerns and significant social institutions have links to religion. For example, religious communities have played integral roles as we have grappled with the COVID-19 pandemic and the racism ingrained in American society. Additionally, the entertainment industry—from Hollywood films to Harlem hip-hop lyrics—continues to dialogue with images and ideas from various religious traditions. Religion continues to permeate every level of American life.

PINN: The grammar and vocabulary we associate with religion are present in the popular imagination of the nation. However, religious language and symbolic content lose their "charge" in this popular use. In other words, religious language and symbols in popular usage serve the "horizontal" or mundane dimensions of life. The transhistorical claims of religion are often not evident unless the film, or book, or lyrics are meant to directly impinge into the world of a religious tradition. The shifts between frames of reference—religion and secularity—can have detrimental effects on both. I'm sure you'd agree, yes?

BRAXTON: Before I can agree or disagree, let's clarify how we understand the "horizontal" and "vertical" axes in our respective understandings of religion. Religion, in my estimation, involves both vertical and horizontal axes.

Many religions posit a vertical axis, namely the relationship between people and some form of transcendence. This transcendence might be a profound inner enlightenment or power defined as an external and invisible source or force (e.g., deities or ancestral spirits). Popular appeals to religion often ignore the considerable concern in many religions about the horizontal axis. By horizontal, I mean human behaviors that foster either just or unjust relationships between individuals and groups.

Let me be folksy and proverbial. In African-centered cultures, some of the best "theoretical" work occurs in proverbs and pithy sayings. When I was growing up in Salem, Virginia, the spiritual elders often said it like this: "We don't care how high you jump when you shout in the Spirit. We wanna know how straight you gonna walk when your feet hit the ground." In other words, the vertical dimension of religion (e.g., *a Spirit-inspired ecstasy* manifest in ritual performance) is meaningless without a corresponding horizontal dimension (e.g., *a Spirit-led ethic* manifest by right relationships with people).

These same spiritual elders regularly cited 1 John 4:20–21 in the New Testament: "Those who say, 'I love God,' and hate their brothers or sisters, are liars; for those who do not love a brother or sister whom they have seen, cannot love God whom they have not seen. . . . Those who love God must love their brothers and sisters also." Tony, how do you understand the relationship between the vertical and the horizontal in your definition of religion, or do you find the metaphors of the vertical and horizontal axes problematic or challenging in some way?

PINN: I appreciate your appeal to folk sayings and the wisdom they contain. As you know, I grew up in Buffalo, New York, raised by folks with immediate roots in North Carolina and Virginia who used similar sayings. Thinking back on those days and those sayings helps me address your question.

I agree that the conversation within religious circles often moves in two directions: vertical and horizontal. The saying you provide—"We wanna know how straight you gonna walk when your feet hit the ground"—measures religious principles and claims in relationship to their application in the mundane world in which we live. In a way, vertically situated claims only make sense in relationship to horizontal practices, thus highlighting the ultimate significance of horizontal relationships. This is another reason for claiming religion involves an interrogation, framing, and presentation of human experience within the context of human history (i.e., the horizontal dynamics of life).

Additionally, folktales like some of the Brer Rabbit stories suggest this horizontal priority. Maybe you remember the story of the rabbit wanting a long tail. It's been a long time since I thought about this story. So please forgive me if I omit parts of it. However, the gist of the story is something like this.

The rabbit wants a long tail to help swat flies away. So the rabbit goes to the "big house" and asks God for a long tail. In response, God gives the rabbit a list of items to secure and says that, once this is done, the rabbit will receive the tail.

The rabbit goes about the tasks, comes back victorious, and wants the reward of a long tail. However, in response, God gets angry and throws lightning. As the rabbit runs away, he hears God say, "If you so smart, get your own long tail." There are many ways to read this, but for me it points out the centrality of horizontal relationships and a horizontal perception of the world and what moves it. What is certain is the capacity of embodied beings to act on their own behalf.

Now, this story doesn't necessarily advance a humanist agenda. Yet it offers additional evidence that some black folks have always understood religion as horizontal interactions expressed at times through expansive theological language, which capture the implications for the individual in relationship to the larger community. The religious priority is the horizontal geography of life, and this means theology is anthropology.

BRAXTON: That's right. "Theology is anthropology." What we *do* "in the name of God" speaks volumes about who we *are* as humans. Even as religious people have done good things, they also have caused unspeakable harm to many, and the process of repairing the harm is ongoing. It's incumbent upon us to examine the tension between the helpful and harmful effects of religious communities in public life. In your extensive writings and incisive comments in the public dialogues we have shared, you have rightly insisted that respectful attention to religion both appreciates religion when it is most creative and holds religion accountable when it falls short of its noble aspirations.

PINN: You hit on something that's important to me—a balanced and lucid critique. We should equally challenge the harm that theism does in the world *and* the harm that humanists and other disbelievers do in the world. I see the same appreciation for a dual mode of critique in your work, ministry, and conversation, and I appreciate that.

I want to comment on the history of religious involvement that you highlight. I don't dispute what you've said concerning the long-standing tradition of religious involvement. Yet religion in the United States is often expressed through performance of competing claims and sensibilities that, at their best, offer different approaches to the enhancement of life opportunity, well-being, and deep and abiding obligation to others. In addition, you're correct: cultural production has borrowed from the grammar and vocabulary of religiosity (particularly Christianity) and used its imagery and sensibilities to craft responses to the circumstances of life. As you note, this is certainly the case with hip-hop.

But there's another element to consider. Cultural production has also critiqued the assumption that religion belongs in public because it has an inherent ability to advance the best of human interests and concerns. There is certainly an acknowledgment of religion's presence, but figures like Tupac Shakur often scrutinized this presence, highlighting the ways that religion regularly safeguards the very structures of oppression that it speaks against. This is one way of reading Tupac's persona of "Black Jesuz," the patron saint of thugs. Also, the assumed need for religion in public falls victim to Scarface's critique in tracks like "Mind Playin' Tricks on Me '94."

These hip-hop artists, and others like them, raise something worth considering: Is the public presence of religion more than historical? In other words, is there merit in the presence beyond the fact that it exists? Is religion's public presence something that should be continued? Does this existence entail a particular obligation or mode of accountability that extends beyond just the merit of religion "being there"? What is the benefit over against the risk? Perhaps you view this differently.

BRAXTON: Religion has a role to play in the public sphere. When religious communities behave and embody their noble aspirations, they contribute immeasurably to "public health." Religious communities—from congregations to faith-based community organizers—are frontline "doctors of the soul" seeking to dispense healing balm in hurting communities. Whether registering voters, supporting climate change initiatives, creating art to inspire social protest, or mobilizing congregations against corporate injustice, religious communities are compassionate and courageous creators of the social change the world needs.

Similarly, we must not shy away from exposing how religion motivates violence. Religiously motivated violence erodes public well-being in many ways. Some religiously motivated violence occurs in intimate spaces beyond public scrutiny. Yet it diminishes public well-being nonetheless. For example, many misogynistic men justify the physical and emotional abuse of their spouses, partners, and children with words from the Holy Bible about women "submitting" to men. This raises issues about just how "holy" the Holy Bible is at times, which is certainly a topic we have examined in this book.

PINN: Are you suggesting that this justification of disregard and violence is a misread of scripture? Or is there something about scripture that supports these behaviors? In other words, does the biblical worldview assume forms of engagement we now critique?

Maybe the lessons we learn from Job's wife (who exhorted Job to curse God because of Job's suffering) or Lot's wife (who mysteriously dies as she views God's destruction of her city) reveal scripture's inability to articulate the types of relationships we value. Perhaps embedded within the scriptural story of salvation is an "insider versus outsider" dynamic that can be shifted but not removed. There will always be those on the margins who, based on their positioning, are exposed to harm.

I ask these questions so that you can explore further your intriguing last line: "this raises issues about just how 'holy' the Holy Bible is at times."

What do we do with this? Should we begin by reassessing what we mean by "holy"? Should we rethink the distinction we make between violence and biblical values?

BRAXTON: Allow me to explore more fully a critique of religious traditions and their public import by focusing on my tradition—Christianity and its scriptures. Along the way, I'll comment on transcendental claims and Tupac's concern in "Black Jesuz."

Let's consider, for example, the so-called Lord's Prayer (Matthew 6:9–13). Many Christians recite the Lord's Prayer as an almost mindless ritual of personal piety. Yet biblical studies colleagues such as Obery Hendricks Jr. and Amy-Jill Levine have demonstrated how politically provocative Jesus really was when our interpretations of Jesus are situated in thicker cultural frameworks. Their culturally nuanced readings of Jesus unveil the missed correlation between piety and politics in the Lord's Prayer. Jesus invites his followers to pray: "Our Father in heaven, hallowed be your name. Your kingdom come. Your will be done, on earth as it is in heaven."

In the patriarchal idioms of his day (which should be interrogated in the name of inclusive justice), Jesus invites his followers to consider the political power of a transcendental claim. Caesar in Rome was considered the "Father" of the kingdom, and Caesar's name was to be revered in ritual worship.

In a bold, anti-imperial move, Jesus insists that the true "Father" or "Leader" of the world's kingdom is God (once again the patriarchal metaphor "kingdom" is problematic). The appeal to transcendence ("Our Father") in the Lord's Prayer is not about personal piety or political passivity. Instead, the appeal to God creates a matrix of metaphors and meanings by which the community can galvanize itself for struggle against Roman imperialism. Jesus—and many ancient communities that formed in his name and memory—resisted the vicious power of Rome, seeking instead more peaceful forms of community.

I want to say something now about Tupac's "Black Jesuz." Arguably, Tupac's profane lyrics are sacred and tap into the kind of cultural critique that historical figures like Jesus raised against their own religious and cultural traditions. We're avoiding long citations of external references in this book, but c'mon, Tony; it's Tupac. Let that brother and his crew grab the mic. Yaki Kadafi, Tupac's close friend and fellow rapper "spits" these lyrics in "Black

Jesuz" (apologies for the explicit language; these brothers were known for keeping it "real" and "raw"):

> *Brainstorm on the beginnin'*
> *Wonder how shit like the Qur'an and the Bible was written*
> *What is religion?*
> *God's words or a curse like crack?*
> *Shai-tan's way of gettin' us back*

These lyrics reveal a keen awareness that sacred texts and traditions, amid any claims to divine authority and transcendence, must still give an account of their situatedness in the messy power dynamics of culture. In the New Testament, there are stories about Jesus being tempted by Satan (or to use this song's Arabic-based lyric "Shai-tan"). In those stories, Satan quotes scripture to Jesus. So ancient scriptural texts, like the contemporary scriptures that Tupac and his crew are writing, are aware that scripture is not inherently right or useful just because it claims to be scripture.

PINN: Okay, I'm with you on that.

BRAXTON: The authority of scripture is not about its claims to have a sacred author (God). The authority of scripture is about its ability (or, at times, inability) to create sacred people and communities who are godlike.

By critiquing sacred traditions in a blasphemous way, Tupac and his crew might mediate the sacred irreverence of the historical black Jesus/Jesuz. I mean the Jesus who according to scripture cursed and called some religious leaders "sons of snakes" (perhaps akin today to calling someone a "son of a bitch."). I mean the Jesus who was "somebody raw" enough (Tupac's words) to have in his crew a sword-packing, holy thug like the disciple Peter. I mean the Jesus who liked to party so much that his enemies called him a "drunkard and a glutton" to use the antiquarian prose from the King James Bible. LOL.

PINN: While not trained in biblical studies, I agree that there is an anti–status quo and revolutionary way to read the Lord's Prayer. But it isn't a necessary interpretation. There are likely some Trump supporters who claim Christianity who would agree with the revolutionary take on the prayer, but they might disagree with the target of the revolutionary impulse. Even if, for the sake of argument, I agree with the depiction of Christianity's revolutionary potential, there is still too much about the tradition that advances marginalization and disregard and undercuts the impact of critique and correction.

With Tupac, you're downplaying his deconstruction of tradition. The equating of God's word with crack is a damning critique—one that sees little distinction between the death-dealing consequences of illicit drugs and the Bible's principles and values. However, turning to his depiction of "Black Jesuz," he raises questions concerning the moral and ethical codes inherited from the Christian tradition and celebrates the way of life of the "thugs."

Tupac is "signifying" or providing a brutal satire on black Christianity. I particularly have in mind two tracks, "Blasphemy" and "Hail Mary," although others are applicable. In "Blasphemy," he encourages a position contrary to Jesus's suggested moral code. The track begins with a process of salvation familiar to Christians. One must accept Jesus to secure eternity. This Jesus is "Black Jesuz," who authors a new set of commandments or, as Tupac announces, "rules to the game" that sound Machiavellian in nature. In "Hail Mary," the depiction is even more graphic—despite your intriguing depiction of Jesus in the New Testament as "thuggish."

You mention that the importance of the Bible isn't the author, but what it encourages. Does it encourage godlike people? The question is: What do you mean by "godlike?" Tupac, at certain points, claims to be Jesus. Yet this salvific figure operates in counter-distinction to dominant sensibilities that raise questions concerning the nature and meaning of "sacred"—as in "sacred people."

I appreciate your attention to Tupac and your willingness to read him through his lyrics as opposed to through the creeds of the black church. However, I wonder if the effort to make him "recognizable" from a Christian vantage point damages both his intent and the church? Perhaps some perspectives are simply oppositional.

BRAXTON: Keep "droppin' science," Professor Pinn. Given your extensive work on hip-hop, we could spend the rest of the book riffing on the complex interactions between hip-hop and religion. But for now, let's return to the broader topic of religion in the public.

While religion can positively impact the public sphere, it unfortunately can also erode public well-being. For example, some religious people are ignoring public health advice about wearing face coverings during the COVID-19 pandemic. Their "faith" supposedly will protect them from the coronavirus. What some people call faith, I call foolishness. Ah, there's the rub. Religious motivations and teachings, like many other human experiences such as "art" and "love," invite wildly diverse interpretations.

PINN: This doesn't tie in fully to your point, but I'm going to say it anyway. Here's the problem for me. While religion has both harmed and advanced human aspiration—as has humanism—the challenge is the way that religion ultimately projects the rationale for activity to a source beyond the grasp of human reason and accountability. When the fallback religious position places the rationale for behaviors on a divine presence beyond the scope of human interrogation, how is a firm sense of accountability and responsibility secured?

Humanism has faltered, for sure, and has produced harm, but we can critique and challenge it using tools available to us. Religion's transcendent claims prevent full accountability. How does one counter the claim of divine authority? What criteria or values can effectively cancel these transcendent claims? The responsibility in humanism is horizontal rather than vertical.

Some might argue that this is a matter of interpretation, and religious people who jettison reasonable measures of accountability are misusing religious traditions. This may be the case, but what is there beyond interpretation? Also, in response to destructive religious practices, too many people say, "That's not my Christianity," or "Those people aren't *really* Christian." While I understand what they are trying to say, this claim of religious otherness prohibits useful critique of the actual role that religion can play in harming collective life.

There is some value in the involvement of religious organizations in public activities: for example, black churches serving as communal locations for distribution of supplies and information. However, my concern is with the theological filter through which information is presented. Theological grammar has a limited reach for capturing the complexities of the public arena and the wide-ranging issues that impact public life.

In some measure, the church arises from theological sensibilities that project difference as a problem to be solved (often through some mode of conversion). How does a theologically sanctioned articulation of "difference as a source of despair" serve as the grammar and vocabulary to articulate the inclusive reach of democratic possibility? There is an intrinsic logic to theism (e.g., Christianity), which undercuts the complex and messy nature of collective life and fails to appreciate the paradoxes and tensions that are beneficial to public discourse and exchange.

BRAXTON: I share your concern about the limitations of "theological grammar" with respect to the "complexities of the public arena." Those limitations, however, aren't unique to theological grammar or theism. As I suggested earlier, all cultural practices and their associated intellectual discourses are prone occasionally to overstatement and exclusionary tendencies. Therefore, other practices and discourses must correct those problems and limitations. Arguably, the public arena in democratic societies is strengthened by more, not fewer, cultural practices and grammars—each one contributing to, and complexifying, public discourse and the overall practices of debate, ethical discernment, and the respectful accommodation of robust difference.

PINN: There's a problem: the dominance of Christian tendencies has prevented this type of expansive public grammar and vocabulary. Examples of this are numerous and are depicted graphically by Christian nationalism, which is not new but certainly is more aggressively advancing in the twenty-first century.

The goal isn't simply a more pluralistic—but still religious—framing of the public space. Rather, we need to develop a new grammar and vocabulary that take seriously "difference" as an opportunity, that wrestle with opposition and conflicting views on life, and that are mindful of the United States' past, as well as its current relationship to the world.

BRAXTON: I want to challenge your characterization of Christianity's rendering of "difference" and "insider/outsider" status. In your words, Christianity "undercuts the complex and messy nature of collective life." The evidence from early Christianity calls your description into question.

I won't delve too deeply into the social intricacies of how the Christian Bible came into existence (a process referred to as canonization). However, even some basic knowledge of this complex process reveals that people, politics, and power played a key role in the Bible's production. As I say often in my lectures on the Bible, even if people think the Bible is a "celestial" book, its composition and canonization were quite terrestrial. Permit me to offer a synopsis.

Many early Christian texts—which began as stories, sermons, and letters—were preserved and circulated among diverse communities for decades and even centuries before they officially became a part of the Bible or "scripture." Communities in various parts of the world considered these texts valuable because they were *useful.* By useful, I mean these texts often directly addressed the complexities of communal life to which you allude. Sometimes, these texts provided beneficial examples; other times, the examples they offered were detrimental to communal well-being.

In this regard, some of the apostle Paul's letters in the New Testament are instructive. I have devoted more than thirty years of my life to critical examination of Paul's writings, and still, his texts delight, baffle, and anger me. Like many black interpreters of Paul, I have had a love-hate relationship with him.

In *True to Our Native Land,* the historic one-volume African American New Testament commentary, black biblical scholars such as Boykin Sanders, Monya Stubbs, and I demonstrated how black people have found motivation for social liberation in Pauline letters such as 1 Corinthians, Galatians, and Philippians. Irrespective of whether one believes the transcendental claims in Paul's writings, Paul's intense grappling with the social boundaries and ethical mores of his fledgling communities are worthy of exploration. Paul's writings have significantly impacted global civilization for centuries. Thus, I approach his writings less as "scripture" to be venerated and more as "classic cultural texts" to be interrogated.

We often read Paul as if he were a dispassionate, systematic theologian who was hell-bent on reinforcing oppressive norms. Instead, Paul was a passionate and pragmatic pastor and community builder. Paul was not a supporter of the status quo. On the contrary, he was attempting to express through his churches a communal ethic that he believed Jesus wanted us to follow, namely the celebration of ethnic diversity within Christian unity.

Paul pleads for the eradication of *dominance,* not the erasure of *difference.* When believers entered the Christian community through belief in Christ and baptism, they didn't lose the social distinctions that characterized their lives. Thus, Paul was interested in *unity,* not *uniformity.*

The embrace of God should abolish the dominance of one group over the other based on difference. Jews should not dominate Gentiles; free persons should not dominate slaves; men should not dominate women. Christians should foster harmonious relationships characterized by mutuality and respect for social difference. Unity emerges only when the social distinctions that define us are present and acknowledged but never used as a means of domination.

There remains much unfinished work concerning racial/ethnic, economic, and gender justice in Christian communities, let alone within the broader public sphere. For instance, we must critique the gender politics in many Christian congregations. Many congregations perpetuate a patriarchal culture, which assumes that male leadership is "natural." This gender apartheid relegates women to their "proper place," while denying women access to symbols and systems of power (e.g., the pulpit, equal employment opportunities and pay as pastors, and the right to officiate major rituals such as baptism and holy communion). Galatians 3:28 insists that belief in God compels us to dismantle the social barriers that prevent us from truly being siblings.

PINN: Yes, the biblical world was complex, and numerous ways to interpret it present themselves. However, your insightful analysis doesn't counter my claim concerning how Christianity "undercuts the complex and messy nature of collective life." Our world isn't the world that biblical writers encountered. The ability, then, of the biblical text to speak to the intricacies of contemporary life and respond to the nuance of our dilemmas is suspect.

You present a compelling counterinterpretation to dominant ways of reading Christian scripture, but this doesn't negate how the biblical text has been (and continues to be) used to inflict harm. The biblical text occasionally claims a more expansive and egalitarian existence, as you note. However, this sense of equality is framed by the norms of the social world. Therefore, this sense of equality doesn't necessarily wipe out disregard and oppression.

You say, "This gender apartheid relegates women to their 'proper place,' while denying women access to symbols and systems of power." You also claim that the biblical text calls us to remove barriers to brotherhood and sisterhood. However, this doesn't necessarily follow. You assume a twenty-first century sense of "social barriers." Yet the biblical writers could be convinced of the need for social equality and still hold to limited leadership for women. Why? Because the sense of equality is framed by social norms.

Take, for example, the Constitution of the United States. It claims the rights and liberties of all men, and based on the social norm of that time, this excludes women and black people. We reflect on this based on our social norms, and we see a contradiction to correct, along with basic parameters within which to work. But for the authors of the Constitution, there was no contradiction, and the demand for "life, liberty and the pursuit of happiness" was real but restricted.

You might understandably argue that this example demonstrates the ongoing utility of scripture. However, there's a significant difference. The Constitution makes no claims to a higher authority beyond human reason. Consequently, it's much more "pliable" than scripture. Everything about the Constitution lends itself to reworking for the benefit of horizontal relationships. I'm not convinced that the Bible has the same interpretive "pliability."

BRAXTON: Speaking of interpretation, my commitment to Christianity informs my belief in religion's public role. I mean Christianity as interpreted and practiced through the lens of progressive, even radical, black politics. The need to qualify my understanding of the term "Christianity" is telling.

PINN: This might have something to do with the complexity of practice, and the flexible nature of religious values. But please finish.

BRAXTON: Many communities across the millennia have misrepresented the inclusive and revolutionary aims of Jesus, the first-century African-Asiatic Jew who joined the "Jewish Lives Matter" movement at the Jordan River. Jesus was drawn there by the radical teachings of John, a fiery prophet who was calling for people, including the politicians and power brokers of his day, to adopt a more justice-oriented way of life. Both John and Jesus were executed by the state. Both John and Jesus believed that religion had a public role, and the Roman imperial apparatus responded publicly and decisively to this belief by wielding the death-dealing power of the state against both prophets.

Yet before his death, Jesus provided his followers a brief "pocket guide" on how their inner convictions should influence their outer conduct. In this teaching in the Gospel of Matthew, which is referred to as the Sermon on the Mount, Jesus calls for an ethic of integrity: "Blessed are the pure in heart, for they will see God" (Matthew 5:8). The pure in heart are those whose outside behaviors are in line with their inside principles.

PINN: Yet there are numerous ways to interpret Jesus. I don't want to simply trade scriptural texts, but doesn't Jesus's silence on some of the issues impinging on life in our times say just as much? As a secular humanist, I believe that Jesus comes as the solution to a problem of God's making. I read salvation history as tied to a problem of knowledge that is fulfilled by Jesus, but it isn't a problem that is radically deconstructed. Jesus offers reform, not radical deconstruction, based on an implicit acceptance of the "laws" (i.e., the necessity of punishment for salvation). How is integrity defined and performed here?

BRAXTON: Before I say more about integrity, let me unpack a thorny word you just mentioned—"salvation." This is a loaded term that has caused considerable confusion, pain, and social separation. When you speak of "salvation history," are you referring to a kind of Protestant theology (often associated with the sixteenth-century European theologian John Calvin) that divides the world into those who are the "divine elect" and those who are the "damned"? Theological language like this, which creates simplistic and false binaries, has typified a considerable amount of religious belief and practice—especially in Christianity—across the centuries.

PINN: I don't have a Calvinist orientation in mind nor notions of heaven and hell. My use of this language isn't traditionally theological in that sense. By salvation history, I simply mean a measuring of deep transformation over time. But please say more.

BRAXTON: My understanding of salvation is more akin to ideas from the scriptures of ancient Judaism, and we know that African cultures significantly influenced ancient Jewish cultures and Jewish scriptures. The African influence on ancient Jewish culture impacted how ancient Jews understand important concepts like "salvation" or "deliverance." Thus, by grounding my understanding of salvation in the Hebrew Bible, I'm probably closer to some black ways of thinking about "salvation" than when we define salvation from the perspectives of a sixteenth-century white theologian.

PINN: This point is debatable, if one takes into consideration the thinking of many black evangelicals who are influenced, sometimes unbeknown to them, by the theories of sixteenth-century white theologians. Sorry, I've interrupted you again.

BRAXTON: Tony, I'm as far removed now from black evangelicalism as you are from the black Christianity of your youth. So you'll have to debate that point with black evangelicals. LOL.

The Hebrew Bible often depicts salvation or deliverance as the removal of people from tight, troublesome, real-world situations—situations that restrict them. For example, the writer in Psalm 107:13 declares: "Then they cried to the LORD in their trouble, and God saved them from their distress." The Hebrew word translated as "trouble" (*tsar*) means "tight place." This word also can mean "hard pebble."

We could poetically render Psalm 107:13 this way: "Then they cried to the LORD in their tight place or rocky space, and God saved them from their distress." In other words, salvation is not about whether my invisible "soul" is washed clean from my individual "sins." Salvation is about pragmatically delivering people who are stuck in tight situations—social, economic, political, familial, and personal situations.

Thus, in my estimation, salvation is about prophetic religion and not just religion in terms of personal piety. This understanding enables me to interpret Jesus not as my "personal savior" but instead as a religiously motivated and fully human (not divine) prophet. Jesus believed that God sent him to interrupt an unjust status quo so that more people might experience peace and prosperity. Jesus presented his central theme in *social* and *political* terms. He preached and taught consistently about the "kingdom of God"—God's beloved *community*, where social differences no longer divide and each of us has equal and unrestricted access to God's abundance.

PINN: I wouldn't disagree with that, but the biblical writers' sense of beloved community and of social differences isn't the same as ours. The cultural norms and sensibilities in that world are not easily translatable into ours. It seems to me you are making Jesus a twenty-first century progressive rather than a marginalized Jew from a radically different time.

BRAXTON: I beg to differ. I'm not making Jesus a twenty-first century progressive. Instead, I'm probing the implications of Jesus being a first century radical or even revolutionary. His radical practices and critiques of the religious traditions and political configurations of his day led to his execution.

Billions of people across the millennia have been animated, for good and ill, by Jesus's ministry and teachings. Thus, interpreting texts about Jesus's ministry and teachings is for me a meaningful exercise in *humanities* scholarship, irrespective of whatever assertions about his *divinity* these texts might make. I read biblical texts about Jesus with this question in mind: What can we discern about this particular human being and the movements he inspired, especially since these movements have enthralled large segments of humanity for an appreciable portion of recent human history?

Furthermore, when interpreting texts that are substantially removed from us in time and culture, we must acknowledge the real and perceived differences and similarities between the horizons of that text and the horizons of our contemporary world. The ancient concept of the "kingdom of God" and the contemporary concept of the "beloved community" are not identical. However, by analogy, we might clarify points of resonance and dissonance between these concepts. The resonance and dissonance enable us to have a thicker rendering of both concepts and might also point to different frameworks and practices more appropriate for our times.

Having alluded to prophetic religion, let me return to that topic. Prophetic religion honors the real experiences, messy details, and stubborn questions in people's lives, as they encounter joy and sorrow, suffering and celebration. Relevance is key to prophetic religion. The most compelling prophets and prophetic movements have not been prognosticators of some murky future but instead instigators for a more righteous present. Thus, prophetic religion encourages the wise, relevant use of resources to provide serious solutions to the world's serious problems.

Hatred and violence batter every part of the globe. Economic downturns constantly threaten the security of families. The COVID-19 pandemic, cancer, and diabetes continue to send people prematurely to the cemetery. Many children in our schools are failing, even as billions of dollars are spent to strengthen the prison system. Environmental toxins poison precious natural resources. These dilemmas do not allow religious or secular people to remain locked in their "ivory tower" abstractions.

PINN: I agree. There are many issues that must be addressed, and we need a language of life—a grammar of compassion—robust enough to harness justice work. But I don't think we find this in scripture. We need source material drawn from our cultural world that reflects our contact with the world.

BRAXTON: A "grammar of compassion"—that's a beautiful phrase. The world surely needs more compassion. I won't begrudge people about whether their motivation for compassionate problem-solving arises from religious or secular sources. We just need to address these public problems.

When teaching in divinity schools and seminaries, I remind students that prophetic religion involves more than simply naming social problems. Constructive and imaginative activism articulates and embodies promising possibilities beyond the problems.

Nonviolent cooperation between diverse religious groups can heal gang-ridden neighborhoods and unite war-torn nations. Strategic philanthropy can enhance employees' job skills and encourage employers' job creation. Congregational partnerships with medical institutions can provide more low-cost, healthcare options for uninsured or underinsured persons. Children's minds can be liberated, instead of their bodies being incarcerated. Regulations to ensure the environment's clean bill of health can be enacted. The aim of prophetic activism is abundant life for all forms of life on this marvelously diverse planet! My comments about integrity are buttressed by a fulsome understanding of real-world "salvation."

PINN: My sense of salvation is also consistent with the "real world." As a secular humanist, I wouldn't advance a Protestant theologically derived view of the human and the human in the world. I also appreciate what you are saying concerning "prophetic religion." Individuals and communities should have the right to dedicate themselves to a religious orientation. The Constitution safeguards this personal relationship to faith.

However, this is different from saying that a prophetic religiosity can shape the public arena. True, Christians, in this case, might be motivated by their prophetic sensibilities, and they might vote accordingly. But this should remain a matter of personal—and religious community—engagement. The public arena should be more robust and more reflexive of democratic ideals.

My aim isn't to prevent people from being religious. Also, to the extent that people are religious, the more progressive and prophetic they are, the better. However, I am advocating for a public space and public policies that are grounded in democratic ideals as opposed to being driven by religious—even the most progressive—religious ideals. Democratic ideals aren't synonymous with Christian—or even "religious"—ideals.

BRAXTON: Don't get it twisted. I'm just as interested as you are in diverse, *secular,* democratic public spaces and public practices. I'm simply trying to articulate how people with progressive and prophetic religious commitments might contribute to, not dominate, those spaces and practices.

As we mentioned earlier, Jesus exhorted his followers to be "pure in heart" and operate with integrity in private and public spaces. People who are "pure in heart" still stumble and fall. Their lives still bear the marks of hand-to-hand combat with temptation.

According to Jesus, the pure in heart strive to make their outward practices embodiments of their inner principles. People of integrity know that the profession of one's lips and the production of one's life ought not be in radical disagreement. Religion has a role to play in public, especially if religion has *integrity* and thus enables piety and politics to embrace in ways that enhance life for as many people as possible.

PINN: You say, "If religion has integrity . . ." The "if" here is too substantial for me. I believe that new mechanisms of discourse and delivery can offer whatever benefits religion might offer in public without the theological pronouncements and assumptions.

The United States has operated with an assumption that religion—and particularly the Christian church—has a unique quality, that there is something about the Christian church that imbues it with capacities unmatched by other institutions, that the Christian church is in public because it is uniquely qualified to guide the moral and ethical steps of the nation. I wouldn't deny the right of folks to practice their faith on the level of individuals or even in communities of the like-minded. Still, I'm not convinced it is necessary (or useful) to charge those communities with public responsibilities and authority.

BRAXTON: We've disagreed about many things in this book. Yet I completely agree with your critique of the unwarranted privileging of Christianity in the United States. Neither theism in general nor Christianity in particular has a unique or inherent capacity to provide moral guidance, especially for a broad, diverse public.

In authentically democratic spaces, a plethora of religious, spiritual, and ethical traditions should be welcomed into the public sphere to make their respective cases about their possible contributions to our collective well-being. I respect your opinion about permitting the practice of religion in individual and communal spheres, while "restricting" religion's influence in the broader public sphere. However, within the guardrails of legal statues about "religious freedom" (e.g., prohibiting religious practices that harm others), each religious, spiritual, and ethical tradition should be allowed to determine what public engagement its adherents might (or might not) pursue. A public sphere devoid of religious people is no better than previous Christian attempts, for example, to "rid" the public sphere of secular people. As a publicly engaged black Christian theologian and pastor, I'm interested in principles and practices that enable fellow Christians to be humble, morally aware (not morally arrogant) contributors to public well-being.

I began the chapter by raising the question: What happens when piety and politics embrace? My father's remarkable life offers a practical answer to the question. During the seventy-five years he lived, he embodied the noble struggle of bringing piety and politics together.

My father was a Baptist pastor in Virginia for more than forty-five years. He was deeply committed to Jesus and to civic engagement and social justice. On most Sundays during my childhood, my father passionately preached to a warm congregation of earnest black people in the Blue Ridge Mountains of southwest Virginia.

Yet I have equally vivid memories of my father's passionate commitment to the Citizens League, a group of people in my hometown who met regularly on many Mondays to discuss and enact tangible ways to improve civic life—from poverty eradication to voter engagement. The faithful piety my father exhibited on *Sunday* compelled him to engage in freedom-expanding politics on *Monday*. While I've made mistakes aplenty in my life, I'm trying to acquaint my "Sunday" with my "Monday." I want my piety to embrace my politics.

PINN: I appreciate the personal narrative. It reminds me of the power of the personal to provide orienting moments. I also see through the compelling example of your father how—on the personal level—connections between faith and politics are mapped. My concern is with scaling up from the individual to the organizational. I'm okay with individual Christians, for example, being guided by faith as they move to the ballot box. I, however, wonder about the church claiming space in the public arena. I'm not convinced it's a good move.

When and where has such a public presence of the church benefited those outside the "grace" of the church? What about people in the public arena who adhere to other traditions? Are they to bracket their religiously inspired framing of life to participate in a "Christianized" public? What about the most despised—atheists and humanists? How does this religiously positioned public speak a democratic possibility that is inclusive and robust?

BRAXTON: Black people are a "tribal people" who deeply appreciate community. Thus, I expect black people, and in this instance black Christians, to scale up religiously motivated civic engagement from the individual to the communal. The scaling up can create synergies and coalitions that produce public goods from which diverse groups can benefit.

Thus, in my father's example, his religiously motivated public engagement galvanized him to participate in a civic group that enhanced the quality of life for a larger segment of the community, not just a narrow group of citizens who professed religion. Consequently, religion can play a public role without it necessarily mutating into an exclusionary theocracy, where people only have access to power and social goods if they submit to a litmus test of religious belief and practice.

I detect hyperbole as you question whether the public presence of churches has benefited those outside the "grace" of those churches. Our colleagues in social sciences, religious studies, and history have provided documentable evidence about the positive impact that religious communities, and more specifically black churches, have had on public life.

PINN: Some of this is a matter of perspective. In other words, to whom is credit given? For example, do we credit the church with the civil rights movement—despite King's complaints about a lack of financial support and involvement from many churches? Do we think in terms of the civil rights activism of more secular students and leaders such as A. Philip Randolph? Perhaps, it's the more "secular" dimensions of the church (e.g., buildings/facilities, communication networks, resources, and person power) that are important here.

Yet we often confuse those dimensions with the theologically derived dimensions of the black church. If what we gain from the church in terms of public aid involves these secular dimensions, we should build new organizations with these resources, without the liability of religious doctrine and creed. I'm not certain the public presence of churches advances the type of diversity our democracy calls for.

BRAXTON: In fairness, the motivations of certain religious communities have been more insular and self-serving when they have engaged the public. On the other hand, the motivations of other religious communities have been more universal and altruistic. However, in your hyperbole, I hear a helpful cautionary note: we should not automatically assume that the presence of religiously motivated individuals or communities is inherently good for the body politic. I second that motion and cosign that idea!

PINN: I want to be clear. I'm not opposing religious people in public using their beliefs to ground their actions. I'm opposing religion providing the language and codes that shape the public. The public, I'll say again, should be a secular space.

BRAXTON: Let me say again, I gladly embrace a *secular* public sphere. Yet in a secular public sphere that is *democratic,* no singular person or group should decide what language and codes will shape public discourse and practice. As diverse individuals and groups engage, debate, and persuade one another, decisions about religion's public role should be made in public by the public.

As we listen to and talk with many beautifully diverse people in the public sphere, all of us will have more opportunities to appreciate our similarities and celebrate our differences. In the creative tension of this appreciation and celebration, we all might become better humans.

IN THIS MASTER CLASS, WE ALL HAVE HOMEWORK

When you were growing up, you might have occasionally received the same gentle reprimand that we received from family members, teachers, and mentors: "it's not just *what* you said; it's also *how* you said it." While what is said could land you in serious trouble and place you in a "world of hurt," the wisdom in those words is that there are more than simply words to consider. A major lesson we learned in writing this book is so straightforward, and so vital: *how* we communicate with each other matters. When we adopt antagonistic approaches to communication, especially toward people with whom we differ or disagree, we miss and diminish many opportunities for mutual enrichment.

Differences in perspectives, practices, and worldviews are beautiful. Yet when we encounter differences in people across the table, down the block, or around the world, it can be frustrating and frightening. Prodded by frustration and fear, conversations between diverse groups of people often "fly off the handle," forcing people to duck and run from each other, rather than inspiring them to lean in toward each other with curiosity, humility, and respect.

Reflecting on the experiment of fostering exchange amid significant differences, we realize how the electronic nature of our exchange and the constant threats of the COVID-19 pandemic impacted the dialogue. The pandemic fostered in us a hyper-awareness of the body—its vulnerabilities, limitations, and communicative capacities. Writing this book through email amid the social isolation of the pandemic reduced the "presence" of our bodies in the dialogue.

Let's put it a different way. So much human communication is *body language,* but some of that is hard to gather by simply reading words on a computer screen. How was Brad reacting to a comment meant as a joke? Was the intended humor or camaraderie evident in the word selection? Did Tony get the playfulness of a statement when expressed by quotation marks or italics as opposed to a perceptible smile or a salient pause if we were leaning back in our chairs at that coffee shop? Some "technicolor" communication dynamics cannot be captured in the "black and white" of the written word.

Furthermore, the pandemic foisted upon us a new kind of fatigue. As we wrote, we grappled with this question: How do we name and address this bone-deep weariness when limited to the written word and when bereft of the ability to see how the pandemic is affecting each other? We reduced ourselves to one way of knowing what the other meant to say—the written word.

Limiting the dialogue to the written word—rather than an embodied discussion in a shared space with written words as secondary—required a different level of trust and comfort with communication. Instead of inferring ill will, we assumed good will. This good will enabled us to respectfully probe deep thoughts and delicate feelings upon which each of us has built our personal and professional lives.

The nasty frictions between Christians and secular humanists are entrenched in long-standing and alternative visions of life. Thus, conversation alone is unlikely to alter the animosity between these groups. Nevertheless, conversation is *something.* It is at least an opening.

Recalibrating the meaning and positive possibilities of difference will not solve all our problems. Yet it will help us better identify what is at stake so that we can more effectively address our problems. Amid our distinctive philosophies of life, human connections can be more meaningful and human communities can be more peaceful if difference is not a weapon of warfare but a catalyst for compassionate and courageous conversation.

We hope this book will motivate you to expand your range of conversation partners. Take some chances and "calculated risks." Connect with people who have different worldviews and identities and explore why and how they engage the world. In the process, you will probably learn something unexpected about someone new, and you also will likely gain a refined understanding of your identities, commitments, and behaviors. Courageous engagement with diverse dialogue partners is an effective exercise for strengthening the empathy muscle. Empathy—the use of head and heart to positively relate to the identities and experiences of others—is needed now more than ever, as divisive forces are using any mean necessary to sever the fundamental bond connecting us—our mutual belonging in the human family.

Enhancing our perspectives on others and ourselves can improve how we speak to each other about the world and how we express our disagreements and moral and ethical similarities. The key here isn't a "I must win" posture toward conversation, but rather a "I should learn" approach to exchange. It's an opportunity to clarify and refine, to grow and better appreciate a diversity of perspectives and opinions. And so, why do we have these difficult conversations? Well . . . because we might just learn something that helps us to better understand the diverse human community of which we are a part. And in this learning, we might better understand and appreciate the humanity of the other—not because they agree, but simply because they are. Our value, our importance, isn't found in our ability to "win" arguments—both theists and nontheists have been too concerned with this—but in our ability to expand the scope of our concerns to include those who disagree with us.

This approach to conversation might reduce the violent nature of so much disagreement and increase our comfort with "knowledge discomfort." There are too few spaces and places that strengthen the capacity to engage—let alone learn from—diverse people who question our cherished beliefs. Knee-jerk, visceral responses to difference frequently short-circuit the learning process.

We are not issuing a naive call to forget about difference—to pretend we all want the same thing. No, it is exactly the opposite. This is a thoughtful call to appreciate the instructive potential of difference, especially when we purposefully transgress traditional boundaries and communicate across appreciable dimensions of diversity.

This approach will not work in all contexts. Some positions are so rigid and dependent on the destruction of the "other" that conversation is not possible or even worth the effort. However, people so "fundamentalist" in their thinking are not likely to read this book.

Certain Christians and secular humanists will consider our effort to talk and encourage conversation as "surrender." Those people might label us as "sellouts" who have lost sight of what matters: converting nonbelievers and making the world safe for believers or belittling and minimizing believers to render the public sphere safe from religious influence. For those people, there can only be *one* way.

There are, however, many others who are more comfortable with questions, more open to diverse encounters, more aware of our collective human circumstances, and more willing to give earnest conversation a try. We have written for those folks, and we count among them the growing number of people who claim no particular religious affiliation but whose commitment to promoting restorative justice draws creatively from a range of religious, spiritual, philosophical, and ethical perspectives.

Speaking of ethics, the ethicist Emilie Townes encourages people to ask essential questions about the human experience: What is the society we are trying to create? What does it look like? Is there a common vision?

As we grapple with these and other pertinent questions, we should develop a new grammar and vocabulary to bring people together, not despite our differences but because of our differences. Townes further contends that the ethical task is to work toward "a society that respects the rights and humanity of all peoples."

As seasoned classroom teachers, we have written many lectures and lessons plans. Thus, we know a superb assignment when we hear it: respecting the "humanity of all peoples." That is it! That is the "learning goal" of *A Master Class on Being Human*.

We appreciate your valuable input, instruction, and classroom participation. Until we gather for the next class, we all have a homework assignment: respecting the *humanity* of all peoples. Ding! Ding! Class is dismissed.

ACKNOWLEDGMENTS

BRAD R. BRAXTON: This project has been a treat, but we can't forget all those who opened us to this opportunity and who nurtured our work.

ANTHONY B. PINN: That's absolutely right. Of course, there are those we hold in common, but also people within our personal circles we need to acknowledge.

BRAD BRAXTON: Let's begin with our shared "thank-yous." Without these folks, we never could have made the pilgrimage from the inchoate ideas that we shared in an initial email exchange in the summer of 2020 to the codification of our refined thoughts in this volume.

BRAD BRAXTON AND ANTHONY PINN: Prior to our dialogue at The Open Church of Maryland in July 2020 that launched this book, the Smithsonian Institution curated two events that fostered the book's development. First, we are thankful for the Smithsonian Center for the Study of African American Religious Life's Teddy Reeves, Eric Williams, Kim Moir, Donna Braxton, and Nicole Fuller. They invited us to serve as "village elders" in the Smithsonian's "gOD-Talk" initiative—a national dialogue examining religious diversity among black millennials—in Dallas, Texas, in January 2020. During the event, we had an engaging conversation that provided the scaffolding for our dialogue during another Smithsonian event later that year.

Second, we thank the Smithsonian Center for Folklife and Cultural Heritage's Michael Atwood Mason (former director), Sabrina Lynn Motley, James Deutsch, and Diana Baird N'Diaye. As an inaugural event for the 2023 Smithsonian Folklife Festival on religious diversity, these colleagues invited us to present an online dialogue titled "Reconstructing Hope: Black Religions in the Age of Black Lives Matter" in June 2020.

In a sense, we wrote this book "backward." Authors typically execute a contract with a publisher and then write the book. The exigencies in the summer of 2020 demanded that we "get on" immediately with writing the book. Consequently, we decided that after the book was written we would find the right publisher, or the right publisher would find us. As the book neared completion, we contacted our friend Eboo Patel, founder and president of Interfaith America, who graciously introduced us and the book to Amy Caldwell, editorial director at Beacon Press. Amy's immediate and abiding enthusiasm for the book and her expert editorial guidance have immeasurably refined the book's clarity.

BRAD BRAXTON: I count it a privilege to serve as the founding senior pastor of The Open Church of Maryland. For eleven years, this remarkable congregation (or "merry band of misfits," as we jokingly refer to ourselves) has provided an innovative laboratory for exploring the meanings and methods of radically inclusive love, courageous social justice activism, and compassionate interfaith collaboration. I especially want to thank The Open Church's board of directors, whom we affectionately call the "Dream Keepers," for giving me permission to dream: Florine McCready Lewis (board chair), Marco Merrick, La Tanya Simms, Heather Cronk, Greg Murrill, and Tanya Page. A special shout-out to La Tanya Simms, whose comment in the Zoom chat during that July 2020 dialogue with Tony inspired the title for the book.

We wrote the book during my service as chief diversity, equity, and inclusion officer at St. Luke's School, a coeducational Episcopal school in New York City. This hospitable community of administrators, educators, students, and parents graciously welcomed me and fashioned opportunities for me to use my gifts, even as I learned brilliant lessons from them about the art and science of learning and leading. Bart Baldwin (head of school) and Holly Fogle (board chair) secured resources and established an administrative structure that enabled me both to contribute to the daily life of the school and to have meaningful moments for contemplation and writing. Chiarna Morton, my friend and co-conspirator in the DEI Office at St. Luke's School, was an invaluable dialogue partner as Tony and I hammered out each chapter.

The aforementioned Eric Williams of the Smithsonian Institution and Terrence Johnson of Harvard University cared for my soul with priestly attentiveness as I wrote and as we all endured the vicissitudes of the COVID-19 pandemic. Their friendship is a priceless gift.

During the later phases of editing the book, I assumed the position of president and professor of public theology at Chicago Theological Seminary (CTS), a progressive theological school on the vanguard of social justice and interreligious engagement. The CTS community has warmly embraced me, and I appreciate my partnership with the board, faculty, staff, students, alumni, and community partners. I am especially grateful to Brian Clarke (former board chair) and Janet MacLean (board chair) for regarding my role as a public theologian as an integral aspect of my leadership. Additionally, Kim Johnson, my outstanding executive assistant (whom we affectionately call "General Johnson"), manages my schedule and administrative tasks with finesse and humor.

My parents—James and Louise Braxton; my parents-in-law—Melvin and Dorothy Rainey; and my siblings and extended family have been, and are, a ceaseless wellspring of love and encouragement.

Finally, the joy that I feel in completing the book pales in significance to my unspeakable joy and boundless gratitude for having my wife, Lazetta; our daughter, Karis; and our four-legged "son," Sampson (a retriever/terrier) as my closest companions on life's journey. Lazetta's unending love, unrelenting loyalty, and sage counsel are a compass that keep me moving toward true north. Karis's incessant energy, keen insights, and raucous humor keep the fires burning on my altar. Sampson's regal presence, watchful eyes, and quiet companionship in many midnight writing sessions nudged me to keep on keepin' on. By God's grace and your support, we did it, y'all. In the words of our family motto: One clap! I dedicate this book to Karis. To paraphrase the writer Madeleine L'Engle, keep disturbing the universe, Karis, for the sake of righteousness.

ANTHONY PINN: I must thank my friends in the Unitarian Universalist Association for opportunities to stretch my thinking and to further recognize the options available for a more expansive sense of community. Thank you to the UU Panel on Theological Education and the UU Service Committee for wonderful conversations and opportunities to work in new ways. I must thank, in particular, Susan Frederick-Gray, who, as president of the UUA, invited me to serve on the panel, and Mary Katherine Morn, executive director of the Service Committee, who extended an invitation for me to join the Service Committee. I can't fully express my appreciation for those invitations, and what that work has meant for me and how it has influenced my thinking.

In addition, Marc Loustau and the selection committee invited me to give the Minns Lectures through the Unitarian Universalist Association. And, while those lectures aren't explicitly found in these pages, writing them did offer me an opportunity to think about some of the commitments and strategies that inform my conversation with Brad. Furthermore, my conversations with Meadville Lombard Theological School faculty and students have been invaluable to me as I've thought through what it means to theologize as a humanist in a social world still decidedly theistic.

The American Humanist Association—particularly former executive director, Roy Speckhardt, and current executive director, Nadya Dutchin—offered opportunities for me to present ideas that led ultimately to my thinking reflected in these pages. It was also through the American Humanist Association that I had the good fortune of meeting and working with some fantastic thinkers and activists whose engagement in/with the world speaks to the ability to hold one's beliefs and respect those who think differently. Thank you to Anne Klaeysen, Dale McGowan, Chris Stedman, Greg Epstein, Sikivu Hutchinson, Colin Bossen, and John Hooper, among others. My work as director of research for the Institute for Humanist Studies has given me an important opportunity to present humanism beyond the assumptions of "tradition" in relation to pressing social issues, and in light of a larger community of concern. The late Warren Wolfe was key in what the institute was able to accomplish. I still miss his insightful comments and support.

Rice University has given me the space and resources needed to have the types of conversations important to me and to conduct the type of research that energizes me. Thank you to my colleagues for support and encouragement and thank you to my graduate students—DeAnna Daniels and Hassan Lott—for their intellectual challenge and theoretical push. My colleague, and friend, Maya Reine has helped me manage my campus responsibilities and has provided important feedback on my work.

Finally, family and friends are an ever-present source of support and encouragement. I think my mother, the late Rev. Anne H. Pinn, would have been proud of this project, and my extended family provides much-needed encouragement and time away from the madness of academic life. Holidays with my extended family, as well as the unplanned moments, are precious— and I am grateful. My friends—really part of my extended family—push me on my ideas and never fail to inspire me. I dedicate this book to my great-niece, Ava Santana. Her view of the world is delightful and speaks the persistence of possibility.

REFERENCES

Alexander, M. Jacqui. *Pedagogies of Crossing: Meditations on Feminism, Sexual Politics, Memory, and the Sacred.* Durham, NC: Duke University Press, 2005.

Blount, Brian K., ed. *True to Our Native Land: An African American New Testament Commentary.* Minneapolis: Fortress Press, 2007.

Boesak, Allan. *Running with Horses: Reflections of an Accidental Politician.* Cape Town: Joho, 2009.

Braxton, Brad R. *No Longer Slaves: Galatians and African American Experience.* Collegeville, MN: The Liturgical Press, 2002.

————. *Preaching Paul.* Nashville: Abingdon Press, 2004.

Camus, Albert. *The Plague.* New York: Alfred A. Knopf, 1948.

Cannon, Katie G. "Wheels in the Middle of Wheels." *Journal of Feminist Studies in Religion* 8, no. 2 (Fall 1992): 125–32.

Clifton, Lucille. "Won't You Celebrate with Me." In *The Book of Light*, 25. Copper Canyon Press: Port Townsend, WA, 1993.

Coates, Ta-Nehisi. "The First White President: The Foundation of Donald Trump's Presidency Is the Negation of Barack Obama's Legacy." *The Atlantic* (October 2017), https://www.theatlantic.com/magazine/archive/2017/10/the-first-white-president-ta-nehisi-coates/537909.

Craddock, Fred B. *Preaching.* Nashville: Abingdon Press, 1985.

Crenshaw, Kimberlé. *On Intersectionality: The Essential Writings of Kimberlé Crenshaw.* New York: The New Press, 2019.

Douglas, Kelly Brown. *Sexuality and the Black Church: A Womanist Perspective.* Maryknoll, NY: Orbis Books, 1999.

Du Bois, W. E. B. *The Souls of Black Folk.* Chicago: A. C. McClurg and Co., 1903. Repr., New York: Dover Publications, 1994.

Ehrenreich, Barbara. *Nickel and Dimed: On (Not) Getting By in America.* New York: Henry Holt and Co., 2001.

Felder, Cain Hope, ed. *Stony the Road We Trod: African American Biblical Interpretation.* Minneapolis: Fortress Press, 1991.

Fish, Stanley. *Is There a Text in This Class? The Authority of Interpretive Communities.* Cambridge, MA: Harvard University Press, 1980.

Floyd-Thomas, Stacey M. "Writing for Our Lives: Womanism as an Epistemological Revolution." In *Deeper Shades of Purple: Womanism in Religion and Society,* ed. Stacey M. Floyd-Thomas, 1–14. New York: New York University Press, 2006.

Foucault, Michel. *Discipline and Punish: The Birth of the Prison.* New York: Vintage Books, 1979.

———. *The History of Sexuality, Volume 3: The Care of the Self.* New York: Vintage Books, 1988.

———. *The History of Sexuality, Volume 2: The Use of Pleasure.* New York: Vintage Books, 1990.

Garza, Alicia. "A Herstory of the #BlackLivesMatter Movement." The Feminist Wire, October 7, 2014, https://thefeministwire.com/2014/10/blacklivesmatter-2.

Harding, Rachel Elizabeth. "You Got a Right to the Tree of Life: African American Spirituals and the Religions of the Diaspora." *CrossCurrents* 57, no. 2 (Summer 2007): 266–80.

Hendricks, Obery M., Jr. *The Politics of Jesus: Rediscovering the True Revolutionary Nature of the Teachings of Jesus and How They Have Been Corrupted.* New York: Doubleday, 2006.

hooks, bell. *Where We Stand: Class Matters.* New York: Routledge, 2000.

hooks, bell, and Cornel West. *Breaking Bread: Insurgent Black Intellectual Life,* 25th-ann. ed. New York: Routledge, 2017.

Hughes, Langston. "I, Too." In *The Collected Poems of Langston Hughes,* ed. Arnold Rampersad, 46. New York: Vintage Books, 1994.

Hurston, Zora Neale. *The Sanctified Church: The Folklore Writings of Zora Neale Hurston.* Berkeley, CA: Turtle Island Foundation, 1981.

Johnson, James Weldon. *God's Trombones: Seven Negro Sermons in Verse.* New York: Viking Press, 1927.

Jones, William R. *Is God A White Racist? A Preamble to Black Theology.* Boston: Beacon Press, 1973.

King, Martin Luther, Jr. "A Tough Mind and a Tender Heart." In *Strength to Love,* 13–20. Philadelphia: Fortress Press, 1963.

Levine, Amy-Jill. *The Misunderstood Jew: The Church and the Scandal of the Jewish Jesus.* New York: HarperOne, 2006.

Lorde, Audre. "The Master's Tools Will Never Dismantle the Master's House." In *Sister Outsider: Essays and Speeches.* Berkeley, CA: Crossing Press, 1984.

Martin, Luther H., Huck Gutman, and Patrick H. Hutton, eds. *Technologies of the Self: A Seminar with Michel Foucault.* Amherst: University of Massachusetts Press, 1988.

Oduyoye, Mercy Amba. "Three Cardinal Issues of Mission in Africa." In *Mission in the Third Millennium*, ed. Robert J. Schreiter, 40–52. Maryknoll, NY: Orbis Books, 2001.

Orsi, Robert A. *Between Heaven and Earth: The Religious Worlds People Make and the Scholars Who Study Them*. Princeton, NJ: Princeton University Press, 2005.

———. "The Study of Religion on the Other Side of Disgust." *Harvard Divinity Bulletin* 47, nos. 1–2 (Spring–Summer 2019): 21–30.

Patterson, Orlando. *Slavery and Social Death: A Comparative Study*. Cambridge, MA: Harvard University Press, 1982.

Paulsell, Stephanie. "Writing as a Spiritual Discipline." In *The Scope of Our Art: The Vocation of the Theological Teacher*, ed. L. Gregory Jones and Stephanie Paulsell, 17–31. Grand Rapids, MI: William B. Eerdmans Publishing Co., 2002.

Pinn, Anne H., and Anthony B. Pinn. *Fortress Introduction to Black Church History*. Minneapolis: Fortress Press, 2002.

Pinn, Anthony B. *Why, Lord? Suffering and Evil in Black Theology*. New York: Continuum, 1999.

———. *Terror and Triumph: The Nature of Black Religion*. Minneapolis: Fortress Press, 2003.

Proctor, Samuel DeWitt. *The Substance of Things Hoped For: A Memoir of African-American Faith*. New York: G. P. Putnam's Sons, 1995.

Ross, Rosetta E. *Witnessing and Testifying: Black Women, Religion, and Civil Rights*. Minneapolis: Fortress Press, 2003.

Schüssler Fiorenza, Elisabeth. *Rhetoric and Ethic: The Politics of Biblical Studies*. Minneapolis: Fortress Press, 1999.

Shakur, Assata. "To My People." Third World Women's Alliance's *Triple Jeopardy* 3, no. 2 (November/December 1973).

Sharpe, Christina. *In the Wake: On Blackness and Being*. Durham, NC: Duke University Press, 2016.

Simmons, Martha, and Frank A. Thomas, eds. *Preaching with Sacred Fire: An Anthology of African American Sermons, 1750 to the Present*. New York: W. W. Norton and Co., 2010.

Smith, Andrea. "Native Feminist Theology." In *Liberation Theologies in the United States: An Introduction*, ed. Stacey M. Floyd-Thomas and Anthony B. Pinn, 149–67. New York: New York University Press, 2010.

Stendahl, Krister. "Ancient Scripture in the Modern World." In *Scripture in the Jewish and Christian Traditions: Authority, Interpretation, Relevance*, ed. Frederick E. Greenspahn, 202–14. Nashville: Abingdon Press, 1982.

Taylor, Charles. *A Secular Age*. Cambridge, MA: Harvard University Press, 2007.

Thurman, Howard. *Footprints of a Dream: The Story of the Church for the Fellow-ship of All Peoples.* New York: Harper and Brothers Publishers, 1959.

Tinker, George E. *Missionary Conquest: The Gospel and Native American Cultural Genocide.* Minneapolis: Fortress Press, 1993.

Townes, Emilie M. "Living in the New Jerusalem: The Rhetoric and Movement of Liberation in the House of Evil." In *A Troubling in My Soul: Womanist Perspectives on Evil and Suffering*, ed. Emilie M. Townes, 78–91. Maryknoll, NY: Orbis Books, 1993.

———. *In a Blaze of Glory: Womanist Spirituality as Social Witness.* Nashville: Abingdon Press, 1995.

Walker, Alice. *The Color Purple.* New York: Houghton Mifflin Harcourt, 1982.

Webb, Joseph M. *Preaching and the Challenge of Pluralism.* St. Louis: Chalice Press, 1998.

Webb, Taurean J. "Troubling Idols: Black-Palestinian Solidarity in U.S. Afro-Christian Spaces." *Journal of Palestine Studies* 48, no. 4 (Summer 2019): 33–51.

Williams, Delores S. *Sisters in the Wilderness: The Challenge of Womanist God-Talk.* Maryknoll, NY: Orbis Books, 1993.

Wright, Richard. "The Man Who Lived Underground." In *Eight Men: Short Stories*, 19–84. Originally published 1961. New York: HarperPerennial Modern Classics, 1996.

———. *Black Boy (American Hunger): A Record of Childhood and Youth*, 60th-ann. ed. New York: HarperCollins, 2005.

———. *Native Son.* Originally published 1940. New York: HarperPerennial Modern Classics, 2005.

INDEX